CAMPFIRE STORIES

VOLUME II

CAMPFIRE STORIES

VOLUME II

Tales from
America's National Parks and Trails

Edited by
Dave Kyu and Ilyssa Kyu

Foreword by
J. Drew Lanham

**MOUNTAINEERS
BOOKS**

MOUNTAINEERS BOOKS is dedicated to the exploration, preservation, and enjoyment of outdoor and wilderness areas.

1001 SW Klickitat Way, Suite 201, Seattle, WA 98134
800-553-4453, www.mountaineersbooks.org

Printed in South Korea
Distributed in the United Kingdom by Cordee, www.cordee.co.uk
26 25 24 23   1 2 3 4 5

Copyeditor: Laura Whittemore
Design and layout: Melissa McFeeters

Illustration on pages 20-21 by Simone Martin-Newberry; illustration on pages 68–69 by Dominique Ramsey; illustration on pages 106–107 by Levi Hastings; illustration on pages 150–151 by Sarah Gesek; illustration on pages 194–195 by Pavonis Giron; and illustration on pages 246–247 by Lauren West. All illustrations used with permission.

Library of Congress Cataloging-in-Publication data is on file for this title at https://lccn.loc.gov/2018015725.

Mountaineers Books titles may be purchased for corporate, educational, or other promotional sales, and our authors are available for a wide range of events. For information on special discounts or booking an author, contact our customer service at 800-553-4453 or mbooks@mountaineersbooks.org.

Printed on FSC®-certified materials.

MIX
Paper | Supporting responsible forestry
FSC® C140526

ISBN (hardcover): 978-1-68051-550-3
ISBN (ebook): 978-1-68051-666-1

An independent nonprofit publisher since 1960

For Lula and Isla.
In memory of our Pops, Sheldon Shapiro.

Contents

GRAND CANYON NATIONAL PARK
A Chasm of the Sublime

EVERGLADES NATIONAL PARK
A River of Grass

OLYMPIC NATIONAL PARK
A Forest for Seeking

GLACIER NATIONAL PARK
Backbone of the World

JOSHUA TREE NATIONAL PARK
Where Two Deserts Meet

APPALACHIAN AND PACIFIC CREST NATIONAL SCENIC TRAILS
A Path to Walking It Off

Foreword

FOR MANY, THE IDEA OF A NATIONAL PARK conjures up visions of the faraway wild: beasts of immense shaggy proportions and ferocity. Birds soaring on broad wings, or in still-abundant flocks wheeling above landscapes only they have the privilege of visiting at will. It is snowcapped peaks almost higher than imagining and canyons so vast, deep, and grand that time seems trapped within them. It's blue haze on the rounded shoulders of Appalachia making those mountains smoky. It's New England forests turning brilliant hues in autumn and Southwest deserts being painted by sunrises. It's badlands that make us feel good or dust devils in great basins that slake our thirsts for wonder though there's not a drop of water in sight. It's the sweep of tall grass on Midwestern prairie and the sway of tall grass in Floridian wet glades. It's getting our wandering priorities straightened out in big bending places. Millions of acres that give grizzly bears enough space to get lost and moose that are made to feel small under the gaze of glaciers. Fathomless depths that help us breathe more deeply. Whale song we dance to. It is the opportunity to love the wild, at a respectable and safe distance, while we get ever closer to discovering our innermost selves.

For every park there are stories.

Our national parks are, at first glance, a collectively good idea, but they're not without some issues that still need to be faced. As we reckon today with how white-written history has given short shrift to aboriginal occupancy by First Nations and Indigenous people and the subsequent expulsion and genocide to occupy their lands as "new and wild discoveries" or how names on mountains matter, we need to more carefully examine park stories. At the same time, we must wrestle ethically with how Black people guarded sacred wild spaces in the beginning, but were then excluded from them, or how other people of color have been seen as unworthy of this "best idea." Our parks become complex and sometimes cloudy places rife with sins we thought absent from the grand vistas.

These places, though visited by millions, often hold highly personal stories that singularly define their value beyond any policy ever written on paper. There is an opportunity in the natural world to reconcile the bitter past and present predicaments with opportunities for a better future. I believe this to be one of the great undiscovered, or at least untapped, functions of wildness in our national parks.. For all the wondrous superlatives of height, depth, expanse, and abundance, it is the intensely personal relationships with land and space and time that offer opportunities for recognition of what was, is, and might be—reconciliation of past, present, and future desired conditions and, ultimately, eco-reparation in understanding that our place as humans is just as another cog in the wild wheel of nature. That is my hope anyway.

Ilyssa and Dave Kyu searched across the country to find the writers and stories herein. And they provide a large step forward in the Three R's Process: to recognize, reconcile, and repair, in these desperate times of upset and angst with one another and the natural world, through some relationship with wildness. Through our place in and responsibility to the parks too, but even more so with the greater park we all inhabit called Earth.

So sit close by and melt some s'mores or lift a tin cup of whatever goes down best. Read with eyes, ears, and heart wide open to absorb these stories. Recognize a bird call but then, too, the call for seeing identity of those different than you. Reconcile your speck-of-dust insignificance in the shadow of a stone monolith, but then know that you are singularly worthy of all the wildness we share, no matter your color, hue, love preference, or faith. Repair from within what's been torn apart. Find space to be quiet under a throw that will warm and cover a new collection of those gathered around the campfire. Snuggle up y'all. Let the frogs and night birds interrupt as they will. It's okay to pause for falling stars. Enjoy.

—J. DREW LANHAM

Introduction

IT WAS NOT STANDING BELOW sheer vertical granite walls or watching waves crashing along shorelines that fueled the inspiration for this second volume of *Campfire Stories*. It wasn't the enormity of glaciers, the otherworldliness of geysers, or expansive barren deserts that pushed us to seek more stories from our national parks. In fact, it was quite literally the opposite.

From within the safe bounds of our home, isolating ourselves from a microscopic virus wreaking havoc on the world, we couldn't help but think of . . . well, *anywhere else*.

Like the rest of the human population, we found ourselves overwhelmed with fear and uncertainty of what was to come, determined to keep our two young kids safe as news of the COVID-19 pandemic traveled across the globe, becoming our reality. They tell you to expect the unexpected when you become a parent, but this was taking it to a whole new level.

Just a couple months before the pandemic, Ilyssa happened to pick up *Station Eleven*, a post-apocalyptic novel about a traveling symphony and civilization in the aftermath of a flu outbreak. But she couldn't even get through the opening scene because the thought of it ever being reality felt too scary, especially now as a parent.

And then it did become reality.

We found ourselves in this strange new role we didn't audition for—a hybrid of modern-day forager and post-apocalyptic survivor, hoarding toilet paper, diapers, whatever nonperishable food was left on grocery store shelves, and so much hand sanitizer. As soon as we realized we were likely in this for a while, we shifted to arranging the puzzle pieces of our lives to get through each day with a baby, a toddler, and full-time jobs. We wanted to protect and distract our kids—and ourselves—from something that was so incomprehensible to *us* that we didn't quite know how to explain it to *them*. A story we didn't want to be part of, a climax we were too afraid to imagine, and a plot whose ending we couldn't anticipate.

Between watching daily news briefings, learning how to regrow scallions and salvaging other kitchen scraps in the event we needed to become homesteaders, and the general monotony of our new everyday indoor routines, we found our minds wandering to faraway places—beautiful places, our favorite outdoor spaces, and to no surprise to any of our readers, our national parks.

We wondered what these places might be like in the absence of . . . *us.*

What do the bison and foxes make of all of this? Do they even notice? Are they setting foot in territory that was once too noisy, too busy with people with their cameras and their cars and their buses? As businesses, schools, and workplaces shuttered completely, we began experiencing the outside world through social media. We saw glimpses of what was going on in our national parks—now closed to the public to prevent the spread of COVID-19—through posts by rangers and other staff in lockdown within them. We saw images of coyotes and bears wandering desolate parking lots and visitor centers. Scenic lookouts absent the usual throngs of tourists lined up for the perfect picture. Sunshine, blue skies at some of the most highly trafficked landmarks of our national parks—Yosemite Valley, Old Faithful, the rim overlooking the Grand Canyon—completely deserted. Our imaginations lit up thinking about our parks, without us.

The more we saw, the more we were reminded there were more stories to be told about our parks. While we envisioned building on our initial collection in *Campfire Stories: Volume I,* the reality of road-tripping with two very young kids and handling the amount of research and grueling travel felt impossible. Until it didn't.

When suddenly our lives became one big Zoom meeting, we realized maybe creating another book *was* possible. Because many of us were forced to figure out how to work remotely, travel was no longer a requirement for creating this collection, as accessing people virtually became infinitely easier. While we spent a lot of our time in libraries and archives on the road researching the first volume of this book to find source material and works or collections that are only locally accessible, the bulk of our learning and the themes that guided our story selection came from the people who live near, work for, and love these national parks. While many local works and collections were still not accessible digitally, this challenge presented an opportunity.

The intention of this collection has always been to tell stories from a diverse set of perspectives and voices in the outdoors. Relying on what we could find on the shelves of libraries and national park archives made this challenging, as being part of a collection requires people deciding what's worth saving and preserving. And let's face it, past generations have not always gotten this right. Our inability to travel or access these spaces might just unlock a whole new way of creating this collection—to not rely on what already exists, but to seek the stories that have yet to be written. We decided this next collection would feature more contemporary works from contemporary writers. This approach gave us full creative control over who gets to tell the stories of our national parks. And that's *everyone*.

We sent out a call for submissions, seeking writers who identify as part of the BIPOC (Black, Indigenous, and People of Color) or LGBTQ+ (Lesbian, Gay, Bisexual, Transgender, Queer, and all other non-cisgender and non-straight identities) communities. While we invited and selected works from all people, this was a deliberate invitation to people within often marginalized communities who are not always represented or welcomed in outdoors spaces. To address the barrier of access to the parks, we offered travel grants to help writers visit and then write stories about the parks for our collection. As we made story selections based on the merit of the writing first and foremost, we also continued to learn more about each park, discovering the important figures or elements of place that should be conveyed and finding the best writing to do so. In addition, we commissioned artists to create illustrations that allow us to see our parks through the lens of diverse perspectives.

For this book, like the last, we selected a handful of beloved national parks across the United States that represent different regions and landscapes. The Grand Canyon invites everyone to stare into a sublime chasm carved by the mighty Colorado River. In the Everglades lies a river of grass, a place where poetry seems to be the only way to capture its essence. The Olympic rain forest is so thick with mystery that its stories become a place for seeking. Glacier, with its turquoise lakes and technicolor rocks, fights to keep its last remaining namesakes from disappearing in the age of global warming and wildfires. Joshua Tree is the desert that inspires outcasts and rock 'n' roll musicians with its otherworldly, fragile yet resilient landscape. And the Pacific Crest and Appalachian Trails show how finding oneself in nature means finding a community.

While we wish this book had been created in a secluded cabin in one of these parks, the reality is that it was researched, curated, and written in the nooks and crannies of our pandemic parenting lives, while daydreaming of these immensely special places. We always thought of travel being a necessary part of our process, giving us the credibility to share these delicate stories of place. But after hundreds of hours of research, crammed in after full days of work, during nap times, late evenings, and weekends stuck at home, with kids on top of us and bouncing toys off our heads, we came to know and love these places through the words of writers who have experienced them—and we are the richer for it.

This anthology is a collective tapestry of perspectives and experiences in our parks. The stories by over fifty writers in this collection, from seven national parks and scenic trails, are meant to be read or shared around a campfire—whether quietly to yourself or aloud with the people sharing the light and warmth of the glowing embers. These poems, myths, legends, and personal essays capture the diverse history, culture, and experiences of those who have collectively built, shared, explored, and enjoyed these parks, as well as those whose people have always been there and never left. We sought stories from storytellers with different backgrounds, perspectives, and life experiences to widen the lens of who our public lands are for. These are not the definitive stories of each park, as each one could easily fill its own volume (and often has). Instead, we present a handful of stories of each park that, taken together, provide an overview of place, of the flora and fauna that thrive in each region, of the climates that are threatened, of the people taking in the majesty of these parks and all that they offer to help make sense of the things inside of *themselves*. These stories show you why each place is worthy of protection, and who suffered because of it. While some readers may expect this to be a collection of your "classic" spooky campfire tales, these are not stories just for those seeking to be entertained. Instead, we've selected these stories for those who are curious about how these parks and trails came to be, and why these places continue to mean so much to us. The stories we tell determine our values and shape our future. They connect us to something we all share—these lands were preserved for all of us.

We are proud to present this second collection of *Campfire Stories*. It is a labor of love, and we are deeply grateful to each of our contributors who brought the parks *to us*. We hope you get lost in these stories of past and present, as we did, and find yourselves, or your sense of the wild, in these words.

Storytelling Tips

SOME OF THESE STORIES are for you to read quietly beside a campfire, by lantern light in your tent, or from the comfort of your couch. Others can be shared and read aloud as you bask in the warmth of togetherness around a crackling fire.

Should you decide to share a story, these tips should get you ready if you need a refresher or have never read aloud at a campfire. Keep in mind, they are here to serve as a loose guide. Find what works for you and your audience, and know that you won't be on the spot. A campfire is a perfect place for someone to watch the fire or look at the stars, and not directly at you. Have a sip of water, share the things about a story that you love, keep it simple, and relax. Remember that you're sharing a beautiful campfire with a group of people, and a reading will just enhance this memorable experience.

Choose the right story.

A crucial part of telling a good campfire story is selecting the right story for your audience. Think about whose attention you need to hold, and what they might be interested in. For example, children might be more interested in a bear story than a reflective memoir about geology. Think also about the length of your story. Is this one of many activities or are you settled in for the night? Are you reading to kids with short attention spans or a group of engaged adults? Choosing a story that's too long is a common rookie mistake.

Read it out loud ahead of time.

Don't think of it as practice; reading ahead simply allows you to feel more relaxed later. Reading out loud in advance will reveal the words you can't pronounce, and will give you time to look up words you don't know. For the overachievers who want to memorize or perform the story, reading out loud often helps you memorize better than reading internally.

Set yourself up for a good reading.

Water is magic for any voice. Having water on hand can rescue you from dry mouth or a fit of coughing. Remember that, in a camp setting, you are competing with the chirping of crickets and the crackle of the fire. Make sure you sit or stand straight up, breathe from your diaphragm, and project your voice. As you're reading, don't forget to breathe or you might find yourself gasping for air.

Bring a flashlight.

The campfire provides a warm, flickering light that sets the perfect mood. But if you're relying on firelight to read your book, you're also probably projecting your voice away from your intended audience. We recommend bringing a flashlight so you can read to your audience, and still see the text. If you want to go hands-free, bring a headlamp or a book light that can clip onto the book.

Wait for the right moment to start.

You want to start from a beautiful, perfect silence. If people are fiddling with their sleeping bags or rooting around in the cooler for their favorite drink, it's not the right time. There's a moment when the audience is ready—they are captive, silent, and all breathing together. This is when you want to begin. Don't miss it!

Introduce the story.

But keep it short and sweet. Share the title, author, and the park the story pertains to. If the story is written in the first person, you might share a bit of info about the author. Feel free to borrow a little insider knowledge from the accompanying "About This Story" blurb to get your audience excited!

Find the rhythm—and then break it.

A good performer establishes a rhythm, and then breaks it. Every story has its own rhythm, especially poetry. Stories read out loud should be read slightly faster than you think, but without rushing. Ignoring punctuation like semicolons and hyphens can help keep the momentum. You will want to find the story rhythm that works for you, and then play with it. The volume, speed, and tone of your voice all affect the rhythm of the story. If you can make the rhythm break surprising, this can be very fun for your listeners! A break in rhythm can include a silent pause, but use such pauses sparingly for greater effect.

Don't let performing get in the way.

You want to illustrate the story with your voice, but you don't want to overdo it by being too dramatic. One way to avoid this is to just be you—be authentic. Try to convey your experience with the story as you go. Don't be afraid to laugh, gasp, or ponder a thought. Funny voices are entertaining, but make sure it doesn't slow you down or cause you to lose your rhythm. Most importantly, enunciate and speak clearly.

Say thank you.

Give space at the end of the story. Leave a brief moment of silence by taking a deep breath before saying "The End." Thank your listeners for their attention and allow any reactions to the story to flow naturally. You can also gauge your audience's interest for another reading.

· ✦ ·

We'd like to thank Ben Camp, Artistic Director for Team Sunshine Performance Corporation, a Philadelphia-based theater and dance company, for his advice on telling a great campfire story. In additional to having "Camp" as a last name, Ben is uniquely suited for campfire story magic-making after his love of attending camp as a kid and camp counselor led him to co-found and direct Camp Bonfire, a summer camp for adults in northeastern United States.

GRAND CANYON NATIONAL PARK

A Chasm of the Sublime

A MECCA FOR GEOLOGY NERDS, hikers,
river rafters, and tourists, the Grand
Canyon was carved over 5 million years
ago by the Colorado River in Arizona.
This immense and awe-inspiring
canyon stretches for 277 miles, and
its mile-deep chasm reveals layers
of geologic time.

illustration by
SIMONE MARTIN-NEWBERRY

Dave will never live down skipping the Grand Canyon. With two days to travel from the Rocky Mountains in Colorado to Yosemite in California, Ilyssa, who had already seen the canyon, gave Dave a choice: visit the Grand Canyon or stop by Las Vegas. Dave chose . . . Las Vegas. Let's just say, some regrets linger.

At that time, we had already visited Great Smoky Mountains and Rocky Mountain National Parks to begin research for volume one of *Campfire Stories*. For two months, we had been living out of a tent, fueled by sunrises and campfire breakfasts and had a couple more months ahead of us yet, with three more parks to go. Did we need to see another national park? More appealing was the chance to gawk at neon lights and spend a night in a Gothic art–themed hotel and nightclub.

More importantly, the immensity of the Grand Canyon loomed in Dave's imagination. For the parks on our research trip, we planned to spend at least two weeks in each: to visit both the popular and less crowded places, to speak with the people that champion these parks, and really let our bodies soak them in. The prospect of adding six hours to our route, only to stand at the North Rim for one, maybe two hours, just didn't feel like a visit that could possibly do justice to a canyon that's been named one of the seven natural wonders of the world.

"You cannot see the Grand Canyon in one view," says explorer John Wesley Powell, "as if it were a changeless spectacle from which a curtain might be lifted, but to see it you have to toil from month to month through its labyrinths." Powell, a geologist and one-armed Civil War veteran, led the first American exploration of the Colorado River and Grand Canyon in 1869, in which an ill-prepared party faced calamities, and Powell referred to the canyon as "our granite prison." Two years later, backed by the US Congress and the Smithsonian Institution, with a crew that included several scientists, Powell led another expedition into the canyon, on a trip that would produce the first reliable maps of the Colorado River.

Powell's accounts of his expedition would make the Grand Canyon popular around the world, and inspire conservation efforts for Grand Canyon National Park. The Grand Canyon became a park in stages, first as a forest reserve in 1893, then a national monument in 1908, and finally a national park in 1919. "Let this great wonder of nature remain as it now is," President Teddy Roosevelt declared in a 1908 speech. "You cannot improve on it. But what you can do is keep it for your children, your children's children, and all who come after you, as the one great sight which every American should see."

But Powell's expeditions were not just daring forays into the wilderness. In the 1800s, the science of geology was tied to Manifest Destiny, the idea that God had always intended for the United States to expand across North America to the Pacific Ocean, and mapping these territories meant identifying valuable resources and clearing out Indigenous tribes. Powell's expeditions and reports were political arguments to justify colonization.

The lands that comprise Grand Canyon National Park encompass territories that once were the homelands of the Hualapai, Supai and Havasupai, Navajo, Hopi, Diné and Zuni tribes. By the mid to late 1880s, as Americans began entering the canyon, tribal members were well aware of Indian removal happening across the continent. Instead of fighting, tribal members negotiated to keep some of their land, establishing the Navajo Nation in 1868, the Havasupai Reservation in 1882, the Hualapai Reservation in 1883. Each tribe struggled to adapt to their much smaller territories, and after a century of advocacy, have only recently begun regaining their land rights.

"All the lands you are exploring have never been unused wilderness," writes Ophelia Watahomigie-Corliss, contemporary Havasupai tribal member and contributor to this book. "They have all belonged and been taken care of by the Indigenous communities that still exist today." In 1975, Congress reallocated nearly 185,000 acres back to the Havasupai tribe. In 2008, the Hualapai tribe built the Skywalk, a glass walkway that allows tourists to walk over the canyon, on their reservation, which has become the featured attraction of the Grand Canyon West attractions. Continued advocacy, in part by Ophelia, saw Indian Village renamed Havasupai Garden in 2022. Within the same year, the eleven tribes traditionally associated with the Grand Canyon region, in partnership with Grand Canyon Conservancy and the National Park Service, broke ground on the Desert View Intertribal Cultural Heritage Site at the east entrance to the park. "This is an opportunity to tell our stories and showcase our tribes," says Mae Franklin, Navajo tribal member. "The goal is to educate the world community that tribes are still here, we are part of the fabric of our communities, and we have our unique ways of thinking and abilities to think about the land."

Here in the Grand Canyon, we witness the forces of rock, wind, and water working in tandem to create a natural wonder of the world. Time on the scale of the geologic requires us to rethink our own sense of time. To understand how the canyon came to be, the National Park Service (very helpfully) asks you to remember

DUDE: Deposition, Uplift, Downcutting, and Erosion. First is Deposition, in which igneous and metamorphic rock was gradually covered by layers and layers and layers (deposits) of sedimentary rock. Remember that the oldest rocks in the canyon are 1.8 billion years old. The youngest? The Kaibab rock, at 270 million years. Next is Uplift, grinding tectonic plates that lifted those rocks high and flat, creating a plateau. Then come Downcutting and Erosion, which is where our Colorado River comes in. When the river flooded, its fast current and large volume of water carved away at the rock to create a channel, which was further eroded by weather, wind, and rocks carried by the river. In an arid landscape, exposed rock is weathered and susceptible to deeply dramatic carvings, like say, a grand canyon.

The beauty of this place also conceals extreme danger. For as lush as the river seems and as awe-inspiring as the views can be, this is still an unforgiving desert landscape. Many take on the canyon with exuberance, descending into the gorge to test their limits, without realizing the difficulty of the return trip. And in the age of the camera phone, one misstep while staging the perfect selfie at the canyon's rim may lead to injury or death. Between 2018 and 2020, there were a reported 785 search and rescue incidents in the Grand Canyon. An author in this collection, Mary Emerick, worked as a search and rescue ranger there one summer. "I went thinking I was going to fight fires," she recalled. "Instead, I picked up the dead and dying from the canyon's blazing interior—the foolish, the unprepared, and the plain unlucky."

From the safety of wherever you're reading, enjoy these tales from Grand Canyon National Park.

Another View from
Point Sublime

LAURET SAVOY

We had entered Grand Canyon National Park before sunrise, turning west onto the primitive road toward Point Sublime. This was in those ancient days when a Coupe de Ville could negotiate the unpaved miles with just a few dents and scrapes. My father had driven through the Kaibab Plateau's forest on Arizona Highway 67 from Jacob Lake, Momma up front with him. No other headlights cut the dark. I sat in the back seat with Cissie, my dozing eighteen-year-old cousin. Our Kodak Instamatic ready in my hands, cocked. For two hours or more we passed through shadows that in dawn's cool arrival became aspen-edged meadows and stands of ponderosa pine. Up resistant limestone knolls, down around sinks and ravines. Up then down. Up then down. In time, through small breaks between trees, we could glimpse a distant level horizon sharpen in the glow of first light.

Decades have passed, nearly my entire life, since a seven-year-old stood with her family at a remote point on the North Rim. I hadn't known what to expect at road's end. The memory of what we found shapes me still.

This was The Move. My parents were returning to a familiar and familial East. My home lay behind us on the sunset coast, where I was born at the elastic limit of my father's last attempt to craft a life far from Washington, D.C. Movement and change had occurred often—from San Francisco to Los Angeles, from rented bungalow to apartment to second-story flat. The last to 1253 Redondo Boulevard. But these were small steps, our lives pacing an unchanged rhythm. Momma worked as a surgical nurse, mostly night shifts. Dad did many things—marketing, public relations, jobs I never really knew. We lived by what I now know were modest means, each home furnished with what was necessary, accented by his ceramics, pastels, paintings, handmade table and lamp.

In a neighborhood with few children, my reliable companions were sky's brilliant depth and the tactile land. The Santa Monica and San Gabriel Mountains shaped the constant skyline north and west.

If a child's character and perceptual habits form by the age of five or six, then I perceived by sharp light and shadows. If a child bonds with places explored at this tender age, and those bonds anchor her, then I chose textures and tones of dryness over humidity, expanses that embraced distance over both skyscraper and temperate forests.

So when my father, nearing fifty years of age, decided to return to Washington, D.C. to try again, I told my parents to leave me behind. We had visited his family there; I wanted no more of it.

But a seven-year-old has little choice short of running away. If I could gather sunlight and stones, if I could keep Pacific Ocean water from spilling or drying up, then home could come with me.

Sifting through memory's remains—of words spoken, decisions made, actions taken—feels like the work of imagination in hindsight. The scaffolding that ordered my world stood on happenstance. That because my father decided we'd drive across country in a leased Cadillac, roomy and comfortable enough for four; because he chose to stop at national parks on the way—because of these things I stood at that edge, a small child with a Kodak Instamatic in hand.

Point Sublime tips a long promontory that juts southward into the widest part of the canyon, a finger pointing from the forested Kaibab knuckle. It was named by Clarence Edward Dutton with other members of field parties he led between 1875 and 1880, first on John Wesley Powell's Geographical and Geological Survey of the Rocky Mountain Region, then under the new U. S. Geological Survey. To Dutton the view from the point was "the most sublime and awe-inspiring spectacle in the world."

The year the Grand Canyon became a national park, in 1919, more than forty-four thousand people visited. Most of them arrived by train to the South Rim. On the higher and more remote North Rim, those daring could try wagon tracks used by ranchers and "pioneer tourism entrepreneurs" over rough limestone terrain to Cape Royal and Point Sublime. Or they could follow a forest service route to Bright Angel Point. Soon roads scratched out on the Kaibab Plateau would replace the old wagon paths, allowing work crews to fight fires as well as infesting insects.

But the summer of 1925 would be a turning point. For the first time, and ever since, visiting motorists outnumbered rail passengers. The National Park Service encouraged and responded to this new form of tourism by building scenic drives and campgrounds on both rims. Auto-tourists often attempted the twisting, crude road to Point Sublime.

The Grand Canyon has drawn well over six million visitors in some recent years. The seventeen-mile route to Point Sublime remains primitive, and sane drivers tend not to risk low-clearance, two-wheel-drive vehicles on it. Sometimes the road is impassable. One year it was reported to have "swallowed" a road grader. Still, the slow, bumpy way draws those who wish to see the canyon far from crowds and pavement, as my father wanted us to do those many years ago.

None of us had visited the canyon before that morning. We weren't prepared. Neither were the men from Spain who, more than four hundred years earlier, ventured to the South Rim as part of an *entrada* in search of rumored gold. In 1540 García López de Cárdenas commanded a party of Coronado's soldiers who sought a great and possibly navigable river they were told lay west and north of Hopi villages. Led by Native guides, these first Europeans to march up to the gorge's edge and stare into its depths couldn't imagine or measure its scale. Pedro de Castañeda de Nájera chronicled the expedition:

They spent three days on this bank looking for a passage down to the river, which looked from above as if the water was six feet across, although the Indians said it was half a league wide. It was impossible to descend, for after these three days Captain Melgosa and one Juan Galeras and another companion, who were the three lightest and most agile men, made an attempt to go down at the least difficult place . . . They returned about four o'clock in the afternoon, not having succeeded in reaching the bottom on account of the great difficulties which they found, because what seemed to be easy from above was not so, but instead very hard and difficult. They said that they had been down about a third of the way and that the river seemed very large from the place which they reached, and that from what they saw they thought the Indians had given the width correctly. Those who stayed above had estimated that some huge rocks on the sides of cliffs seemed to be about as tall as a man, but those who went down swore that when they reached these rocks they were bigger than the great tower of Seville.

The Spaniards knew lands of different proportions.

Writing more than three centuries later, Clarence Dutton understood how easily one could be tricked by first views from the rim. "As we contemplate these objects we find it quite impossible to realize their magnitude," he wrote. "Not only are we deceived, but we are conscious that we are deceived, and yet we cannot conquer the deception." "Dimensions," he added, "mean nothing to the senses, and all that we are conscious of in this respect is a troubled sense of immensity."

Point Sublime holds a prominent place in Dutton's *Tertiary History of the Grand Cañon District*, the first monograph published by a fledgling U. S. Geological Survey in 1882. Lavishly illustrated with topographic line drawings and panoramas by William Henry Holmes, Thomas Moran's paintings and drawings, and heliotypes of Jack Hillers's photographs, it is an evocative work from a time when specialized science hadn't yet constrained language or image. The monograph also shows a science coming of age. For in the plateau and canyon country, aridity conspired with erosion to expose Earth's anatomy. The land's composition and structure lay bare. Though terrain was rugged and vast, equipment crude or lacking, these reconnaissances tried to sketch plausible models for land-shaping forces. Clarence Dutton gazed out from the North Rim at Point Sublime to describe the grand geologic *ensemble*: the great exposed slice of deep time in canyon walls, the work of uplift and erosion in creating the canyon itself. Dutton also brought his readers to the abyss's edge to see with new eyes.

The men on the surveys by and large beheld with eastern eyes, responding at first with senses accustomed to the vegetative clothing of a more subdued, humid land. They saw at a time when various meanings of "the sublime" had become essential to how the educated in Europe and their descendants in America conceived of the world about them. In a Romantic sublime one encountered power greater than imagined or imaginable. One beheld the might and presence of the Divine. On a mountain peak. In a great churning storm. At the brink of a fathomless chasm. To come to the edge of the Grand Canyon and experience the sublime was to feel unsettled, deeply disoriented. To be awestruck. "In all the vast space beneath and around us there is very little upon which the mind can linger restfully," Dutton wrote. "It is completely filled with objects of gigantic size and amazing form, and as the mind wanders over them it is hopelessly bewildered and lost."

But he didn't stop there. Dutton realized that objects disclosing "their full power, meaning, and beauty as soon as they are presented to the mind have very little of those qualities to disclose." After many field seasons he came to see the "Grand Cañon of the Colorado" as "a great innovation in modern ideas of scenery, and in our conceptions of the grandeur, beauty, and power of nature." Such an innovation couldn't be comprehended immediately. "It must be dwelt upon and studied, and the study must comprise the slow acquisition of the meaning and spirit" of the country.

> The lover of nature, whose perceptions have been trained in the Alps, in Italy, Germany, or New England, in the Appalachians or Cordilleras, in Scotland or Colorado, would enter this strange region with a shock, and dwell there for a time with a sense of oppression, and perhaps with horror . . . The tones and shades, modest and tender, subdued yet rich, in which his fancy had always taken special delight, would be the ones which are conspicuously absent. But time would bring a gradual change . . . Great innovations, whether in art or literature, in science or in nature, seldom take the world by storm. They must be understood before they can be estimated, and they must be cultivated before they can be understood.

The author Wallace Stegner wrote his dissertation on Clarence Dutton, later referring to him as "almost as much the *genius loci* of the Grand Canyon as Muir is of Yosemite." Tourists visiting the park might not be aware of the debt owed, but Stegner believed "it is with Dutton's eyes, as often as not, that they see." While residents of eastern landscapes might have spurned canyons and deserts as irredeemably barren, Dutton's words and vision helped change the terms of perception. That is, for an audience acquainted with particular notions of the sublime and nature, an audience with the means, time, and inclination to tour.

What did my family bring to the edge and how did we see on that long-ago morning? I've wondered if the sublime can lie in both the dizzying encounter with such immensity and the reflective meaning drawn from it. Immanuel Kant's sublime resided in the "power in us" that such an experience prompted to recognize a separateness from nature, a distance. To regard in the human mind an innate superiority over a natural world whose "might" could threaten flesh and bones but had no "dominion" over the humanity in the person. In Kant's view, neither I nor my dark ancestors could ever reach the sublime, so debased were our origins. In Kant's view neither could W. E. B. Du Bois, for whom this "sudden void in the bosom of the earth," which he visited half a century before us, would "live eternal in [his] soul."

We had little forewarning of where the Kaibab Plateau ended and limestone cliffs fell oh so far away to inconceivable depth and distance. The suddenness stunned. No single camera frame could contain the expanse or play of light. Canyon walls that moments earlier descended into undefined darkness then glowed in great blocky detail. As shadows receded a thin sliver in the far inner gorge caught the rising sun, glinting—the Colorado River.

I'll never know what that morning meant to my father when he took this detour on his homeward journey. Or to my mother. We traveled together but arrived with different beholding eyes.

Those moments at Point Sublime illuminated a journey of and to perception, another way of measuring a world I was part of yet leaving behind. I felt no "troubled sense of immensity" but wonder—at the dance of light on rock, at ravens and white-throated swifts untethered from Earth, at a serenity unbroken.

The ocean I'd tried to bring across country had evaporated. Sunlight wouldn't be contained. But pebbles came willingly. Limestone joined basalt, sandstone, and granite on the rear window mat. Images of the canyon, Kaibab Plateau forest, and Colorado River thickened the growing stack of postcards.

Erosive forces carved the North Rim's edge. My family crossed many edges that summer. West to East. One childhood home left for another. Before to after. History began for me on The Move. What preceded was a sense of infinite promise and possibility in a world that made sense. What followed promised nothing. Daddy hoped the nearing future would be a return to origins and dignity. My soon constant question to him, "When are we going home?" always met the same response: "We are home."

My bearings lay in memories of bright days, in snapshots and postcards, stones and a salt-encrusted jar. By the age of ten I knew it was better not to want anything too badly.

I've tried to return to Point Sublime many times. Fire danger and an impassable road aborted all but two attempts. The wooden post still stands, but without the carved sign that marked our presence in a photograph from that distant morning. POINT SUBLIME ELEV 7464. Three of us face morning light; our shadows stretch toward the edge, oblique dark columns. Dad leans against the sign, his mouth caught in mid-sentence. Cissie stands next to him, her Uncle Chip. In front of them, in pressed pants and first-grade uniform blouse and sweater, a child looks down and away. She waits for the shutter to click.

Good morning, yesterday. Gazing into this image, I see us as my mother did—then beyond, toward the abyss. I know our future.

Now my father's age then, I am a witness from a later time checking the rearview mirror. Most of my life has taken place in the East for reasons that at moments of decision seemed right. It's impossible to step into that bright summer morning again, attentive to it, to parents alive, to an intact family drawn by hope and promise. Point Sublime remains. I still try to negotiate its terrain. ✦

About This Story

Of African American, Euro-American, and Native American heritage, Lauret Savoy explores the stories we tell of the American land's origins—and the stories we tell of ourselves *on* this land. Her book *Trace: Memory, History, Race, and the American Landscape,* winner of the 2016 American Book Award, explores how the country's still unfolding history and ideas of "race" have marked the land, society, and her through a mix of historical inquiry and personal reflections. In this modified excerpt from *Trace,* Lauret reminds us that everyone who visits the canyon brings their own histories, memories, circumstance, and perceptions through which they view it. Thanks to the creation of national parks, the Point Sublime that early explorers Clarence Dutton, García López de Cárdenas, or Thomas Moran saw is the same one that Lauret and family visit. Lauret shows us how different parties have stumbled upon "the most sublime and awe-inspiring spectacle in the world" over the course of its history, and how each party struggled to comprehend the grandeur of this place.

The God of Monsoon
& Her Clay Ship

LAURA VILLAREAL

Each year the God of Monsoon traveled
through Arizona's deserts on her clay ship

to deliver rain for the season.
She carefully maneuvered around mountains,

stopped occasionally to pick cholla cacti
and ocotillo for her beloved back home. She was happy

when she saw the usual desert creatures, but especially
pleased when the first rains coaxed vinegaroons

from their homes underground.
The troop of arachnids filed one by one,

then arranged their bodies into the word *Hello*,
like they did every year.

The God of Monsoon's winds pushed
its gray cloud sails and her ship dropped rain

bundles. Each one cracked,
their white light illuminating the sky before

the terracotta shatter of thunder.
She had done this since the earth's birth.

It was always the same.
Sometimes she'd set the ship on course & close her eyes.

I'm just resting my eyes for a bit, she thought,
Everything will be okay. And often, it was

until one day she was thrown awake
as her ship crashed into a mountain. The ship's bow shattered

in millions of fragments. All the rain bundles plummeted
to earth. Thousands broke in unison.

The God of Monsoon watched
as the rain became a flood. What could she do

but call out to the Desert God for help,
her voice thick as mud.

All her desert friends were being swept away in the current.
Even the skyline looked like water now.

The Desert God gurgled a reply
from beneath the flood then land divided.

The God of Monsoon watched
as a canyon was born and rain water began to fill it

like a drain. Its walls became waterfalls
and the canyon grew deeper and wider as the days passed.

The Desert God tried to hold the wealth of water
but there seemed to always be more to contain.

Ridges, rims, plateaus, and peaks formed
as the water pushed and pulled against the earth.

It became the largest canyon either god had ever seen.
Soon the flood was contained, the land dried

revealing beautiful canyon walls colored
by pieces of her ship

which resembled an earthen sunset cradled
in the rock and earth. One long river flowed

through along with small creeks.
The flood swept seeds from all over that now grew

in and around the massive canyon.
The God of Monsoon watched seeds

flourish into transforming terrains.
She loved the smell of the ponderosa pine forest,

the lush meadow grasses, and the nostalgia of desert dust.
In the riparian lands, the original waters

of disaster continue to run. Each year
she gathers stream orchids and arrowweed.

When she returns, she measures awe
in the canyon's length and width. ✦

About This Story

As a writer whose work is informed by place, myth, and storytelling, Laura Villareal felt compelled to respond to our call for submissions. She shared a story about a family road trip to San Francisco, stopping along the way at the Grand Canyon as a young girl, where it was snowing—a novelty for her, as it didn't snow where she grew up in San Marcos, Texas. Awestruck by the enormity of the Grand Canyon, how it seemed endless and mythic, she was no longer paying attention and slipped on ice, nearly disappearing under the guardrail and into the depths of the canyon. Her father caught her arm just in time.

Laura was inspired to write this piece after changing directions on a recent road trip from Texas to California, stopping in Arizona for a night and awaking to the sound of heavy rain. She strove to capture the "aliveness" of this landscape and its weather, which she experienced as a kid and now as an adult, in the form of this origin poem.

We Are the Land,
We Are the Water

OPHELIA WATAHOMIGIE-CORLISS

And as the great condor spread open its wings to fly out from the bottom of the canyon, the peoples upon its back prepared for flight. The peoples who remained at the bottom of the canyon would eventually become known as the Havasu 'Baaja, the People of the Blue-Green Water, the Havasupai. Spiraling out, feathered wings glided across the canyon walls, and with every completed spiral upward a new layer of the Grand Canyon was created. Soaring into the sky, Condor began to slow, and the people understood the final time had come. No longer able to live as one tribe, the people began to gather in groups, conversing amongst themselves about which direction they would move into the future.

Condor landed in the north, Condor landed in the east, Condor landed in the south, and Condor landed in the west. These are the four sacred directions where our sister tribes left the safety of Condor's wings and climbed down to the earth. Condor landed in the four sacred directions, allowing the people to climb down, then Condor landed in between these directions, letting the remaining groups of people off, until no one was left. Our relations left the canyon in search of something that was calling them. They knew, one day soon, they would find the land that called for them to protect it, the land each tribe has now been protecting since time immemorial, up to this very day.

These directions created an ancient symbol for my people, representing how we all used to be one tribe and live as one people, and, when we couldn't, we traveled into the sacred directions, to lands we now steward. This symbol resembles the swastika shape the Nazi regime stole, but ours has no borders. It symbolizes the unity we all have, a unity that still exists in modern times: our unity. Its instructions are flawless, swift like the wind, tattooed on our skin, adorned on our baskets, or drawn into earth; it is a strong reminder. You can observe the arms moving to the right on the outside of a basket, while inside the basket, the arms move left. This symbol forever memorializes our ability to adapt, to survive, and to always remember where we came from, where our people emerged: the embryonic life-blood of the Grand Canyon.

My name is Ophelia Watahomigie-Corliss.

I am proud to say that I have an identity and I know exactly where my culture has lived. It is a gift to be a member of the Havasupai Tribe, the only tribe left living at the bottom of the Grand Canyon, the tribe whose lands of Flagstaff, Valle, Grand Canyon, Williams, Parks, Bellemont, Ashfork, Red Lake, and Seligman many other people now call home.

My connection to the Grand Canyon, as a Havasupai woman, is far beyond my visual comprehension of its vastness or my verbal appreciation for its beauty. It has existed in me since I was an embryo.

If you genuinely intend to comprehend what it means to protect a place, this place, the Grand Canyon, and the lands that surround it, your appreciation must go deeper than what your eyes and ears can perceive. Step into the history of its epochs, immerse yourself in its formation, and in the creation of its peoples.

At thirty-nine weeks pregnant it is as clear as day to me what it means to have an umbilical connection to the Grand Canyon. From the Havasupai stronghold, Supai Camp, inside Grand Canyon National Park, where Havasupai people living in Ha'a Gyoh (also known as "Havasupai Garden") and other areas of the South Rim were forcibly relocated, to Supai Village located on the Havasupai Reservation, which has survived colonialism, genocide, and never been eradicated, to Red Butte on sacred land south of the park's southern entrance, our cultural ties here are unbreakable.

We are the land, we are the water.

We are the Havsuw 'Baaja, the People of the Blue-Green Water. We are the land; we are the Grand Canyon. Items we use in the blessings for our newborn children are quite literally earth and water. From birth, we are connected to the Grand Canyon by the water that created Supai life, and by the earth of the red rocks of this land, which our hearts are buried beneath. These practices help ensure we are meeting the expectations to protect the land like our contract with the creator requests of us.

We are guided to protect the land through the blessings of water, earth, and corn; the land will protect us in the same way we are to protect the land. Our lives are imbued in the Grand Canyon through millennia because of our culture; we are of the land and therefore we are the land.

As the need to adapt to the modern world continues, so does the trust that we have the ability to maintain the lands where we live and raise our families. This land holds our entire lives as we have been building them throughout time, from the ancestors who have allowed all of our bloodlines to survive and live life at this very moment. We too are trying to sustain our current lives, and the future lives of our children and relatives, but how do we do this? Where do we look?

The answer is simple: to our Indigenous communities. When you visit the Grand Canyon National Park, remember the Havasupai greeted the railway when they arrived on our land in 1901, Teddy Roosevelt declared it a national monument in 1908, and President Woodrow Wilson signed the bill that declared it a national park in 1919. All the lands you are exploring have never been unused wilderness; they have all belonged to and been taken care of by the Indigenous communities that still exist today. From the time Condor allowed the tribes to travel to the lands they now protect, we must now work together to protect the lands we all travel distances to enjoy with respect. ✦

About This Story

On May 18, 1971, park officials, environmentalists, and Native activists gathered to review the Grand Canyon National Park Master Plan. Near the end of the meeting, Havasupai Tribal Chairman Lee Marshall rose to speak. "I hear all you people talking about the Grand Canyon," he said. "Well, you're looking at it. I am the Grand Canyon!"

As a member of the Havasupai Tribe and a former Council member, Ophelia Watahomigie-Corliss is a torchbearer of Lee Marshall's legacy. It was in part her advocacy that renamed Indian Garden to Havasupai Garden in 2021. She continues to speak out against uranium mining, which affects the water sources for Grand Canyon residents, with renewed urgency after the recent birth of her daughter.

In this essay, you may notice Ophelia uses both *Havasu 'Baaja* and *Havsuw 'Baaja*. She notes that both are correct in her language. One is the English-to-Havasupai translation, and the other is a Supai-to-English translation. Ophelia never passes up an opportunity to preserve the legacies and educate future allies of the Havasupai Tribe.

At the Intersection

THEA GAVIN

Thunder River and Deer Spring, Grand Canyon National Park

"Springs exist at the intersection of geological, hydrological, and biological processes: they are breeding grounds for change."
—*ARIDLAND SPRINGS IN NORTH AMERICA*

Following old rock
and hydrologists, you hike
for days to sit in the mist
of Thunder River,
born of quiet
Kaibab Plateau snowmelt
gathered into caverns
where it waits
to emerge in a roar
from the blind face
of Muav Limestone.

Stonefly, treesnail, monkeyflower,
orchid, cottonwood co-create
an alternate desert reality
that you hike away from full
of questions.

Next you trek boulderfield
miles down the Colorado,
tiptoe past the sacred
slot canyon to where Deer Spring's
origin story unfolds.
Here are stone thrones.
Here you perch and survey
relict biota: the brilliant
maidenhair hanging gardens
just steps away from
sunscorch, cacti,
agave of the ancients.

Their terraces serve as warning
that life in parched places
will remain only as long
as there is something to seep,
gather, make its way to the light
at the intersection
of water and wonder,
where you drink
straight from stone. ✦

Nearly Impossible?

THEA GAVIN

North Kaibab Trail, Grand Canyon National Park

"Hiking the entire North Kaibab Trail in a single day is not recommended, particularly in summer, as it is nearly impossible to avoid hiking in the heat of the day."

—NATIONAL PARK SERVICE

A trail that winds downhill for fourteen miles.
A day that starts inside a puffy gray
jacket. A stroll that leads you innocent
down, down through mile-deep sediments. You smile

until the canyon shadows disappear.
Mid-afternoon: the sun-stoked igneous
re-ignites enough to burn your hand when
you wobble, when the trail drops off, when the

furious cicadas outshriek
Bright Angel Creek, "Furious Cicadas"
reminding you of a middle-school game:
"That would be a great name for a rock band."

An awkward stranger in your mouth, your tongue
wants nothing more to do with lukewarm sips
or slimy ooze of carbs. You would hunker
and shuck your pack if only there were shade,
if only you could make it go away:
tomorrow's re-wind: fourteen miles back up. ✦

About This Story

For most visitors to the Grand Canyon, the view etched into their memory is from the South Rim, staring into an expanse so wide it has inspired awe for centuries, but Thea Gavin's poems take us to trails not everyone will experience. She is a trained barefoot runner, running without footwear, which allows her to feel the dirt, be more connected to and aware of the landscape. "Although they contain thousands of nerve endings, the bottoms of our feet have been cut off from what used to be normal sensory input most of our lives," writes Thea on her blog, *Barefoot Wandering and Writing*. "My running shoe days are over. I step light and soft, ready to shift my weight, reveling in the peace of no-scuff and thud. Dust? Powdery heaven. Gravel? A chance to really relax and realize how capable my feet are. Mud? By far the best."

That perspective permeates Thea's writing. Walking for miles, for days at a time, she gives us a peek into the sounds and the sensations of these (nearly) impossible trails and shows us the contradictions that make the Grand Canyon unique.

Canyon Dreams

DEBORAH JACKSON TAFFA

As we jumped on the freeway to leave the suburban sprawl of Phoenix, I felt a pang of guilt. I was leaving my mother at Chandler Regional Hospital still in recovery and heading north to Sedona and the Grand Canyon rather than southwest toward my homeland along the Colorado River. I was born and raised in part on the Yuma Reservation, and most of my relatives are still located there. I looked out the window as we climbed away from the valley's buzz, telling myself my heart was in the right place. This trip was a return to our spiritual values, a walking prayer for my ancestors, elders, and mother.

My bloodlines are more than half Native American, but thanks to the Indian boarding school era, my elders all came from different tribes. My grandfather was born for the Quechan (Yuma) Nation in southeastern California, and it is his traditions I write about here. We were delta dwellers, fish eaters, and bean growers living along the once-mighty "American Nile." We thrived in an arid desert made fertile by the river's rising. Every spring it busted its banks, and our people planted seeds when the waters receded.

We are a people of dreamers. Our way is the *icama*. Our way is a nonordinary sleep. Our elders teach us that our experience in the world manifests itself in two different dimensions. Daytime experiences offer material gain; the dream world, spiritual. Nature writer Ellen Meloy writes about us as she hikes the canyons of our homeland: "You are sleepers so laden with dreams that all during the day you carry them into waking thick as stones."

My ancestors hovered over the earth in their dream bodies, bringing designs from their sleep into their working day. They crafted routes followed by gods in the time of creation. Our trails are thousands of years old. We walk across a windblown desert, legs pockmarked by dust devils. Our people were whirled into existence from water and the underworld. Into the sandstone we roam, travelers, traders, long-distance trekkers, a people who find their sacred spaces with dreams and song.

I want to hike these tangled paths until I give my fears the slip. I want to exit the rock labyrinth with my peace of mind restored. I want to shake the anxiety of my mother's impending death. Driving between Arcosanti and Camp Verde in the Tonto National Forest, my hospital headache starts to fade. I can't wait to tighten my boots and hit the trail.

We stopped at the Red Rock ranger center to purchase our weekly pass. I didn't think twice about the conservation tool's expense: the sandstone hoodoos—the spires, pinnacles, and cap rocks—are hard to protect. We found the parking lot packed with RVs, a gang of white-haired retirees milling around the information booth inside. The National Park System's centennial celebration had just ended, and I realized I was the only person of color in the place.

Only 23 percent of national park visitors are people of color. The statistics are not surprising given the history of lynching and Native American removal campaigns. We have been squeezed to the edges of our ancestral homelands. To this day, the animalization of our people as a tool for conquest makes many of us loath to share our beliefs about nature. Our earth traditions can be twisted into a stereotype, or appropriated and mangled by New Agers. A lack of privacy can feel belittling, and therefore many of us keep quiet and watch.

My father grew up in the era when mountain resorts, alpine lakes, and soft sand beaches were labeled with signs that read "Whites Only." He recounted a story about a powwow he went to with his family in the early 1950s. The Yuma Tribal Council rented an old school bus to take dancers and Yuma Marching Band members up north for the festivities, but as they passed through Sedona and arrived at Oak Creek Canyon they were pulled over and harassed by the local sheriff and his deputies. "We don't like Indians in these parts," they were told. The bus was turned inside out, their regalia thrown on the side of the road. Dad said they were held up for hours before the White bus driver finally managed to convince the sheriff it was okay to let them go. It was okay to let them go on the sacred land of their ancestors, where the water ran clean and the cottonwood kept watch. It was okay to let them go as long as the kids who were hiding and shaking under the bus seats understood that they didn't belong.

Not me, I thought as I read the statistics. I had spent my adolescence in the 1980s sharing the trail with White hikers and rock climbers all over the Southwest. I had never begrudged anyone's space on the trail. I felt sad that my ancestors had been driven off these lands, but I didn't want to be bitter. I reminded myself that the land was still there and I was still on it. Nothing was going to get between me and my sacred places, except the cost it took to get here once I moved away.

More than twenty years had passed since I last lived in the Southwest, and I was shocked by how much Sedona had changed. The extra fee at the toll booths at the start of the best trails. The price of local real estate and the commercialization of the canyon via vortex seekers, massage therapy businesses, and all-terrain vehicles. The absurdity of the vision-quest workshops and sweat-lodge gurus charging tourists a mint. I realized the desert had been discovered, and the trails I once loved as a child were now crowded and costly.

"It feels like Disneyland," I told my husband. My ancestors had wandered through the land's beauty freely for centuries—it was their place to pray—but now it felt overrun, and I realized the disparities in access were not only racial but economic. My poorest cousins in Yuma would never be able to afford this place. But the prohibitive costs in Sedona transcended culture and race.

I resented the power of money to buy our national treasures and wanted to get out of Sedona. My husband and I mulled our remaining days. "Why don't we hike down into the Grand Canyon early?" I asked. We both knew it was a long shot. Havasu and Beaver Falls have become famous for their aquamarine waters. The waterfalls sit on the Havasupai Reservation, and the tribe only issues three hundred permits a day. Phone lines open on the first of February, and spots for the entire season are filled within hours. On a whim, I decided to call them. I said nothing about being a Colorado River tribal member until after they praised my impeccable timing. I'd called on the heels of a cancellation. I couldn't help but feel like my ancestors were watching out for me.

The following day, we wended our way down the slot canyons and cottonwood-lined washes to get to their tribal land. And as we hiked, I felt reassured that some things hadn't changed: the infinity pools at the top of mesas after an October rain, the sponginess of the wet soil under my boots, the way the ravens' wings made a scratching sound as they flew above me in the canyon.

When we arrived at the Havasupai office, we bought supplies at their store and prepared to start our descent into the national park and canyon. We went to their office to pay for our pass, and once I told them I was an enrolled Quechan (Yuma) member, they refused to accept any payment for the nights we would stay on their land. "This is what Natives need," I said as we hiked, a bit embarrassed to admit I wanted preferential treatment for my people.

But I do. Deeply discounted "senior passes" are offered to America's retired citizens when they visit the great outdoors. Since the inception of national parks, pristine places have been set aside for wealthy individuals who need time off to relax. The concept of vacation—the eagerness to partake in the "wild" and feel a bit of nostalgia for yesteryear—is a privilege and a horror for the elitism at its center. My ancestors saw "wilderness" not as a place to retreat, but as part and parcel of themselves.

Perhaps even more than preferential treatment, I want our relationship to and philosophies about the earth to be recognized, taken seriously, and recorded. I want to use my voice to speak up rather than remaining quiet, but it's harder to say than to do. The earth is our co-creator and she longs for survival. Every violent thing that we do to her gets returned. Every environmentalist who cries, "Save the Earth," is pleading to stay alive herself. We won't kill the planet because she'll buck. If we don't stop kicking and spurring, she'll throw us off and go on galloping herself.

"I don't understand the lack of attention," I told my husband as we hiked from our base camp at Mooney Falls down to Beaver Falls the day after we arrived. Following our first night in the canyon, we decided to leave our tent up and head down the trail another ten miles. We descended a vertical ladder made of chains, a sheer cliff face that had us dangling on the rungs, then followed the creek along a well-trod path.

I noticed the lack of attention to our surroundings when we passed a crowd of hikers who were so busy talking about the photo they were trying to get right that they didn't even see a herd of bighorn sheep below us in a valley. I was torn between yelling for them to look and not wanting to scare the animals away. Afraid to sound scolding, I remained quiet, and the bighorn sheep disappeared around a bend. I felt sorry that the group missed them.

I noted the hubris when a young couple ran by us around mile six, moving as fast as they could. Neither of them were wearing shoes. They were dusty but happy. He was exceedingly tall and she was short, and he bragged about how well she kept up when they passed. He reminded me of the red-bearded Tormund Giantsbane of the Free Folk who live north of the wall in *Game of Thrones*, and I wanted to tell them to be careful. I wanted to say they should put on their boots, which I imagine they had in their packs. But my voice wasn't clear to speak up, and after a moment exchanging bright smiles, they disappeared around the corner while I felt regret.

I don't know how I knew something bad was going to happen, but I couldn't stop thinking about rattlesnakes and fallen logs. It wasn't until we arrived at Beaver Falls and took a plunge in the freezing aquamarine pool that we heard a commotion. A group at the far edge of the water was agitated, and they were looking for a satellite phone or a doctor. They needed warm clothes before a lady went into shock.

I knew immediately who it was and so did my husband. I felt guilty and embarrassed to wander over and hear the story. Why hadn't I said something? Here were two urbanites in a foreign land, a land I knew well. I'd seen them barreling toward disaster, and I hadn't spoken up. They had passed Beaver Falls, perhaps hoping to arrive at the Colorado River and make it back in one day. They had been moving fast, and the woman landed with a foot between two fallen branches stretched across the trail. She fell and broke her ankle. It was a compound fracture, and the bone was exposed.

My husband came back for the sweater in our pack. She was going into shock and needed to stay warm. The people across the way were running up the trail to see, to gather around and watch as a doctor who happened to be in the canyon tried to stabilize her in her pain. My husband wanted to run his sweater up, but I told him to give it to someone else who was already going. She didn't need more gawkers.

I felt embarrassed for her and disappointed in myself. We hiked the long trek back to base camp wondering and worrying about whether she'd be okay. It was nearly dark by the time we arrived at the waterfall near the vertical ladder made of iron. We stood close to it, feeling the spray, and as we dried our feet to put our boots back on, a helicopter appeared in the sky.

"Someone must have run back to tell the tribe," my husband said, as we watched it hover for a moment before listing forward to fly down the canyon.

"They must have carried her to a clearing where it can land," I added, saying a silent prayer that she would be okay.

When we returned to Phoenix after our trip to the Grand Canyon, I stood by my mother's bed and thought of all that my ancestors gave to this country to make it what it is today. I thought of the blessing I received as I swam in Beaver Falls at the Havasupai Campground. I thought of the barefoot runner, likely recovering in a hospital bed herself.

Nature's grandeur is not neutral, I thought. The earth is not for meekness or folly. If I've been taught one thing by my elders, it's that respect is always necessary, because even as the planet is neutral, she is dangerous. My parents and grandparents were made sick by the loss of their land, by the development of the land, by the nuclear testing done on the land. The more we meddle with her, the more she'll meddle with us. ✦

About This Story

A citizen of the Quechan (Yuma) Nation and Laguna Pueblo, Deborah Taffa is the director of the MFA in creative writing at IAIA (Institute of American Indian Arts) in Santa Fe, New Mexico. Her memoir, *Whiskey Tender*, is published by HarperCollins. In this essay, Deborah unpacks a few of the reasons why people of color so often face a barrier to the wilderness: You carry the baggage of your ancestors being driven off these lands, and just one generation before, you might have made a wrong turn into a "Whites Only" sign. And even though the concept of vacation is out of reach, you visit the wilderness because it is a part of you.

Deborah has experienced it all firsthand—the stereotypes, the economic realities, but also the deeper sense of meaning and time, and the moments of connection to others in the struggle. It is this knowledge that can feel like a weight, that prevents us from having the same hubris as others who adventure in the outdoors. But it is this knowledge that also bestows us the wisdom that respect is always necessary when it comes to Nature.

Rescue Below the Rim

≀ MARY EMERICK

When I arrive at the Grand Canyon helibase, the air is still deliciously cool. It is easy to believe that today will not be like yesterday. Today I won't end up a bystander to someone's tragedy. The rescue helicopter will stay at the base instead of dipping below the Abyss to hover along the Tonto plateau, searching for hikers in distress. Nobody will fall out of a raft into the Colorado River. Someone won't die today. I want to believe this even though none of the days preceding this one have borne this out to be true.

It is June, when nobody should hike below the rim, but everyone does.

The four of us on the helicopter crew scatter to do the busywork that keeps us occupied until the paramedics arrive: inventorying supplies, pulling weeds, eyeing the clock. Before noon, even here on the South Rim at seven thousand feet, the temperature ticks toward eighty. Below us in the canyon's yawning mouth, it is much hotter, spiraling over one hundred degrees. It won't be long, I think, and it isn't. I hear our foreman, Mike, fielding a radio call: female hiker, unresponsive, likely hyponatremia, Bright Angel Trail below Three Mile Resthouse. Within five minutes the medics show up, two unsmiling men in flight suits. They spare no greetings; there isn't time for that. Besides, we will see them half a dozen times before our shift ends.

They tell us what they need and I gather the equipment. What they will find is unknown. The rescue information is sometimes passed on by other hikers, second- and thirdhand, so we have to guess. The helicopter is configured according to each mission. If we need a stretcher, the seats are taken out; if the doors need to be off for a short haul, we remove them. I have practiced this in drills, and I know what to do. Everything is preweighed, so I scribble each item down on the pad I carry and add the weights up to ensure we are all right to lift off. I double-check my math; a mistake, loading the helicopter too heavy, could be disaster. The mood crackles through the base, a controlled urgency. Minutes could mean the difference between life and death. I feel the familiar knot of worry in my stomach: Have I missed something? Helicopters have crashed before in the sullen heat of the canyon.

Before I came to the Grand Canyon, I believed everyone could be rescued. I believed this despite evidence to the contrary. In Idaho, I helped search for a little girl who vanished as she walked home on a dark small-town night. She was never found. But most of the rescue missions I had been on resulted in success: a horseback rider with a broken pelvis carried out on a stretcher, hikers bandaged up and sent on their way. As a wilderness ranger, I carry lifesaving equipment in my backpack. I want to believe in rescue. The canyon is teaching me otherwise.

It is my turn to fly so I vault into the right front seat beside Eddie, the pilot, and we lift off from the cracked concrete as I settle the flight helmet on my head. I study the coordinates while Eddie relays our position to dispatch. The rest of the crew watches until we clear the base, then go back to their chores. They know they will be next.

Imagine this: You sit sweating in a sticky flight suit, zipped up to the throat, looking through the bubble of the helicopter's windshield. The thump of the main rotor mirrors your heartbeat. A mix of adrenaline and fear rockets through your veins. Below your feet, separated only by fragile layers of composite aluminum and stainless steel, is the wide expanse of the canyon, terraces and plateaus like giant steps down to the serpentine blue of the Colorado River. This is as close to flying as you will ever get, and as far from safety as you will ever know.

When hikers descend into the Grand Canyon in summer, they are walking into the mouth of the dragon. The canyon breathes like a pair of lungs, exhaling superheated air. The deeper a person drops toward the river, the hotter it gets. In winter, when the South Rim is buffeted by winter storms, it is possible to sit on the boater's beach near Phantom Ranch in shorts. The canyon feels gentle then, friendly even. Not so in summer.

We pass through the layers of time, the remnants of an ancient sea. I register each by its color: Coconino sandstone, a chalky, crumbly white; Redwall limestone the color of its name, a deep blush. The Grand Canyon is a multilayer cake, each section a story. Some days, on rescue missions, we descend through them all.

Eddie hovers the helicopter over the Bright Angel trail. I scan the horizon for threats: other aircraft, even hikers wanting to be helpful but ending up in the way. We are just above Indian Garden, above the cottonwoods, before the trail steepens for the climb home. I lean out from my side, watching as we inch toward the ground. My job is to decide if it is okay to set down the skids. A mistake could be costly: damage to the helicopter or even a flip. "Looks fine," I say into my mike, and he lowers the helicopter all the way down. At his nod, the paramedics and I spring from the ship, heads low to avoid the spinning rotor. We will be loading hot today, the helicopter still running, in a desperate bid to save a life.

A woman is lying on the ground, her boots dusted with red limestone. She is still, not moving. Her pack is abandoned by the side of the trail. A day hiker. I avert my eyes. It is too easy to be drawn in, and I have already learned that I can't be invested in the outcome. I have to shove all of my emotions down deep, where they can't prevent me from doing my job. I need to let the paramedics work while I deal with the husband. He is distraught; they always are.

"Is she going to be all right? We were just hiking, she was fine," he says, climbing into the extra flight suit I brought along and not protesting. The partners of the ones we rescue are combative sometimes, but he seems dazed and compliant. I have no answers as I lead him to the helicopter and the patient is loaded in on the backboard. He is lucky, though he wouldn't believe it right now. Sometimes we don't have room for the rest of the party and they have to hike up, all the way alone, past the resthouses and the happy people coming down. Nobody can hike fast enough to escape their thoughts.

Another name for hyponatremia is water intoxication, as if you are drunk on water. And you are, your body bursting with water but dry of electrolytes. People at this stage act intoxicated, wobbling and stumbling. They laugh. They don't realize the danger. It can progress quickly, as it has with this woman. The stage past intubation, a tube shoved down her throat to help her breathe, can be coma and death.

We lift off quickly. Eddie's face is inscrutable. He has been at this for a long time, and nothing rattles him. He points out the remains of a car embedded in the top layer, Kaibab limestone. An accident? Purposeful? I never learn. But there it is again: someone who could not be rescued.

The husband and I are left unceremoniously at the helibase. He will have to drive to Flagstaff while the helicopter takes his wife to the hospital there. He lingers for a moment, confusion written over his face. How could a simple day hike have turned into someone fighting for her life?

I want to tell him that I don't understand it either, that before I came here, I thought of wilderness differently. Always working in alpine environments, I know about lightning and bears and creeks running high with snowmelt. If you're prepared with the right tools, you can usually save yourself from a tragic fate. But this place, stark and beautiful and indifferent, draws people in. The corridor trails lure them to go just a little bit farther. I have seen these people, in flip-flops and carrying a half liter of water. Before they know it, they are two thousand feet below the rim and have to climb back out.

I think uneasily that this man probably shouldn't be driving the eighty high-desert miles to Flagstaff by himself, but none of us can leave the base. More rescues are being called in and I see one of the crew grabbing a flight helmet. The man leaves, finally. I have never learned his name. I will never know if she lives or dies, though the scale is not tipped toward survival. The helibase is set far back enough from the tourist routes along the rim that there may as well not even be a canyon. But I know better. I can feel its presence. In my mind I can see the trails, red dust rising as I hike, a slender ribbon of river seen far above, a seduction. Soon there will be another call, someone wavering between life and death.

Or it could go this way, and it has: someone fakes an injury to avoid hiking out, or has bitten off more hike than they can chew, and the rim, far above, feels too daunting to reach. When this happens, we hope the rangers have convinced the person to take a breather, wait it out, and gather courage. Flying in the canyon is tenuous at best, sandwiched between walls that narrow down dramatically, our shadow a small bubble on the sun-filtered canyon walls. I have been taught to evaluate the mission before we lift off. Is it worth risking the lives of the crew? We can't rescue everyone.

I am only here to fill in for two weeks before going back north to my regular wilderness job. The rest of the crew is here for the long haul, with three more scorching months to get through. They hunch on their heels passing the time. Malcolm, my favorite because he is soft-spoken and not as hardened as the others, retreats to smoke cigarettes in the narrow shade of the sloping roof. Some of the others play hacky sack. They talk about anything but what we are doing, wiping their minds blank between each mission. I have not yet learned how to do this. The faces of those we have saved, or not, linger.

The next day we respond to a river accident. A raft has wrapped around a rock in Hance Rapids, and we have to get the crew off the water. The rangers work quickly to pull short-haul net screamer suits on the passengers, and one ranger and one tourist fly entwined underneath the helicopter from raft to beach. I stand there to direct the passengers to a safe location. Every time someone is offloaded, the rotor wash creates a tornado of sand that settles deep into my skin and teeth. At night in my room, I scrub ineffectually at the dust left behind. It won't completely wash off. I think that the canyon is settling into my bones.

When it is time for me to leave this short-term assignment, the rest of the crew barely acknowledges my departure. They look up briefly from their chores, but I know that it isn't personal. Malcolm is already gone; he has decided to leave the crew. The constant edge he has to walk in order to do this job has burned him out. The others suit up. The helicopter is already firing up and they have work to do.

Years later I hike in the canyon solo. The heat presses down, an invisible hand, as I walk across Furnace Flats to Tanner Beach. The sun is a hostile beam. It is high noon, and I am the only creature moving in this harsh place.

I am carrying four liters, way too much water for this nine-mile hike, and I think about water intoxication as I pause to drink. I am thirsty but not hungry, the classic setup for hyponatremia. Pulling out my food bag, I force down some trail mix, the salt from peanuts sharp on my tongue. When I reach the Colorado, I fling myself into water so cold it makes me breathless. It is only April and nearly one hundred degrees. Later that year a woman dies on the Tonto plateau; a man ascending the South Kaibab Trail also succumbs to the heat. In the years since I worked on the rescue crew, nothing has changed.

The next day I hike on the exposed, crumbling edges of the Beamer Trail, five hundred feet above the river. There is no room for error here, and I haven't seen anyone since I left Tanner Beach. But the farther I hike, the more the canyon opens its arms into a welcoming embrace. I am a feral creature, sleeping in the sand, hair tangled, river water drying on my skin. I learn why people attempt to know the canyon. It is worth the risk.

Climbing out the Tanner Trail four days later, I come upon several hikers who underestimated the descent. They sit along the trail like wilted flowers. "How much farther?" they ask. They point at the watchtower, visible for miles. "We must be halfway," they say, when they aren't. Some are forced to bivouac partway down, the river in view but unreachable.

I can't do much except encourage them. They are too far down the trail to get back out before nightfall. There is scarce shade. Rest, I say, eat something. You are almost there.

I hope they make it. I know now that everyone cannot be rescued. We all do what we can. ✦

About This Story

Mary Emerick has spent most of her life traveling and moving back and forth across the country working for the National Park Service and the Forest Service—fighting wildfires, giving cave tours, planting trees, conducting wilderness patrols, and leading kayak ranger programs. In 2000, she went to Grand Canyon National Park to help rescue personnel who were short-handed during a particularly dangerous June.

As she describes it, "I went thinking I was going to fight fires, the only reason, I thought, for existence; I was in love with firefighting and the person I was on the fire line. Instead, I picked up the dead and dying from the canyon's blazing interior—the foolish, the unprepared, and the plain unlucky. During that time, I came face-to-face with mortality and risk in a way I had never experienced before. Wilderness, I had always known, was indifferent, but here, it was also unforgiving. At a time when I was trying to figure out my life, single and independent, it showed me the value of having someone to pick you up and, perhaps, save your life."

Grand Canyon has the most search and rescue operations of any national park, with a reported 785 incidents between 2018 and 2020. Many of these—most commonly falls, heat stroke, and dehydration—emphasize the importance of being prepared for the elements, and staying humble in the canyon.

Woven Canyon

MELISA JANE BOHLMAN

The inception
of the canyon began with a drop;
and carving through the rocks, it grew into a river.
It fills up again from the clouds that hang low,
from trickles of snowmelt,
birthing the life source that
cleanses earth

. . . dripping . . .

drip . . . drop!

to greet the seeping soil
and join the blue ribbons and braids
of the Grand Canyon.
The Colorado River is acknowledged by
powerful Indigenous voices as a healing body of water.

Native fish are the Hualapai ancestors.
The Supai are the people of the blue-green waters.
The Navajo deities live on the confluence
of the big Colorado (him) and little Colorado (her) rivers.

A rainbow that reveals itself over the canyon latches its colorful cord from one side to another, like a horseshoe. The vibrant hues of minerals that stain these rocks will shift below it.

The pigments of the rocks, on the palette of the river, with the paintbrush by the wind, whose intentional strokes carve out the depths and dimensions of the Grand Canyon.

The sun pierces through clouds casting spotlights on pieces of the canyon's layers, bringing your attention to new formations every hour. Do not underestimate those powerful rays on a strong summer day in the curves of this land.

The moon and the stars greet the canyon each evening twinkling and sparkling above and illuminating elegance below. This map can be read so clearly here in these skies. There is a quiet intimacy of the moon's light gently tucking away and caressing some of this earth into darkness and leaving only slivers of it visible for curious minds.

Hopi tongues call this place "Öngtupqa"
(Salt Canyon). This landscape is a
monument to their legacy, teeming
with life and culture and spirits.

An amphitheater of endless mountains,
travelling up terraces and down slopes.
These rocks are a dimensional quilt, complete
with pockets of shadows and patches of light.

Find a rock to sit on or next to.
Feel for areas of its warmth and coolness.
What are some textures you observe?
Who is sharing space with the rock?

The Navajo see the canyon
as a place of resilience and
survival, as a spiritual refuge
and a physical safe haven.

The horizon on the canyon is definite and striking:
a solid ceiling of boulders and rock with agave
and cactus sneakily nestled in her crevices. A softness of
pine vegetation adorning the canyon breaks up the harshness.

Take your time to admire the landscape
in every cardinal direction.
Pause at each point and take in what fills your view.
What is closest to you? What is farthest away?

The Hualapai sustain life in the
high, cool plateaus in pine
forests, and the lower banks of
the Colorado River—their backbone.

Peering into the exposed depths of
the canyon is witnessing geologic scale
and time. The sculpting of cliffs, pyramids,
and layers is Earth's art of land formation.

Entrances and exits are in our world
and in our minds. How do you greet a new
nature space that you are about to enter?
How do you show your appreciation when you leave?

The Zuni, true artists, leave petroglyphs behind;
etched and imprinted in the canyon, marking

their long history of transitions, movements, and migrations.

So much of what was experienced in the Grand Canyon
by their Native stewards is written in stone walls,
sung in prayers, spoken in different orations, spun
into textiles and painted in ceramics.

Reflect on a pleasurable encounter you've had with nature.
How do you celebrate its beauty? How can you help
take care of it for the next 7 generations to enjoy it too?

The song of the Grand Canyon
is rumbles of thunder in the
distance; mules trotting through
staircases of rocks; gentle leaves
and firs tumbling softly to earth;
the drafts and gusts
of the whistling air; tall trees sighing;

brave birds soaring;
busy bugs crawling;
the symphony of blooming flowers and
their melodic petals of pinks,
yellows, purples and whites.

These boulders will echo louder than the sky, the water, or your mind.

Echoes of rockfall promise
eternal metamorphosis
of the canyon's exposed surfaces.
Each rock line representing a
signature, counting the beats of
geologic time and following the
rhythm and ancestral beats of the Indigenous.

Be sure to listen closely and carefully
to her, the warrior native Grand Canyon.
Study carefully her library of life,
and of how she was taken care of.
Cross her slowly, with a gentle pace.
Her towering sandstone scars remind
her human guests of their infinitesimal presence here.

The more we learn, the deeper the canyon gets.

Let's protect her beauty, her culture, and her peoples together. ✦

About This Story

To write this story, Melisa Jane Bohlman received one of six travel stipends awarded through our call for submissions. She is an educator that spent much of the COVID-19 pandemic working with youth—who were at the whim of unpredictable lockdowns and restrictions all while navigating becoming an adult. Currently, she teaches with the Udall Foundation's Parks in Focus program, bringing youth outside and connecting to nature through photography, and is also an outreach presenter for elementary, middle, and high school youth on earth science, energy, and climate change with Environmental Education Exchange. In her own upbringing as a mixed-raced Latinx kid, she grappled with her identity through her "mother's colonized history with my father's colonizing history, leaving me in a state of perpetual confusion and a stacked cultural palette."

It's this perspective that immediately drew her toward the tapestry of stories and cultures represented in *The Voices of the Grand Canyon*, a story map created by the Grand Canyon Trust that "highlights the deep and long-lasting relationships of this vast land from members of the Hopi, the Diné, the Havasupai, the Hualapai, and the Zuni." As she exclaimed to us, "There's a unique Indigenous community around the canyon. The Grand Canyon is nature, in and of itself a beauty beyond words, but the ties and braiding of Indigenous People in that place . . . I can't see one without the other." As an educator, Melisa felt compelled to give special recognition to this and draw awareness to Indigenous Peoples of the Grand Canyon in her piece.

After receiving the travel stipend to create this piece and being forced to cancel a summer visit due to fires in the park, Melisa was finally able to visit in September 2021, staying a full week and visiting both the north and south rims of the canyon for inspiration. She describes herself feeling speechless for most of her time there, and even witnessing "self-actualizing squirrels," who were "also staring out at the view, staring out with their mouths agape."

Everything Is Stardust

NASEEM RAKHA

It's a weekday, I think. It's a weekday in December, and I am deep in the Grand Canyon, just thirty feet above the Colorado River. Not far above me is a twisted outcrop of columnar basalt. The hardened lava protrudes right and left, up and down. Some of its columns are as gnarled as tree roots, some shoot outward—spines on a sea urchin, rays of the sun, ion trails cast by dying stars.

I've been in the Canyon for nineteen days now. I began my river journey at Lee's Ferry 16 miles downriver from Glen Canyon Dam, floated under Navajo Bridges, through Marble Canyon, past Redwall Cavern, the Bridge of Sighs, Nankoweap, the Little Colorado, Horn Creek Rapid, Crystal, Kanab. I have eleven more days left in this rocky cleft, eleven more nights to sleep under a sky wrapped by the Milky Way's diaphanous scarf, eleven more opportunities to absorb all I can from this primitive, bare-knuckled world and all it holds.

The desert is my muse, the place I come to learn what lies beneath my skin. Pavement people, deciduous dwellers, cultivators of copious gardens, they do not understand my fascination with the desert. High or low. Cold or hot, its tell-tale surface is poetry to me. Its ambient light a kind of god. *It's pretty,* these city dwellers say. *It's vast and certainly unusual and the sky, yeah, those stars—amazing. But, don't you miss the green?* There's green in the desert, I tell them. *But what about rain? Don't you miss the rain?* There's rain. *Yes, but it's so, well—barren. There's nothing but rock and sand and scorpions and don't even get me started on the snakes . . .* That's when I smile. It's not for everyone, I say.

There are fifteen of us on this river trip. All of us strangers to one another before we met three weeks ago in Flagstaff during a blizzard. The permit holder had cobbled our group together, struggling to find people willing or able to spend a winter month slicing through icy rapids. Now we fifteen are river-mates, working as one to move ourselves, a couple tons of food and gear, four rafts, two dories, and two kayaks down 289 miles of winter river. Short days, long nights, ice-covered dawns—we are a tribe isolated by mile-high walls that keep the chaos and distractions of the rim-world at bay.

There are no cell signals deep in the Canyon, no interpretive waysides, no Netflix or radios. The last time we saw anyone from outside our tribe was ten days ago, on the shore of Unkar's sandy delta, where the Ancient Ones once carved out terraces to grow corn and beans. On that day, a haboob—a desert windstorm—had hit, and the people we spotted were huddled in the tamarisk and mesquite risking the prick of thorns in order to shelter themselves from the assault of wind-born debris: sand, and sticks, even water slashing up from the river and carried by the gale. Our group was on the river, one person at each oar, fighting our way down Unkar Rapid as the wind tried to push us back up. Since that day, we haven't seen anyone but ourselves, so it's easy to imagine we're the only people left on the planet, but for the slash of contrails against the lazurite sky, and, of course, the daily river surges sprung from the turbines at Glen Canyon Dam—tides determined not by nature but by the power demands of far-flung cities.

Still, I've found no better place than the Grand Canyon to separate myself from the friction of the world. The daily rub of sights and sounds that constantly erode. The news and neighbors and needs, always the needs, and the traffic and the crime and the bills and the ills, so many ills, and the Girl Scouts with their cookies, and the Mormons with their missions, and the politicians with their smiles, and all the aisles of things and things and things that end up in land-fills or as plastic islands the size of small countries, floating in a foul-smelling sea. All of this rubbing at my psyche until a numbness sets in. And an apathy. And a kind of modern-age depression born from a sense of powerlessness. A weakness so overwhelming that when a personal crisis hits, it is hard to get up off the ground.

The invitation to join this winter trip came at the right time. My father had died. He died, and there was this hole, you see. A place where my father had been, and now he was gone and I had no idea how to deal with this loss, this hole, this sense of being plunged into a new and far lonelier world. I needed perspective. I needed silence. I needed time. I needed to be in the presence of something larger than my grief. So I accepted a trip to a place that promised to be cold, and dark, and raw—and very, very deep.

· ✦ ·

I pause in my hike to sit on a ledge above the Colorado. Beneath me, boulders are hammered by cascades of white water. The sound is open mouthed and large. I open my backpack, dig out a sandwich and water bottle. As I drink, I watch a raven circle then land on a nearby ledge. His eyes are on my sandwich. I smile. (Ravens are audacious robbers. I've had one break into my backpack, steal a piece of dried papaya, then fly over to me and gloat about it, the pilfered treat hanging from its beak like an orange cigar.) *I'm not sharing,* I shout over the roar of the river. I bite into my sandwich menacingly, and the bird puffs out his feathers and flies up and up the Canyon walls until he is too tiny for me to see.

Once, when I was about four years old, my father woke me at dawn. *Come with me,* he said. Our family lived in Chicago in an apartment with a view of the Loop to the north and Lake Michigan to the east, and as I followed my father into the living room I saw for the first time how the rising sun poured its color into the lake—rose and peach and orange and maroon. I pointed and my father nodded, then he led me out onto our small balcony, and even now I can feel the sensations of standing out there—the smell of the air, the coolness of the spring breeze against my thin pajamas. It felt like we, my father and I, were on the wing of a plane gliding through the pale morning light. But what I remember most about that morning, what has stuck and what I look forward to still, was the sound of birds—hundreds, perhaps thousands of them singing to the rising sun, as my father and I stood there hand in hand, listening.

I pull out my binoculars, scan the layer-cake surface of the canyon walls. It wasn't a huge leap for me, a child who habitually collected rocks, to one day become a geologist. My degree solidified my fascination with the earth's formations. Everything from the tiny creatures that make up the oolitic limestone that lined the shores near my alma mater in Illinois, to these walls now. In my view, nothing lessens the burden of loss more than having it weighed on the scale of geologic time. At Lee's Ferry, where I've begun all my Grand Canyon river trips, the surrounding rock is approximately two hundred million years old. Within a mile, the boater has floated fifty million years deeper into the fossil-rich Kaibab Limestone, created when the region was an inland sea. Eight-tenths of a mile further, and the Kaibab is out of reach as the river carves deeper and deeper into the Earth, through limestones and sandstones and shales and conglomerates: one thousand eight hundred million years, stacked like bricks.

How long would it take to count to a million?
Eleven days—no eating nor sleeping.
How long would it take to count to a billion?
Thirty years.
How long would it take to count out the years of my father's life?
Less than ninety seconds.

I finish my sandwich and pack away my water bottle, zip up my backpack. The basalt I am sitting amid is a relative newcomer in this place. It is part of the Uinkaret Lava Field, a series of more than two hundred volcanoes that reshaped this area between 3.6 million to one thousand years ago. These particular rocks are likely from Vulcan's Throne, a thousand-foot cinder cone which sits on the north rim of the Canyon, just east of where I am now. Vulcan's Throne is thought to have formed a mere 73,000 years ago—barely a baby's first breath—geologically speaking.

Still, I have to wonder what this place was like back then. How wide was the river? What grew here, what prowled, what grazed? What was the first sign that the dome growing on the edge of the north rim was about to release millions of metric tons of blood-red lava into a writhing river? Usually, pillars of columnar basalt either stand in formation like soldiers, or lie horizontally, as orderly as cordwood. Instead, these distorted stones shout pandemonium, clashing forces, disarray. This is lava that danced with water, curled into eddies, pooled in shoals, dammed the river, and was ultimately broken by the water's inexorable flow. The result is what I am standing next to now, the churning, chocolatey froth of Lava Falls. Its twenty-foot waves heave over sharp-toothed boulders, smashing into them with concussive force, while its icy claws slash at anyone foolish enough to try to make their way through.

Long before any Grand Canyon river trip begins, boaters anticipate the moment they will meet Lava Falls, the most dangerous rapid on the canyon. They study rafting books, watch videos, compare notes. Which is better, entering at high water or low? Taking the left run or the right? What about the lateral waves that wait at the bottom? How do you avoid the raft-eating holes?

Just yesterday, we rowed toward Lava Falls. A mile upriver, the water was calm. Silently, we drifted with dread anticipation. A half-mile further, the water was still calm. A canyon wren sang. A heron flew by. But then something subtle occurred. First, there was a shift in air pressure, a tightening around our eardrums. Next, came a subterranean hum which gained strength with each passing moment. By the time we stopped to scout the rapid, the sound of the still unseen falls had grown into a hungry growl. We hiked along the river's edge, climbed up a cliff, and then looked down. Beneath us was a maelstrom. A chaos. A cross between hell, and whatever lives right next to hell. From above, we could distinguish various routes, but all of them were tenuous, and none would be visible once we were back at river level looking out toward the water's horizon. A misjudged angle, an overcompensated drag on an oar, anything at all, and a raft, or dory, or kayak would be swallowed by the hungry water.

We trudged back to our boats silent with our thoughts and plans. We secured our gear, tightened our life vests, and then, one by one, we pushed out from the safety of the shore. Within moments the red silt current drew us toward the break line, the place where the river disappeared. And then we were off, sluicing down a mirrorlike tongue of water into the rust red world of Hades. The rapid sucked us down and tossed us into the air, grabbed at our oars, bludgeoned our boats, knocked us sideways and silly. Someone shouted "High side" as the boat leaned precariously on one edge, another shouted "Punch" as we curved our way up and fortunately over a frighteningly fulsome wave and then, quite suddenly it was over, and the unsatisfied river spat us out still upright. Another group of fortunate fools.

We honored our successful run through Lava Falls with a layover, unpacking the boats in the early afternoon with plans to stay on the beach not one, but two nights. So today, I have hiked back to the falls in hopes of seeing a different group take its turn. In the summer months, this would not be a long wait. Commercial trips embark from Lee's Ferry four or five times a day, many of them carrying three times the number of people as we have on our trip now. Those summer trips are floating parties with young, well-tanned and hardy boat people serving a well-heeled group of tourists as they scream through this Canyon. These groups never have the opportunity to do what I have done so many times already on this winter journey: just sit, just watch, just think, just feel. Just hike up a side canyon to see where it might go. Just watch a rapid, or a raven, or the light move over a stone.

My father visited the Grand Canyon twice in his life. The first time was in 1957, when he and some other students from Purdue University, all of them Indian immigrants, borrowed a car and drove from Indiana out west. The second time was in 2006 when my brother had driven him across the country to come live near me and my husband and our child in Oregon. My mother had died, and my father had been keeping vigil over her memory in their house in Illinois. He would not sleep in the bed they'd shared, could not listen to their classical music without crying. Every week, he would go to the cemetery and lay yellow roses on her grave. My father, whose faith was in curiosity and science and math, the mystery of the stars, the beauty of the human spirit, the songs of birds, went to the Canyon, looked into its ancient abyss, and concluded all things are temporary. A whisper in the wind. A negligible speck of sand.

I stare upriver, willing a flotilla of yellow rafts to appear. But none do, so I turn my attention to the contorted outcrop I'd seen earlier. It is a couple hundred feet above where I sit, so I strap on my pack and start to scramble up a scree slope to get a closer look. But scree is unfriendly terrain, and my footing is poor. I grab a nettle plant to stop a fall, feel its sting; I scrape against a fishhook barrel cactus, feel a spine embed in my thigh. I slip and slide and call myself stupid, but I climb on. Finally, I reach the outcrop and haul myself over the top.

Beside me on this ledge is a dead and desiccated barrel cactus. The living one—the one whose spine is still lodged in my leg—was strikingly beautiful, with four-inch-long yellow and magenta spines. But this one, this dead and desiccated one, also has a certain beauty. Its body is ashen and collapsed in on itself; its spines, no longer alive with color, stick out like rusted nails. In this brittle environment, where decay is slow, the cactus may have died a decade ago, maybe even more. I know from its size it lived at least ninety years, nine decades in a landscape that stills any imagination of time and space.

Three days before we reached Lava Falls, we had stopped at River Mile 136.9, where I climbed several hundred feet above Deer Creek Falls to a soft and sinuous side canyon cut into the 500 million year old Tapeats Sandstone. The chamber walls were tall and warped and layered like coils of hand-worked pottery. The creek, Deer Creek, was small and clear and melodic. It gathered in pools, then dropped. Gathered in pools, then dropped again. Every Grand Canyon river trip I've been on, I've taken time here. It is sacred to me, this cloister. An umbilical link from the Earth's very heart to the outside world. I climbed up, and I sat by myself, thinking of how my father would have loved this place and how he would have pressed me, his geologist daughter, to tell him about its origins. And together we would have talked about time and space and the infinite magnitude of the universe. And while I sat there, a water ouzel—a dull-gray robin-sized bird, John Muir's favorite—played in a pool, and did what it is most known for—sing and sing and sing. That's when I reached into my pocket and pulled out the pill bottle. I had been carrying it every day of the trip, waiting for the right time. And that was it. That moment, right then, with the careening sun slipping through the narrow gap between the canyon walls, lighting the water, the leaves of a lone cottonwood, the ouzel and its spray. That was the moment I opened the bottle, reached over the water, and sprinkled out its contents. Some of my father's ashes sank to the sand, some lapped onto the shore, and some, the lightest, most crystalline specks, swirled around like the numbers in a Fibonacci sequence, the whorl of a nautilus, a spiral galaxy—and then simply floated away.

I came to the Grand Canyon because I needed time, I needed quiet, and I needed the perspective that comes from desert walls. I needed the dry space where the roots of the earth remind me all things are temporary. Heartaches, heart attacks, politics, preachy puritans, guns, laws, dams, disease.

Canyons.

Rivers.

Stone.

Everything is stardust, my father once said as we looked at a night sky. Borrowed pieces of light, elemental and beautiful and bright. ✦

About This Story

While most visitors peer at the Grand Canyon from above, some choose to see it from *inside*. On the Colorado River, you don't see the horizon for days, and you rely on a highly skilled guide to navigate the treacherous rapids. Trips last three to eighteen days with a professional guide, or twelve to twenty-five days if nonguided (but only for individuals who have mastered navigating the rapids). Trip permits are awarded through a weighted lottery, instituted in 2006 when the demand grew so high the wait list was twenty-five years.

New river-runners learn that Mile 24 rapid is named "Georgie Rapid" in honor of Georgie White, founder of the first woman-owned commercial rafting company, Georgie's Royal River Rats, opened in 1953. Quoted as saying, "I fell in love with the river, married it, and I don't plan on divorce," Georgie spent her life leading people through the Grand Canyon until she was eighty years old. According to the National Park Service, she had a "carefree attitude and outrageous demeanor, often sporting leopard print and curse language, which made her well known throughout the country."

Naseem Rakha is a geologist, educator, speaker, author, and journalist and quite possibly one of the most well-suited people to help us make sense of the Grand Canyon, our planet, and our place in the universe. When we first read Naseem's piece about rafting the canyon, in early 2021, we were in awe of her ability to capture and put into perspective the span of geologic time and her own personal narrative with such beauty. The story took on new meaning after Ilyssa's father passed away, and just one month later, her aunt as well. After months avoiding it, knowing its contents, Ilyssa took in Naseem's words as she navigated her own landscape of loss and grief, and sobbed. After Ilyssa reached out with gratitude, Naseem replied with one note of wisdom: "Always look to the sky and remember how very brief and special our seconds are."

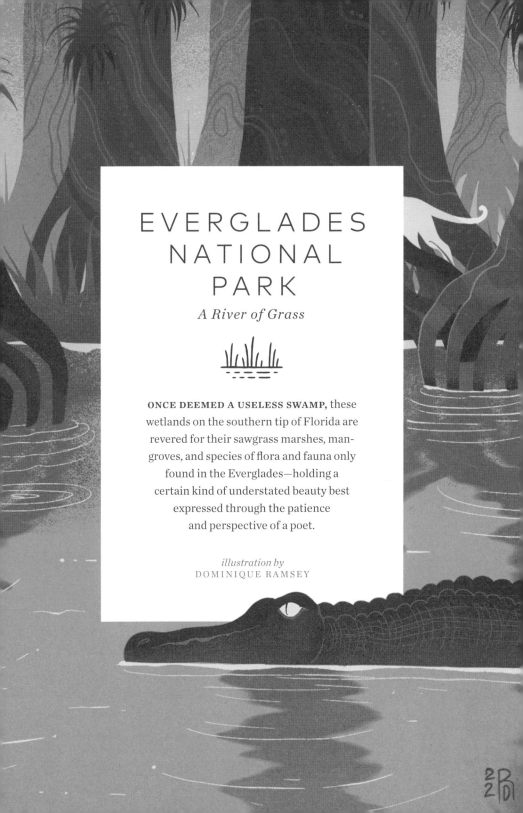

EVERGLADES NATIONAL PARK

A River of Grass

ONCE DEEMED A USELESS SWAMP, these wetlands on the southern tip of Florida are revered for their sawgrass marshes, mangroves, and species of flora and fauna only found in the Everglades—holding a certain kind of understated beauty best expressed through the patience and perspective of a poet.

illustration by
DOMINIQUE RAMSEY

There are no other Everglades in the world, yet even this one has had to fight to exist. Though it is a unique ecosystem of wetlands, many have dismissed this landscape as unimportant. Early conservationist William Hornaday noted the Everglades as a "place of little interest," and Napoleon Bonaparte Broward based his 1904 gubernatorial campaign on draining the entire region.

The opinion at the time was that the Everglades were useless marsh and swampland, uninhabitable by humans. New railroads, canals, and buildings were bringing tourists and residents to booming cities like Fort Lauderdale, Miami, and Fort Myers, and between 1905 and 1910, large tracts of wetland were converted to agricultural to help feed the state's growing population.

One such transplant was landscape designer Ernest Coe, who moved to Miami in 1925 as part of the real estate and development boom, but lost his investment. Coe began taking trips into the Everglades, and was shocked by what he saw: birds being slaughtered by the millions for their feathers, rare orchids and snails being harvested, their habitats burned to increase their value. Concerned that these animals would go extinct, Coe formed the Everglades Tropical National Park Committee in 1928. Joining Coe were Dr. David Fairchild, former head of the US Department of Agriculture's Bureau of Plant Exploration, and Marjory Stoneman Douglas, journalist with the *Miami Herald*.

The group's advocacy coincided with, or perhaps inspired, an important shift in the United States' attitude toward wilderness. Up to this point, conservation had focused on scenery. Yellowstone, Yosemite, Grand Canyon, Mount Rainier—these magnificent western landscapes bolstered the idea of America as a unique and significant land. But the Everglades, the overlooked and underappreciated swamps of South Florida, didn't fit that narrative.

American-Salvadoran biologist George Melendez Wright conducted the first scientific surveys of fauna in the national parks in 1929, eventually forming the Wildlife Division of the Park Service in 1933. Guided by this science-based approach, no longer were we evaluating the quality of tourism but rather the rarity of the plants, the diversity of biological species, and the uniqueness of the ecosystem as the key measures of a place. The establishment of Everglades as a national park in 1947 marked a key turning point for environmentalism. No grand views? No problem.

But as is often the case, conservation was preceded by erasure. Both the Seminole and Miccosukee tribes trace their lineage to the Creek Indians from

Georgia and Alabama. In the 1700s, tribal members migrated away from European settlement into a Florida region controlled by Spain. But the US government under President Andrew Jackson wanted that land and came after the Seminole in 1818, 1835, and 1855—the three Seminole Wars. Many Indians were moved out west after the Indian Removal Act, but others preserved their culture in their ancestral lands by escaping into the swamps of the Everglades, never ceding their land or signing a treaty with the government. To this day, both tribes take distinct pride in calling themselves the "Unconquered People."

Both the Miccosukee and Seminole tribes remain economically independent sovereign nations, even providing a monthly dividend to all tribe members. In addition to casinos, tribes have developed unique industries like alligator wrestling and airboat tours to take tourists deeper into their culture and view of the Everglades. The Love the Everglades Movement is a preservation project founded by Indigenous activists to advocate for cleaning up the water and respecting Miccosukee sovereignty. "We recognize this water that binds us all. Be mindful that the water you're drinking today is the same water your ancestors drank."

The tension between development and preservation is obvious. Just outside the park are industrial farms, gated communities, shopping plazas, a military base, and federal prisons, all within a half hour drive. The park boundary divides these two forces: the Napoleon Browards of the world who yell, "Drain the swamp," and the Marjory Stoneman Douglases who yell, "Be a nuisance when it counts . . . but never give up."

More than any other park in this collection, poems tell the story of this place. Here, beauty needs not just a witness but an explorer willing to endure and persist in discovery. The beauty is not on the surface, not immediately recognizable in grand vistas, but is in a one-of-a-kind ecosystem whose beauty is revealed to those who take the time to read its stanza and understand how species rely on and thrive alongside one another. This is a poet's park, and we welcome you into its verse.

The Nature of
the Everglades

MARJORY STONEMAN DOUGLAS

There are no other Everglades in the world.

They are, they have always been, one of the unique regions of the earth, remote, never wholly known. Nothing anywhere else is like them: their vast glittering openness, wider than the enormous visible round of the horizon, the racing free saltness and sweetness of their massive winds, under the dazzling blue heights of space. They are unique also in the simplicity, the diversity, the related harmony of the forms of life they enclose. The miracle of the light pours over the green and brown expanse of saw grass and of water, shining and slow-moving below, the grass and water that is the meaning and the central fact of the Everglades of Florida. It is a river of grass.

The great pointed paw of the state of Florida, familiar as the map of North America itself, of which it is the most noticeable appendage, thrusts south, farther south than any other part of the mainland of the United States. Between the shining aquamarine waters of the Gulf of Mexico and the roaring deep-blue waters of the north-surging Gulf Stream, the shaped land points toward Cuba and the Caribbean. It points toward and touches within one degree of the tropics.

More than halfway down that thrusting sea-bound peninsula nearly everyone knows the lake that is like a great hole in that pawing shape, Lake Okeechobee, the second largest body of freshwater, it is always said, "within the confines of the United States." Below that lie the Everglades.

They have been called "the mysterious Everglades" so long that the phrase is a meaningless platitude. For four hundred years after the discovery they seemed more like a fantasy than a simple geographic and historic fact. Even the men who in the later years saw them more clearly could hardly make up their minds what the Everglades were or how they could be described, or what use could be made of them. They were mysterious then. They are mysterious still to everyone by whom their fundamental nature is not understood.

Off and on for those four hundred years the region now called "The Everglades" was described as a series of vast, miasmic swamps, poisonous lagoons, huge dismal marshes without outlet, a rotting, shallow, inland sea, or labyrinths of dark trees hung and looped about with snakes and dripping mosses, malignant with tropical fevers and malarias, evil to the white man.

Even the name, "The Everglades," was given them and printed on a map of Florida within the past hundred years. It is variously interpreted. There were one or two other names we know, which were given them before that, but what sounds the first men had for them, seeing first, centuries and centuries before the discovering white men, those sun-blazing solitudes, we shall ever know.

· ✦ ·

Yet the Indians, who have known the Glades longer and better than any dictionary-making white men, gave them their perfect, and poetic name, which is also true. They called them "Pa-hay-okee," which is the Indian word for "Grassy Water." Today Everglades is one word and yet plural. They are the only Everglades in the world.

Men crossed and recrossed them leaving no trace, so that no one knew men had been there. The few books or pamphlets written about them by Spaniards or surveyors or sportsmen or botanists have not been generally read. Actually, the first accurate studies of Everglades geology, soil, archaeology, even history, are only just now being completed.

The question was at once, where do you begin? Because, when you think of it, history, the recorded time of the earth and of man, is in itself something like a river. To try to present it whole is to find oneself lost in the sense of continuing change. The source can be only the beginning in time and space, and the end is the future and the unknown. What we can know lies somewhere between. The course along which for a little way one proceeds, the changing life, the varying light, must somehow be fixed in a moment clearly, from which one may look before and after and try to comprehend wholeness.

So it is with the Everglades, which have that quality of long existence in their own nature. They were changeless. They are changed.

They were complete before man came to them, and for centuries afterward, when he was only one of those forms which shared, in a finely balanced harmony, the forces and the ancient nature of the place.

Then, when the Everglades were most truly themselves, is the time to begin with them. ✦

About This Story

Marjory Stoneman Douglas wrote a wildly popular column for the *Miami Herald* that promoted responsible urban planning and supported women's suffrage. She helped pass a law requiring toilets and bathtubs in all Miami homes, and set up an interest-free loan operation for Black residents of the neighborhood Coconut Grove. But it was when she and Ernest Coe established the Everglades Tropical National Park Association that the fight of her life started.

Challenging the notion that the Everglades were a useless swamp, Douglas spent five years researching the unique ecology of the area. Her 1947 book, *The Everglades: River of Grass*, galvanized the public to protect the Everglades, the same year they became a national park. In later years she continued her fight, founding the Friends of the Everglades in 1969 and taking up causes like opposing an airport in Big Cypress, fighting sugarcane growers polluting Lake Okeechobee, and even speaking against the Army Corps of Engineers for diverting water away from the Everglades.

Her inspiring words still resonate today: "Be a nuisance when it counts. Do your part to inform and stimulate the public to join your action. Be depressed, discouraged, and disappointed at failure and the disheartening effects of ignorance, greed, corruption and bad politics—but never give up."

Naming the Everglades

ANDREW C. GOTTLIEB

I could talk about the biology, the taxonomy,
the scientific names of things—
delicate biodiversity of Latinate costume—
but all I really know is the acres and acres of sedge
stretching away to the eyes' horizon,
so much of it untouchable,
the plains that make these glades,
and the way I'd like to walk out among them,
stepping wetly wild, brushing the side
of one distant, vase-like cypress: leaning greenery
of grey slightness. So much of the world
holds itself at a distance, the woman
with binoculars walking alone off the path,
the teacher who never made eye contact,
the quiet chat you had before your grandfather
disappeared into an Iowan sky,
the moon, the stars, (*what are they?*)
and perhaps we need Latin names
to aid us, Linnaeus with his intricate system,
labels that assist with listing, specificities,
but not with wandering hungrily in the mud
of things, the urge to slather it over skin,
to grab at other people and hold them to our body
with an unfashionable grasping
that doesn't ease in any way the sense

with which we're left, a recurring awareness
of insignificance when confronted
by a vast landscape of hammock and sawgrass.
Or by a call, the hidden hawk, red-shouldered
and solitary, offering an uncategorized cryptography
we can only translate as awe, richness,
epiphany about so many boundaries,
none of which will ever be grammatical
or constellate, but always slipping invisibly away
to the drifting grass that seems just inches
from your fingers, the humbling limits
of your outstretched, hoping hand. ✦

About This Story

Through a partnership between Everglades National Park and AIRIE (Artists in Residence in Everglades), Andrew Gottlieb spent the hot month of June as a writer in residence. June is relatively quiet in the Everglades, as the heat, humidity, and bugs are enough to keep most visitors away. But if that doesn't scare you, you're rewarded with solace and wildlife encounters that make the constant bug swatting worth it.

Andrew recounts long hikes alone in the pinelands, nighttime drives to find snakes and owls, and alligators congregating in water holes. He shares of his experience, "There's a real vastness to the glades, a special sense of space. And yet, a lot of it is untouchable, unless one's willing to wade. So, the Everglades is an experience of witness. For me that translates into an awe and a longing. It's a special ecosystem that's threatened in many ways by a lack of freshwater and an encroachment of saltwater." We were drawn to the longing and respect for place that Andrew infused into his poem.

Slough Slogging in the Dry Season

JEN KARETNICK

We plant our poles in Pa-hay-okee peat
—some like fragile seeds we wish to see grow,
some as if to reach the layer of oo-
lite—and follow with dense, tentative feet
dressed in the skins of animals we hope
to avoid in the sheetflow where we are
not the enabled apex predator.
Sun-swaddled, we grapple with poise, grope
the air for miniature enemies,
wade toward the shadows of the cypress dome,
where the panther makes her diurnal home
and alligators stake their territories.
There we post selfies to prove bravery,
leave behind the whiff of chicanery. ✦

Searching for the Florida
Panther, I Find Only Signs

JEN KARETNICK

Catamount. Cougar. Mountain lion
of the prairie, subspecies of the puma.
Prowler, predator, killer of dormant
cattle chewing on hay reaped from
the rough soil fertilized by ancient

oysters. Taker of tiny dogs who have
wandered too far from ranch houses
stretched on limestone foundations,
who have always traveled in the seats
of a manufactured way of life. I lay

all the names I've been told to fear
on my tongue like paint, thick and dry
as if improperly stored, the animal
I long to hold up at the other end of
a cell phone camera or capture safely

in the rearview mirror of my car. But raw
umber ghosts of the hammocks coming
back to growth after a fire, they offer
no gifts aside from scat and shadow.
Rumor and innuendo. And this framing

of their forms en plein air, stamped as if
in charcoal on cautionary metal, staked
every few miles on the shoulder of
a highway gripping the River of Grass
with the invisible tentacles of canvas. ✦

About This Story

The Everglades mystique is best captured in the spirit of the Florida panther. Panthers were heavily hunted in the nineteenth century after a bounty was put on them because of their threat to livestock, game animals, and humans. After nearly going extinct in the 1950s, perhaps fewer than one hundred panthers now live in South Florida. One of the biggest threats they face today is habitat destruction to make way for industrial farms, commercial development, and residential sprawl.

If crossing paths with a panther has you worried about visiting the park, you might be relieved to learn that the Everglades population is much smaller. They prefer to spend their time in mature uplands dense with hardwood hammocks and pinelands, not slough slogging their way through the glades. Slough slogging is a unique way to explore the park, taking you "off trail" in designated areas and deep into the heart of a cypress dome, a type of freshwater forested wetland, or . . . *swamp*. Slogging is a hands-on, up-close, and *wet* way to experience the park, but it does involve trudging through mucky waters in bug-infested areas. So pack your sturdy close-toed, lace-up shoes, long pants, long-sleeved shirt, sunscreen, *and* bug spray!

Living Jewels
of the Everglades

RACHEL LURIA

The fire starts at the edge of the hammock and eats its way to the center. The sound is surprisingly gentle. Like rain on a metal roof. And the smell is lovely and inviting, like sitting by the hearth. It is only the orange-red heat and the black smoke that betray the danger. Standing beside the hammock in Everglades National Park, the heat roasts your cheeks. Your throat burns. Animals run from the wood in terror. Not all will survive.

Fires like these are common enough in the Everglades. Some fires are meant to save lives. A prescription to preserve the health of a wood grown too wild for its own good. Some fires are meant to destroy. A gamble meant to silence a wood and keep its secrets. Rumor holds that greedy, secretive collectors burned these hammocks to protect their own interests. That once they'd found a particularly beautiful or rare variety of the desired animal, they would set a fire so no one else could collect there.

The animal that may have inspired such destruction lives in this hammock and nowhere else. Small, easy to miss, these animals nestle against the smooth bark of the hardwood trees. If you were to spot one, you might gasp, shocked by its colorful beauty. Their shells are swirls of yellow and pink or brown and black or white and blue—fifty-two combinations of vibrant color. They live only in southern Florida and parts of the Caribbean. Fully grown, they are about the size of your thumb. The babies are called "buttons." Finding one feels like a child's joy at uncovering an Easter egg. Or, for some, a pirate's delight at finding treasure. These creatures are so like treasure, in fact, that they are often called "living jewels." These rare jewels are so prized, so special that they were once chosen to represent the state of Florida in the 1940 World's Fair. The *Miami News* gushed, "Florida Exhibit Director Brown is sparing no effort to make this state's exhibit at the New York World's Fair outstanding. He has just ordered 150 live [tree snails] to add color to the orange grove now blooming on the Flushing flats. In addition to orange blossoms, New York's cliff dwellers will see real snails, transplanted bodily from South Florida's hammocks to the city's citrus grove."

These "outstanding" ambassadors for the wonders of South Florida are the Liguus tree snail, or "ligs" to the enthusiasts. Habitat destroyed by development, collected nearly to extinction, the snails remain a subject of fascination and obsession. Does this hammock burn for the sake of the snail? Either to protect it or to keep it secret? Depends on who you ask. You will have to decide what kind of story this is.

The snails move slowly, silently along the bark. They eat lichen and graze a slimy, serpentine trail. In the dry season they estivate, sealing themselves into their shells, suctioned to the tree, and sleep much of their life away. In the rainy season, they peep out to take in the moist air. Their faces are wet and blobbish, and it is hard for you to imagine a snail, even these colorful specimens, inflaming anyone's passions. Some say that love of these snails and a desire to preserve their habitat is the reason that Everglades National Park even exists. But a sign in the park claims that "after gathering many of one variety, collectors sometimes burned the hammock, destroying any left. This made their collection more valuable. Today at least four kinds of tree snail no longer exist."

Collectors swear that isn't true. But they also admit to being terrific liars. In the old days, collectors would return from the field and stop at a bar called Mac's Place. They'd guzzle cold beer and tell each other nothing that was true about where they'd been or what they'd found there. They'd each amassed collections of thousands or tens of thousands of shells. Many they'd keep, many they'd sell. Some they would sell to museums, but some they would sell for jewelry or home decorations. It was said that the most fashionable women of Miami would wear the shells on necklaces. You can imagine such jewelry hanging beside a snowy egret feather hat—a fashion once so prized that an ounce of feathers was worth more than an ounce of gold—and some American alligator boots. All three fashions stolen from the Everglades, pushing the animals to the brink of extinction.

It's illegal to collect living snails now, and it's illegal to take anything from the park. But you can still find some shells for sale online. You hope these are old collections, passed down by parents or grandparents. But if you walk the hammock and see the glittering shells dangling from the branches like forbidden fruit, you may wonder if, for some, temptation remains.

No one knows for sure how the ligs arrived in South Florida. They might have floated over on tree trunks or they might have been carried by birds. Or Indigenous peoples might have rowed them over from one island to another. Or they might have blown over on the winds of a hurricane. No one knows who was the first to see their rainbow shells dotting the canopy and think: mine. But by at least the nineteenth century, collecting had become a popular hobby. A 1960 article in the *Fort Myers News-Press* proudly showcases one woman's collection of thousands of snails and offers this advice for processing the shells: put the snail in the refrigerator overnight and "the animal comes by without difficulty." A 1961 article in the *Orlando Sentinel*, however, cheerfully instructs collectors that "processing the shell is quite simple: place the snail in a pre-heated oven for five minutes, then pluck it from its shell with tweezers, wash the shell in plain water, and polish with a soft cloth." More recently, collectors turned preservationists who are still obsessed with the beauty and purity of the shells report "stomping" snails who have traveled from their own hammock to a neighboring hammock, thus avoiding crossbreeding and color hybridization.

Stomping, freezing, baking of living snails. Razing, developing, depleting living habitats. You may not know how these snails arrived in our world, but you have an idea of how they might depart.

Like the snails, Everglades National Park is a hidden beauty. Or perhaps you could say its beauty is hidden. Most park historians agree that the park was not created to preserve its beauty, what beauty it possesses being of a much subtler nature than that of something like the Grand Canyon. It was preserved for more practical reasons: people need its water and wanted its resources, like orchids and snails, to survive. There are no breathtaking mountains, no towering monuments, no volcanoes. The colors can seem muted, the views subdued—brown and green and flat to the horizon. A one-star review of the park describes it as "miles and miles of nothing." But for some, like park founder Ernest Coe, it is not miles of nothing but a "great empire of solitude," its landscape one that invites introspection, that allows you to gaze inward as much as outward, its subtlety something to cherish and celebrate.

If you look closely, even briefly, you will see eruptions of color and life everywhere. Great blue herons. Snowy egrets with their prized white plumes and delicate yellow feet tiptoeing across the sawgrass. Bright pink roseate spoonbills with their prehistoric faces. At least five kinds of orange butterflies, some making a royal court of queens and monarchs and viceroys. Pink and green orchids dotting the trees. Red-winged blackbirds. Iridescent blue gallinules. Shiny black gators basking in the sun.

The park is full of music. Crickets singing. Frogs creaking in rhythm. Manatees surfacing and gulping air in wet, friendly chuffs. The air tastes of vegetation and salt and water. The park will fill your every sense if you let it.

If you have a bit of the pioneer about you, you may venture off the park's paved trails and slosh out into the marsh on your own. You may go searching for hidden hammocks, rare snails, but you won't get any help from seasoned collectors. None will share their secrets with you—they went out and earned the right to witness these rare beauties, now you will have to do the same.

You will need a good walking stick. You will want to test each step before you take it, lest you break an ankle in a solution hole, the deep erosions in the porous limestone. Bring a camera. A picture is the only way to carry the snails out with you.

Bring your memory. The wet adventure, the sense of being farther from home than you have ever been before may remind you of your childhood. You might remember summers spent exploring similar brown-black waters. You could remember mosquito bites and the dreadful pleasure of scratching their raised bumps until they bleed. That time at camp that you yawned and a mosquito flew right down your throat, and you feel as if it lives there still as your belly jumps and tingles at each rustle from the grasses, each burble beneath the water.

Bring your imagination. As you know, the wilderness before you is secretive. It has been buried beneath the ocean and it has stretched across half the state. It is just a fraction of the size it once was. It's been hacked and carved into submission, but it remembers when it reigned over man and beast. It remembers when it was so dense and wild that early explorers couldn't—or wouldn't—brave its depths. They just stood at its edge and wrote made-up accounts of dragons and kangaroos. It wants you to imagine it as it was then, a seemingly untamable wilderness, an inexhaustible Eden. It will want you to imagine because it wants to be that Eden again, impossible though that may be.

You will stand in the marsh and watch the blue sky and white clouds reflected in water that sparkles with light and water lilies. You will imagine yourself as one of nature's creatures. You will feel water seeping into your shoes and you will lift your foot like an egret, spread your arms to the sky and dig your toes into the muck like you're a cypress. You will wish that you could open a portal in time and step through, find those explorers and warn them of the future. Convince them to tell the true story of this new world, that it is a treasure to protect and cherish, not a monster to slay.

You may think that the story of the Everglades has already been written. It's too late to change anything now. Where once there was a mighty river of grass, now there are theme parks and city streets. Once there were peoples who lived here long before European explorers "discovered" it, and now they exist only in the names of coastal resort towns. Entire histories, arts, stories, lives—all now just blood salting the water. And those waters are rising higher each day. One day we may all be buried in ruins beneath the ocean.

But I remember a time before now. I remember when alligators were endangered and the sight of them rare. Now one lives in my backyard. The snowy egret, once hunted nearly to oblivion by humans, is on the rise, its status listed as "least concern." They too are frequent backyard visitors.

We have the capacity to change.

I spent a month living in the Everglades. Here is a poem I wrote then:

> The water is so clear and still, it is a perfect mirror of the sky. Even the stars can't tell one from the other. They begin to argue. "Our home is above," some say. "No, our home is below," say others. At last, they ask the sun, the wisest and brightest star among them. "Where do we belong?" they ask.
> "Where is it most beautiful?" she answers. "That is where you belong." And so they choose below.

It was inspired by water lilies on the marsh, but I could have just as easily written it about the tree snails. They glitter in the trees like fallen stars or captured drops of sunlight.

What story will you tell about the Everglades? About its living jewels? Will it be a story of obsession? Of mad collectors burning hammocks and hoarding their treasure like dragons? Or will it be a story of hope? Of fire as rebirth? ✦

About This Story

The preservation of the Everglades marked the first time in the Park Service story that land was protected not for scenic views, but for the ecosystem and all the plants and animals within it. It represented the culmination of a movement that asked conservationists to adopt a nonhuman-centric view of wilderness. Imagining the socialite with the snowy egret feather hat and American alligator boots, Rachel shows us why the Everglades needs protection, but also invites us to look just a little closer, and specifically at the Liguus tree snail.

The snails can be found pretty easily if you know when and where to look. First, make sure you are visiting during Florida's wet season, typically mid-May through mid-October. This is when you'll find snails cruising the tree trunks and munching on lichens. Pull up your rain boots, and walk the Gumbo Limbo Trail, Pineland Trail, or the Mahogany Hammock Trail to spot any of the fifty-two color varieties.

Signs of Wildlife

SYLVIA JONES

Tropical hammock, cigar-shaped
periphyton. The great white heron

flew and landed in the borrow pit
a hundredth of a second faster

than the egret
on the billboard

Sometimes when we do not see
an animal, we still see signs

of its presence, tracks show
in uncovered soil, like acres

of abandoned skunk cabbages.
All animals have tracks. Those

of the racoon, are slight lookalikes
to human handprints. Feathers too

can be used to identify birds
a cohort of brown pelicans facing the Gulf of Mexico

or a gaggle of sweet bay magnolias plume
hunting in rest stop camo gear near

Lake Okeechobee, where there was a little bit of sidewalk
and then there wasn't.

To wall off the wharf blight of an ocean highway
floating over a river of clumps of life

Mangrove bend, Bald
Cypress, we saw the sun revolving

we saw the planets
revolving around the sun. ✦

About This Story

Sylvia Jones is a queer Black writer and first-generation college graduate from Baltimore, Maryland. When we first connected with Sylvia, she was in the process of converting her MFA thesis into a debut collection of poems that deals with notions of class inequality, ancestral memory, environmental racism, and the human toll of diaspora. She is the recipient of one of our travel stipends, and had applied to write about Olympic National Park. Drawn to her work but having already selected somebody to travel to Olympic, we asked Sylvia if she would be open to taking a journey down south to Everglades National Park. Luckily, she agreed and took her first ever trip south of Orlando, staying in Miami after her lodging near the park fell through, and arrived right as Cuban protests erupted, a condo collapsed in nearby Surfside, and on the anniversary of the death of legendary fashion designer and LGBTQ+ icon Gianni Versace. Her intense arrival into Miami didn't sound much different from the shock of entering the Everglades.

Sylvia was struck by what she saw: farm animals along the highways you'd expect in the Midwest, abject poverty, correctional facilities, gated communities, and Indigenous reservations. She did not know what to expect once she got into the park. Arriving in the heat of summer, she shared she had "never been so swarmed in such a quiet way": the mosquitoes, the "freaky" huge orange grasshoppers, the turkey vultures staring down at her from above, the mud and muck, the thick, humid air. Despite this overwhelming sense of being immersed in it all, Sylvia shared with us, "When you think of national parks, you think of something prolific in its own right. The Everglades are marshy. It's a thing you can't translate into photography.

That's what makes me want to get back there. There's a real specific feeling of the flatness of it. It's longevity. I always think about birds being related to dinosaurs. That's the cradle of society. I felt so humbled and enamored to be there."

What Used to Be
the Everglades

LEAH CLAIRE KAMINSKI

The sky takes on a greenish-black hue before a hurricane or tropical storm. An eerie quiet descends, followed by winds that unfurl the palm trees' fronds and blow the Spanish moss hanging from live oaks like curls of gray hair. The rustling of a million leaves and the whisper of gumbo limbo's peeling bark. The windblown rain.

When Hurricane Andrew spawned dozens of small twisters in its wall, knocking down mangroves, defoliating and killing hardwoods, snapping slash pines in multiple directions, I started dreaming of tornadoes. It might be the gray-black thickness of them, solid air turned weapon, that sticks with me. It might be the mindlessness, the capricious destruction, that sows them through my nightmares.

Tornadoes aren't a normal part of South Florida's weather, but one of the area's strongest and most dangerous magics is that it feels like anything can happen here, in what used to only be the Everglades.

I want to weave you a net of words to hold this place's shining mystery—black skies heavy in storm, hard snouts of gators patient in the parching sun, dark water studded with cypress knees, humid shade of mahogany trees clacking with inch-thick pods. The flat, glinting plate of the still-yet-moving River of Grass.

But the net of words would need to hold us, too. Because we surround the Everglades, press into it. We run into it and it through us. I can't talk to you about the Everglades without talking about us, without talking about its ruin, and our own.

As Miami-Dade County began to rise up in the eighties and nineties, colossal and peninsula-spanning, my family and so many others were left clinging to the edges of its fantastic wealth. When they were young hippies, my parents had chosen to live in a sepia-toned semirural area called Princeton, at the far edge of Dade County, on an acre of land filled with slow-growing spindles of slash pine. In 1992, when hundreds of homes and thousands of protected pines were crunched to shards by Hurricane Andrew's teeth, developers had their excuse to throw up townhome after townhome after townhome on zero lot lines, paving over any remaining pockets of wilderness. Human tragedy and environmental tragedy were bound up together. The wealth concentrated further, and the population swelled, choking the Everglades.

Half of the River of Grass was already gone, of course. We cut it off at the hip more than a century ago, and we've been poisoning it ever since. Napoleon Bonaparte Broward in 1903 stumped he'd "drain that abominable pestilence-ridden swamp." Drain the wide, flat tongue of shining sea moving through glade to mangrove, from clear north Florida stream to Okeechobee and down the slope of Florida's toe. Canals drained it, then Big Sugar poured phosphorous through the whole system. And ever since, the mythos of money and palm trees, the glamour hiding the reality of a broken ecosystem, has kept us pouring down the country like runoff, to make new homes in what used to be the Everglades.

I grew up in a little cypress house, on a limestone ridge that juts up a few feet from land that was once the Everglades, that was close enough to feel their slow pull. Phantom limb of them.

In Princeton, we often called our piece of land a hardwood hammock, which is an ecosystem unique to the Everglades region: a small limestone island covered with rich soil, rising just a few feet above sawgrass prairies or pineland. Hammocks are dense, clumped acres of subtropical and hardwood trees—live oak, gumbo limbo, royal palm—and near the bottom, sharp saw palmettos clamp down, weaving sawed blade into sawed blade. Our land was laced with slash pine trunks, cut with gumbo limbo, dotted with fat thumbs of oak, palms, mahogany, and fern.

But a hammock is an island, its edges carved out by alligators thrashing holes in the sawgrass-jeweled mud during the dry season. Our little Princeton acre was surrounded by nothing but strip mall and tract house. So it turns out it was just unmaintained pineland rife with invasives—with the full 30 percent of Florida plant species designated as such, ornamentals thoughtlessly planted decades ago. On or near our land: Johnson grass and Florida holly, Australian pine and the shaggy, spreading melaleuca, soaking up what used to be the moving water of the Everglades.

Pineland is the driest land in the Everglades. It's dominated by a single species of South Florida slash pine clamping down on the limestone that shoulders up through sandy soil. Pineland requires fire, and the trees live in ways that both promote and resist it. The dry, sandy floor of true pine forest is covered with flammable pine needles. The occasional fire, so freely stoked by the needles, allows undergrowth to burn off and cones to open and germinate, while the trunks themselves are insulated by their thick bark.

A period without significant fire, usually due to human control and misunderstanding of fire, can begin to turn pineland into hammock as larger trees overtake the slash pines. Add invasive species and you get overdense, underburned land: in other words, tinder.

The year I went to college, our fire, which was not a maintenance fire but deformed, grown huge from years of denial, destroyed every tree in our square mile. But it took just one house: my house, the house my family wrapped our sadness in, the house I never let my prep school friends see. At night, in the park for my artist residency, I wonder about the fire: Was it payback, for perching a small cypress house in what used to be the Everglades?

I missed that fire. Had run up the coast, to college and away from my childhood's dark heart. I miss the fire this time, too. The morning they do a controlled burn in my quadrant of the park, I leave as the crews arrive and drive out to 232nd St. and 120th Ave. to show my baby nephew where I grew up. I think all day of the fire and I return that night to smoke filtering in through the wall air conditioner.

Next morning the smell of wet, charred pine forest mingles with my coffee. The dew-wet window screens make it look like it is still smoking, but when I walk out, wind my way through blackened saw palmetto and barely singed pines, the ground is only warm to the touch, the fire extinguished completely by dew. Pine cones lie on the steaming ground open and gleaming like jewels.

It's hard to reconcile the need for this kind of destruction. Hard to trust that what hurts us saves the land. The Everglades are a fire-dependent ecosystem. Human homes and possessions aren't. But this is part of the mystery, too. How we can live our human lives in what used to be the Everglades, and still protect what's left.

Walking alone is scary on Old Ingraham Highway, the deserted carriageway to Flamingo that cuts through savanna and cypress domes on the east side of the park. I'm five months pregnant, worried that I'm getting too hot. I came for my residency in February so that I could avoid the heat, but it's been the hottest year on record. Normal averages in the high sixties balloon to the high eighties, and summer-afternoon thunderheads roll across the horizon every day.

Records will be smashed again the next year, and the next. In 2021, we will have such strange weather that a "falling iguana advisory" is issued for when the nonnative but now-common creatures fall from the trees during a rare freeze.

But right now, it's the hottest February on record, and I'm worried about the small kicking thing inside of me.

For my first time back in Florida in over a decade, not only the heat has shocked me. Mosquitoes mean I can't go out at night, especially not pregnant, especially not with the Zika scare. I didn't remember, not really. The buzzing disgust and maddening whine of thousands of mosquitoes crawling through the air, how you can feel them tickle your skin.

The alligators and crocodiles haven't changed, though my tolerance for them has. I am nervous at even the sight of one of their trails, flattened sawgrass and cattail bowing down to a gator's ferocious weight. I keep close watch on the edges of this empty track.

Alligators rarely attack humans, and as usual what's really dangerous here is what's dangerous to the Everglades themselves. Since the last time I came, invasive species have taken over. Aggressive, feral wild boars, 150 pounds and six feet long, traveling in groups. Not seeking humans out, but trampling native plants. Or the pestilence of invasive Burmese pythons, who have never hurt a human in the park. But every ranger tells me of the python whose stomach split wide open after eating a gator.

The pythons have all but wiped out the small mammals of the ecosystem. On this visit, I've heard no chittering in the pines, no rustling of leaves, seen not one single rabbit, squirrel, fox, raccoon, opossum, bobcat. On the way to Old Ingraham today, I did see a single Key deer bound across the road. Otherwise, just gators, birds, and silence in the emptying stage set of a once-bustling Everglades.

I'm here soon after Irma, and when I visit Flamingo on the southern tip of the park, I walk through acres of cracked and splintered mangroves, plastered white with smothering mud flung in from the ocean. Irma killed or damaged 40 percent of the park's mangroves, those stilt-walking salt-drinking umbrellas of trees that create a net to hold in South Florida's coastline. And climate change is causing more and stronger hurricanes.

But the more direct threat is when we simply chop down the mangroves. One of my former classmates' parents chopped down their protected mangroves to get a better view of Biscayne Bay, taking advantage of a recent hurricane to claim they'd been felled by wind. They were ordered to replace them, but that feels like a thumb in the dam. Rich people aren't ordered to do much in South Florida, not even when they're squatting on what should still be the Everglades.

The Everglades ecosystem has held up under more than a century of strain, under everything we've done to it, everything we continue to do. As I watch water streaming with bladderwort, dotted with apple snails, anhinga, zebra longwings, and gators, as I paddle past mangrove nurseries harboring infant fish and manatees and watch kites swoop over the wetlands, as I walk into green-shadowed hammocks stalked by rare panthers, I am grateful. Grateful that I've caught myself in this shining net, cheek to cheek with the river of grass and its ghosts.

Once I leave again, back north, I wrap the net around me; it gives me cold comfort, for what remains of the Everglades depends on what is already lost, or nearly so. The fish won't last long without the mangroves, the snail kite without the native apple snail. And we won't last long without any of it. Who has the forbearance to wrap their own arms around what remains?

There's a reason people don't think to protect the Everglades, don't think twice about pouring into the bursting cul-de-sac of the peninsula and stressing this unique ecosystem ever further.

My brother-in-law visits the park for the first time while I'm here as artist in residence. Through his eyes, I see it new: flat, monochromatic, hot, and buggy. Somehow both intensely humid and scorchingly dry. Marl hangs from sawgrass like the foam of a slurped-up sea. The sawgrass prairies are sharp and unpassable.

Even summer's lush greenery, or the bright white beaches in the south and southwest, strung with slender palms, circled by clear turquoise water—there's always more to it. The canals leading into those turquoise waters stacked with crocodiles, that white sand swarming with mosquitoes. The greenery up close becomes sharp and rough, harbors insects, snakes, poisonous plants. Deep, dark solution holes sink into the limestone.

The Everglades denies us full entrance, invites skirting around. This intractable discomfort lets us ignore that in this relationship, we wield the power. So when you next visit what used to be the Everglades (the highways and townhomes, the farms and gas stations, strip malls, clubs, manmade beaches), may you let it shake off the region's flimsy glamour, may you see what aches underneath: that here—right here—once flowed a great river of grass. ✦

About This Story

Born in Homestead, just outside the entrance to Everglades National Park, Leah calls a lifetime of observation into her writing. In a changing landscape, we appreciate her invitation to imagine what once was here, even as we grapple with a place that she calls "somehow both intensely humid and scorchingly dry."

In addition to constant threats from hurricanes—more hurricanes land in Florida than in any other state—South Florida has been subject to multiple waves of development. The appeal of oceanfront land, business-friendly policies, and a lack of understanding of the ecology of the Everglades have led to repeated drainage of the swamplands in order to create new inhabitable lands. Some estimates say that 50 percent of South Florida's original wetland areas no longer exist today, and wading bird populations have dwindled by 90 percent.

Today, groups like Love the Everglades join together to preserve the Everglades landscape. Founded by Miccosukee grandmother Betty Osceola and two-spirit Miccosukee activist and poet Reverend Houston Cypress, Love the Everglades seeks to revitalize community participation to protect and revitalize this sacred land. The group hosts prayer walks around Lake Okeechobee, the primary water source of the Everglades, to pray for the waters of the lake, and for humanity to reconnect to the natural world again. "This prayer walk will be most arduous and will test you physically and mentally," Betty warns. "We welcome and encourage prayer warriors from near and the world abroad to join us daily with prayer from the safety of your homes." As Marjory Stoneman Douglas asked before, and as Love the Everglades brings into focus again, "What are *you* doing to save the Everglades?"

Dear National Park Service,

HANNAH ROGERS

I would like to read a story about a lone park ranger in a tower.
I know these are american rocks, and american egrets, and american waters.
These beloved american rocks, beloved american egrets, beloved american waters.
These damn american rocks, damn american egrets, damn american waters.
I know my life would be different without these american rocks, egrets, waters,
but I know also that when the government shuts down you are "nonessential."
So you call your friends and you sit in wooden clapboard lighthouses and
fake adobe kiosks and you wait for some other Americans to come shoot ducks
or pick off pieces of native heritage and most of you were wildlife
studies majors mixed with a couple of archeology minors and you didn't
sign up for this part. So I'd like to hear a few stories about lone park rangers
because I know even when you've stamped all the tickets, and played the film
on the half hour, and have a breath to look out of the tower, you know that
those american rocks, american egrets, american waters need you. ✦

About This Story

What drew us to Hannah's work was her ability to provide a glimpse into a side of the park that many of us don't get to see—the park as . . . well, *your job*. Working in a national park offers the opportunity to spend most of your time in some of the most iconic and often downright beautiful places, an ability to fulfill a passion for the outdoors, to preserve and protect these places, and though these roles may not be the most lucrative, many rangers have described the job as being "paid in sunrises and sunsets." But, believe it or not, there are sometimes some pretty unglamorous aspects to having one of the most revered and romanticized jobs in the American lexicon—a park ranger.

Park rangers spend long days out in the elements on their feet, sometimes in grueling environments and weather conditions. Many times rangers are at understaffed parks, have limited access to housing, have to deal with sometimes annoying and misbehaving tourists, and point people in the direction of the toilet *constantly*. Through government shutdowns and global pandemics, park staff generally remain on site, whether because they live there or they play an essential role in keeping the park safe, even in the absence of visitors. At the end of the day, many park rangers we've met along the way can't imagine anywhere else they would be and feel a strong sense of service and responsibility in protecting and educating others about the land.

The Corn Lady

AS TOLD BY BETTY MAE JUMPER

"This is the legend of how the corn came to the Tribe. I can remember my grandmother telling us this one at night by the campfire. Sometimes we were under the mosquito net ready for sleep. Other times we were eating sweet potatoes and roasted oranges. On a cold weather night, those hot oranges were real good."

There once was a family living at the edge of the Big Forest, a wonderful place with swamps full of meat and fish. The family had places to grow vegetables, pumpkins, potatoes, beans, and tomatoes. They also raised pigs and cows. These were happy people with no worries—they had everything!

The children could be seen running about everywhere, playing around and swimming in the ponds nearby. But sometimes, when the older children were playing really hard, they would forget to keep an eye on the younger children.

One day an older sister put her baby brother down to play with the little children while she played with the older ones. They played a long, long time and she forgot about her baby brother. When she finally went to check on him, he could not be found anywhere. She called and called and called his name but could not find him.

The big sister ran home to tell her mother. Soon, all of the women in the village were out looking for him. They kept looking until sundown but were unable to find the baby. When the men of the village returned from their Big Forest hunting trip, they all looked for the child well into the night. But no baby was found.

A few days later, the men returned to hunting and fishing. The father of the baby sent for the wise medicine man. Since he lived quite a distance from the village, it took the medicine man two days to get to the village at the edge of the Big Forest.

When he finally arrived, he asked everyone to sit down. He told them about the "unseen people" that lived on small islands deep in the swamps.

The medicine man believed that one of these unseen people had picked up the baby and run off with him. He told the village people that they could not find these unseen people. But, the wise medicine man believed that the baby was still alive someplace in the Glades. The family was very sad at this news and gave up looking for the baby and all hopes of ever seeing him again.

Years went by. The missing boy's family still lived in the same village. The brothers and sisters had grown up and some were married. Then one day a strange thing happened out in the jungle in the heart of the Everglades on a little island. No one had ever been there before, nor had anyone ever seen the place.

On the island was a beautiful camp with three chickees: one for the campfire, one for sleeping, and one for eating. An old witch lived there, and she had a young boy living with her. Every day she would prepare corn sofkee and vegetables for the boy. He soon grew to be a strong teenager.

The old witch was so ugly that it made you wonder where she came from. But her love for the boy was great and she raised him well. She knew that someday she would have to tell him the truth about himself. This made her very sad because she knew this day was near.

The boy noticed that the chickees were old and falling apart and often asked why he was not allowed to repair them. The witch would never give him a reason. The boy questioned where she got the corn she prepared for him, but she would never tell him. All he knew was that there was always plenty of corn to eat.

The day came when the boy decided it was time for him to follow the old witch. She would always get up very early, check to make sure the boy was asleep, pick up her basket, and walk toward the swamp. One day the boy pretended to be asleep until she had gone, and then he followed her. She walked quite a distance to a running stream where she stepped in and scrubbed her legs until they were very clean. A little farther away, she sat on a log, dried her legs, and started rubbing them from the knees to the ankles until beautiful yellow corn fell and filled her basket. She continued doing this until her basket was full.

On the way back, she stopped and filled up another basket with white sand. The boy was watching her all this time. He ran back in front of her and quickly jumped in his bed and pretended to be asleep when she returned. She built a fire and parched the corn in the sand in an iron pot. She then placed the corn in a log about two feet from the ground. The log was about seven feet long and twelve inches around. She pounded it up and down until it was ground into cornmeal.

When breakfast was ready, the old witch called the boy to come to eat. But he refused. The old witch went to where he lay and said, "You know, don't you?" The boy didn't answer, and she asked again. Finally, he told her that he had followed her that morning and saw everything.

"I knew this day would come," the old woman told the boy. She began to cry. "Yes, my son, you have given me much happiness all these years, but it is now time you returned to your people."

She then told him the story of how she had taken him years ago when he was just a baby. She gave him the name of his family and told him where they lived. She also told him it would take at least two and a half days to reach his home. She then gave him the necklace he was wearing at the time she stole him away.

"I am an old woman and my time is drawing near," she told him. "You must do as I say: Leave and don't turn or look back. Just keep going! Tonight when the sun goes down, you must go to bed and sleep. When you wake up past midnight, you must get up and get ready to go.

"Go east toward the sun, and go past two big forests on the other side of the Big Lake. This is where your people live, and you will find them there. Now, sleep, my boy, you have a lot of walking to do. When you get up, pick up the fire and throw it all over the chickees and run.

"Follow the trail we have walked many times and go. Run! Run! Run! Don't cry! We have had many wonderful years together, and I have enjoyed seeing you grow into a fine boy. Get yourself a pretty girl and marry among your own people."

Somehow, the boy knew she meant well for him. She had been good to him and taught him everything he knew, including how to hunt. Past midnight, the boy got up, sadness in his heart. But he did as the old woman had requested. He threw the fire on the chickees and started running. He ran until he was very tired and started walking. He walked all through the night.

At daybreak, he passed the first big forest and continued walking until that evening, nearing the second big forest. He was very tired and wanted to rest because he knew he was near his village. He wanted to be rested before he saw his people.

The boy found a large oak tree and climbed up about midway to a large branch that looked like a saddle. He could sleep here without falling out of the tree. He awoke at sunrise with the birds singing all around. Feeling hungry, he climbed down from the tree to look for berries to eat. After eating the berries, he found fresh water to drink.

He continued walking until he reached the Big Lake the old woman had told him about. The men from the village were on their way hunting, and he quickly jumped out of sight as he didn't want to meet them yet. He knew the village was very near.

The boy continued walking until he saw many chickees. He climbed up in a large tree and watched the people until almost sundown. He wondered what he would say to the people about where he had lived for the past years. After a while he climbed down from the tree and started walking to the edge of the village.

The children saw him and started yelling, "New man. New man. Visitor." The older men of the village came out to shake his hand and talk to him. When he told the old men about himself, the old men remembered the story of the little boy who was lost long, long ago.

The boy then gave an old man the necklace he was wearing when he disappeared. "Yes, yes!" cried the old man. "I know your family." They slowly walked to the other side of the village, where a man and woman sat talking.

The old man placed the necklace in the old woman's hand. She stared at the beadwork for a long time and then looked up to say she knew the work. The old man then told her that this was her son, returned from being lost a long time ago.

The story was told over and over to everyone that joined the happy family around the campfire. They sat and listened all night long to the boy's stories. After many months, the village men decided to go and see where the boy was raised.

They left early one morning and were gone for about a week. When they returned, they told of finding the place where the boy was raised. Only now it was a patch of beautiful green corn that stretched all over the island. Soon, everyone went to see the corn, which was so yellow and pretty. The men gathered all the corn they could carry and took it back to the village with them. They saved the seeds and planted them year after year.

After the boy returned home and the corn was discovered, a Green Corn Dance was held every year to thank the Great Spirit for his blessing. And this is where the Indians got their first corn. ✦

About This Story

This Seminole campfire story captures the origin of the Green Corn Dance, an important spiritual event held each spring in undisclosed locations in southern Florida. In the early days, this marked an important occasion where Seminoles gathered with different camps and has since evolved into ceremonial events that include settling tribal disputes, separating men and women into different camps according to their clan, and purification and manhood ceremonies.

According to the Seminole Tribal Council, this gathering includes "hours and hours of 'stomp dancing,' the methodical, weaving, single file style of dancing traditional to Seminole Indians. Following behind a chanting medicine man or 'leader,' a string of male dancers will 'answer' each exhortation, while women dancers quietly shuffle with them, shakers tied to their legs." While Seminole Stomp Dancers occasionally appear at public events, very few non-Indigenous people have witnessed this celebration.

This story's orator, Betty Mae Jumper, is a formidable figure in Seminole history. She was the first and so far only female chief of the Seminole Tribe of Florida, the first Florida Seminole to learn to read and write English, and the first to graduate from high school and a nursing program. She also cofounded the tribe's first newspaper in 1956, *The Seminole Tribune*, and served as the director of communications for the Seminole Tribe of Florida. In a tribe wary of outsiders, Betty Mae Jumper went against the grain to share the stories, and the values, of the culture she held so dear.

Beggar in the Everglades

DIANA WOODCOCK

It pierces my heart till I rejoice when the mosquito pricks my finger for blood to nurture her eggs, initiating me into the life cycle of this place to which I've come like meeting someone for the first time and feeling I've known her all my life. They tell me their life story, and I'm converted—born again—their waters, slow-moving shallow river rising with summer rain, baptize me. And I'm forgiven—sins of omission (failing to do the little I could do to protect and restore them)—draining, bull-dozing of their sawgrass prairies. Washed in the blood of a million plume birds, I offer my body to be bitten, slashed, burned, but they neither punish nor scold; they are gentle, delicate even in their pain, in their sentient struggle to regain their rightful place. Sovereign in tenacity, endurance of extremes: drought, deluge, plenty, starvation, disaster. They are the sisters I never had—graceful, brave, beautiful. Symbol of fortitude, rainbow after the storm. Stasis in the mangroves, pivot of manatee and speedboat. I walk softly, silently—afraid of killing, injuring, disturbing anything in this fragile place. Red-winged blackbird taking over my favorite post and alligator dozing on my path remind me I'm the intruder—here today, gone tomorrow; they have been, will be, here forever. I lift up my cup and bowl for them to fill, walk humbly through sword-sharp sawgrass by the slough, admiring the slender beauties heaven-made: egret, heron, anhinga, ibis, wood stork, bittern, limpkin. Bowing before them, I pray for their flame that I might burn through the dark night and give light. Their flight and calls like alternations of Koranic recitations and mystical music. Let a green bird—heron preferred—descend on my head if indeed I am the elect. Let me make collyrium for my eyes from the dust kicked up by the alligator, that I might see more clearly and die pure. Let the master mixer of the red sulphur elixir, the roseate spoonbill, transform my soul into pure gold. Then, great egret white and delicate as falling snow, send me forth as arrow to pierce hearts set on destruction. ✦

In the Company
of Alligators

DIANA WOODCOCK

They were the last thing
I went to see—could not
imagine what the attraction
could be. I went for birds:
anhingas, spoonbills, egrets,
herons. And swamp lilies.
Manatees and dark, steamy
mangroves. Maritime fauna.
Palmetto palms and pig frogs.
Whispering of wind across
sawgrass prairies.

But I was hooked the moment
I spotted that first one dozing
along Anhinga Trail. Hearing
the bellowing of two echoing
across the slough—a sutra—I knew
they were saints if not prophets,
beyond good and evil, soul-readers
seeing by God's light, wildly created,
audacious, hypnotic, driven
forward by practicalities—not
hostilities, in control—rulers but
not dictators of the slough, kings
of the vast river of grass, a dark

tense presence, unadulterated motion
among soft-shelled turtles, garfish
and fallen ripened pond apples.

Sinking deep into my awareness,
triumphantly fulfilling my need
for distinct, unabashed wildness.
Even here, back now in my desert,
the Everglades flows through my days,
bellows of alligators like plain chants
echo in my ears—rhapsody, love song
so endearing, drowning out the
groaners of this sad world.

Hosanna to the alligators
in the highest: Glory be
to their Maker. ✦

About This Story

Diana Woodcock's work in the Everglades felt like the ultimate embodiment of what so many have described as being impossible to convey through image. To give a reader a glimpse into life in the Everglades that only sloughing through the muck or pulling back the sawgrass can reveal. And that she did. Diana is an award-winning poet and teacher of creative writing, environmental literature, and composition at Virginia Commonwealth University in Qatar.

While being an artist in residence in the Everglades, Diana reflected on her time living in an oil-rich desert sheikdom, observing the landscape much like she does in the Arabian Desert where she lives, and created these lush poems that are alive and vivid in intimate detail—radiating curiosity, respect for our natural world, and joy in discovery. Through her work, she wanted to "represent how deeply I was inspired by the Everglades and how much it is ingrained in my consciousness." Interested in local and global conservation issues, she focused on conservation efforts in the Everglades during her time there, specifically homing in on the flora and fauna "so that I can represent them concisely yet vividly in poetry to inspire readers to a greater commitment to protecting the environment." Diana hopes that her chapbook *Begger in the Everglades* (Finishing Line Press) helps to "tell the Everglades' story (past and present) and proclaim its wish list for the future."

OLYMPIC
NATIONAL PARK

A Forest for Seeking

INITIALLY PRESERVED to protect its
dwindling forests and population
of Roosevelt elk, Olympic is home
to diverse ecosystems that boast
glacier-capped mountains, old-growth
temperate rain forests, alpine forests,
and over seventy miles of wild coastline.
Here one can traverse varied landscapes
on or off trail, through forests and
along rocky Pacific coastlines.

illustration by
LEVI HASTINGS

t was in Olympic National Park that we came face-to-face with a band of mountain goats. How we reacted forced us to face the truth of who we are.

At first they were far down the trail. Far enough to wonder, "Is that . . . a cloud? On the trail?" But soon, they wandered closer into view. Two mountain goats and their two kids, ambling toward us. We couldn't believe it: our first encounter with the mascots of the park, and here they were going for a walk, on the trail, just like us! We took picture after picture, amazed and delighted they were moving closer in frame. But at the last moment, we looked up from our cameras to notice just how big they were, and how sharp those black horns looked. And they showed no sign of altering course—were they briskly walking . . . toward us?

Ilyssa turned and ran the opposite way. It was fight or flight, and Ilyssa chose flight. Dave just . . . stood in place. "What do we do?" shouted Ilyssa. As the goats closed the gap, Dave remembered reading about what to do in this scenario, so he pulled out his Olympic guide and flipped to the index. "Okay, where's M, where's M, not Mount Anderson, Mountain GOAT, here we go, okay, okay, page 9 or 135?" With just a few feet now between him and the goats, Dave had to pick one. Flipping to page 9, he read, "Mountain goats cause enormous damage to fragile alpine plants . . . " With no time left, and no wiser than a moment before, Dave tiptoed off the trail and hid behind a tree. He watched as the mountain goats, with one eye on him, continued right along the path.

Once we knew they had no interest in attacking, we watched the mountain goat family continue their hike, eventually veering off the trail, climbing up and down steep cliffs. They tramped over the landscape, hopping over tree roots and one another. As they began attracting a crowd, we noticed the parents walking a wider perimeter, as if to protect their young so they too could explore this landscape.

Olympic is a place that rewards the curious. Its diverse landscape includes glacier-capped mountains, old-growth temperate rain forests, and over seventy miles of wild coastline. There is no road that takes one through the heart of Olympic, and 95 percent of the park, over 1 million acres, is managed as wilderness. It can take you three-plus hours to get from one side to the other by car. "It's magical how you pop into one ecosystem and suddenly you're in another," says Anja Semanco, recipient of a Campfire Stories travel stipend. "If you're in the rain forest, you wouldn't know there's an ocean twenty miles from you. One landscape disappears into another. This place is thick with mystery."

Let's start with the Hoh Rain Forest. Here it rains most of the time, averaging 140 inches each year. The region is also fed by the Hoh River, which itself is fed by glacial runoff from the neighboring mountains. With Sitka spruce, bigleaf maple, and Douglas-fir trees that create a thick canopy, that sheer amount of wet also feeds a dense undergrowth of mosses and ferns.

This forest represents different things to different communities. For naturalists, the beauty of the unique temperate rain forest was one reason to preserve these parks. For the growing timber industry, the forests of this region were a source of income, fed by the demand of American expansion. Responding to the growing concern over the area's disappearing forests, President Grover Cleveland declared this area the Olympic Forest Reserve in 1897. The forest's continued disappearance also contributed to a steep decline in the elk population. Alarmed, President Teddy Roosevelt in 1909 designated a part of the reserve as Mount Olympus National Monument. The Roosevelt elk native to the park still bear his name today, after his cousin, President Franklin Roosevelt, declared it Olympic National Park in 1938. Still, tension with the timber industry remains. When we visited in 2016, we saw many "TREES = JOBS" signs along roads on the outskirts of the park. Preservation still faces off with profit, depending on who is looking at these forests.

Temperate forests soon give way to subalpine forests, then alpine forests, as they climb up the mountain peaks of Olympic. These U-shaped valleys were carved by frozen glaciers, which settled into the rock bed being lifted up from the floor of the Pacific Ocean, as the North American and Juan de Fuca tectonic plates underneath crashed into one another. These forces together created the stunning mountains and wide meadows of the Olympic landscape. Today, Mount Olympus reaches 7,980 feet, and continues to lift up as plates move. These mountains are so large that they create "rain shadow" effects in other areas of the park, literally blocking rain clouds from reaching areas behind them.

Next is the third ecosystem of Olympic, where many of these mountains were born—the rugged Pacific coast. The seventy-three miles of undeveloped coast are the longest protected coastline in North America. Just as forests transition moving up the mountain, this ocean has many tidal layers moving out to the Pacific. The splash zone is never submerged but is wet from spray, while the high-tide zone is covered only during high tide. The mid-tide zone is exposed during low tide, and the low-tide zone is submerged most of the year. The various tide zones and the cold, nutrient-rich water of the Pacific support hundreds of animals adapted to this unique marine ecosystem.

This beautiful but rugged coastline is preserved for the animals, at the expense of human visitors. Certain hikes along the coast require close attention to tide charts, as various tides make return paths inaccessible. Fierce storms and rocky coastlines have resulted in 180 documented shipwrecks here, earning the nickname "Shipwreck Coast." Just off the coast are over 450 sea stacks (tall islands once part of the coastline), that are important refuges to tufted puffins and other bird species, but off-limits to human visitors. Only scientists and research divers can access much of the marine ecosystem that makes up a large area of the park.

Humans have sure made their mark in the parts of the park they can visit. The grand Lake Quinault Lodge, built in 1926 by Seattle architect Robert Reamer, references the rustic style pioneered at the Old Faithful Inn at Yellowstone, another Reamer classic. The Lake Quinault Lodge was added to the National Register of Historic Places in 1998. Lake Crescent Lodge was originally built in 1914 as Singer's Lake Crescent Tavern. Built using locally milled timber, the resort consists of a main building and ten additional buildings situated amid an old-growth forest. All of the buildings were added to the National Register of Historic Places in 2007. For many, visiting these lodges is akin to stepping back in time. But before these lodges, eight Indigenous tribes called this place home.

The Klallam, along with the Makah, Quileute, Hoh, Quinault, Skokomish, Port Gamble S'Klallam, and Jamestown S'Klallam all have ancestral ties to this land. Migration of white settlers during the Oregon Trail era in 1842, and establishment of the Washington Territory in 1853, brought increasing conflicts with an expanding American territory. In 1855, the Point No Point Treaty was signed by Governor Isaac Stevens and representatives of the S'Klallam, Skokomish, and Chemakum Tribes. But soon, in 1856, many Puget Sound Indians fought Americans in the Indian Wars for suitable land. Weakened by smallpox and other diseases, the Coast Indians struggled to remain on their homelands.

The history of the Elwha River Dam is a fitting metaphor for the relationship between colonizers and Indigenous people. Connecting mountains and sea, the Elwha River was once a thriving ecosystem that supported eleven species of salmon and trout. With so much variety, the river was an important fishing ground for the Lower Elwha Klallam Tribe. But as the growing American timber industry sought new sources of power, the Elwha was blocked by the construction of the Elwha Dam in 1912, and Glines Canyon Dam in 1927. These dams generated power for nearby Port Angeles's lumber mills, but were disastrous for the ecosystem, blocking salmon migration and sediment flow, and flooding sacred areas of the Lower Elwha Klallam Tribe.

Fast-forward to the 1980s, when mounting evidence pointed to the Elwha and Glines Canyon Dams as the cause for dwindling salmon populations across the Pacific Northwest. After decades of advocacy by the Lower Elwha Klallam Tribe, the US Congress passed the Elwha River Ecosystem and Fisheries Restoration Act in 1992, which called for federal acquisition of both dams, and full restoration of the Elwha River ecosystem. In close collaboration with the Lower Elwha Klallam Tribal leaders, Olympic National Park officials removed the Elwha Dam in 2011, and the Glines Canyon Dam in 2014. The following decade saw a stunning recovery of the ecosystem, with salmon populations increasing steadily and the count of adult chinook salmon at over seven thousand in 2019. Olympic National Park officials continue to work with the Lower Elwha Klallam Tribe until full restoration of the river is achieved.

In this region, native people were marginalized in their own lands, and their way of life threatened by new ideas of conservation. But through continued advocacy, ecosystems are being restored. Olympic enjoys a reputation of being one of the only national parks where Indigenous people still live on the land and even hold the right to close down areas of the park to visitors, so that tribes can conduct private ceremonies. "Just as the earth can be transformed for the worse," writes Rena Priest, enrolled member of the Lhaq'temish (Lummi) Nation, "it can transform itself for the better."

Olympic is a forest for seeking. In the stories we've collected, we follow people who are searching for baby elk, searching for Glukeek (also known as Sasquatch or Bigfoot), or searching for silence. We invite you into their curiosity in the hopes that you, too, will reap the rewards of Olympic National Park.

Under the Spell of
the Roosevelt Elk

ROSETTE ROYALE

never thought I'd be awed by the magical genius of Roosevelt elk, but that began to change in the summer of 2011, when I worked as an editor for a Seattle weekly newspaper called *Real Change*. As its name implies, *Real Change* is a different kind of paper, one sold by people referred to as "vendors"; most vendors are houseless or have experienced homelessness. One day, a coworker suggested I interview a vendor named Bryant Carlin, who, along with living in a city park, is also a nature photographer. Bryant saves money from paper sales to help fund photographic journeys into the backcountry of Olympic National Park, where he often focuses his camera on the park's temperate rain forest. His trips, hardscrabble solo excursions, can last weeks, sometimes months, as he presses deep into the lush, tangled landscape.

Our interview was great, and the moment we finished and I turned off my recorder, Bryant invited me to accompany him to the rain forest. I burst out laughing. Me, go backcountry camping? Sure, it sounded amazing, but, in my midforties, I didn't know squat about the woods. He couldn't be serious. But he was, and over the course of several years, he followed up that invitation with at least a dozen more, every one of which I shot down. I didn't have the heart to tell him the wilderness terrified me, or more to the point: the *idea* of the wilderness terrified me. Along with being queer, I'm Black, and I've been told, in ways subtle and not, that the backcountry was no place for someone like me. While I respect the great outdoors, appreciate its wonder and beauty, it seemed safest to do all this from a distance. What if I went and something happened?

Of course, something always happens no matter where you go, and when Bryant invited me again, in February 2015, I realized the something I was worried about might not be terrifying. Indeed, it might be extraordinary. So, once I finally said, "Sure, let's go," and Bryant recovered from his shock, he asked when. I suggested late May. He lit up. That's perfect, he said, because that's when female elk give birth, and maybe we'll see a baby elk. This time I beamed. Baby elk? All I could imagine was a bundle of cute, a dappled ball of fur cavorting on four spindly legs. Whenever fears about the approaching trip arose, I repeated an incantation: You're gonna see baby elk, you're gonna see baby elk.

On one level, I couldn't have chosen a better place to do it. The park's signature animal is the Roosevelt elk, the largest elk in North America. Their name honors President Teddy Roosevelt, who designated Mount Olympus National Monument in 1909, to help protect the region's elk; in 1938, the monument was redesignated Olympic National Park. A Roosevelt elk bull can top out at half a ton, while a cow can attain seven hundred pounds. Calves are born in late spring, when pregnant cows retreat to calving areas, woodland maternity wards situated near water, often obscured by dense vegetation. An estimated five thousand Roosevelt elk live in Olympic, making it home to the country's largest unmanaged herd, so the odds of seeing at least one baby, out of the dozens or hundreds likely to be born, had to be good.

Or so I thought. But elk, I soon learned, don't play by human odds, especially when their playing field consists of a dense rain forest that spans tens of thousands of acres. On the first day, we had a fleeting encounter with a small herd of females, each of whom eyed us with an unblinking amber gaze. There wasn't a calf in sight. For most of day two, elk remained AWOL, though by midday, my attention was focused on keeping my balance in a river. Like almost every experience on the trip, fording a river was new, and after a practice ford of the Bogachiel River, the northernmost of the rain forest's four major waterways, I staggered onto shore. Still humbled by the river's raw power, I followed Bryant up trail. A former Marine Corps reservist, Bryant, a white man with a Southern drawl, moves through the wilderness with military efficiency. Though I tried to keep up, I was hampered not only by the tricky terrain, but by my feet, which sloshed and slurped inside my boots. We undoubtedly passed under the moss-draped branches of bigleaf maple, and we likely walked past Douglas squirrels scurrying up trees like furry, russet-colored missiles, but I was too busy lamenting my waterlogged Gore-Tex footwear to notice.

Then Bryant's right fist rose to shoulder height. *Stop.* He pointed in front of us.

"What?" I asked.

"Elk," he whispered.

Elk? Where? I squinted. All I saw was sword fern in a field of green, an extension of the field where we stood. There was nothing else—until there was. A female elk lowered her head to forage. Another elk moved behind her. As the second bowed her head, the first looked up to survey the surroundings. Behind the second, a third appeared, a front hoof hovering above the ground. Against the verdant backdrop, the first, with her chestnut-brown flank, pulled off a master illusion and disappeared, while the second elk took a step and the third stood statue-still. From behind a tree a fourth elk materialized. As Bryant snapped photos, I watched, mystified, as the elk demonstrated they were so at one with their environment, it was difficult to separate them from it. They seemed to dissolve into, then emerge from the rain forest like a troupe of four-footed Houdinis: there one second, gone the next—then back again.

And if that's how the adults performed, I figured the calves must do the same. All I had to do was bide my time.

As any performer will tell you, timing is critical, and spring 2015 was a critical time for the temperate rain forest. The rain forest receives, on average, roughly ten to twelve feet of rain from October to May, making it the wettest place in the continental United States. But that spring, the Olympic Peninsula, home to the national park, experienced a drought, one that would eventually encompass all of Washington State. Snowpack in the Olympic Mountains was 7 percent of normal levels. Mountain snows replenish the rain forest's four major rivers, and the drought placed the trees, the rivers, the moss, and, of course, the elk under stress.

But seeing how the drought affected the rain forest was almost as difficult as seeing an elk. Often, the area seemed a landscape in balance, a wonderland in eye-popping shades of green. When we forded the Bogachiel, the river crested midthigh, and its tributaries appeared robust, as did the waterfalls—though we never would've found the waterfalls if it weren't for the elk.

As a rule, stepping off established trails is prohibited in national parks. Olympic National Park is different: off-trail hiking is permitted. This allows rain forest visitors to explore the backcountry, and it's an allowance Bryant adores. Day after day, we'd strike out in the morning, and at some point, Bryant would veer off trail and surge into the green thick. With the downed logs that crisscrossed the earth and the red alder saplings that stood in tight formation, exploring off trail was arduous. And confusing. Bryant seemed to decide to bushwhack on a whim. Why here? Why now? These sudden route changes happened so often that, midway into our nine-day trek, when, once again, he charged off the established trail, I couldn't keep quiet.

"Bryant, what are you doing? Why'd you just walk off the trail?"

"I *am* on the trail."

"What trail? Where?"

"The elk trail. You're standing on it." He pointed in front of my wet boots.

This had to be a joke. There was nothing around us but grass and moss-clad logs, until—presto: the elk trail materialized. Barely as wide as my boot, it meandered past Bryant, through a pocket of sword fern and into the woods. When I turned around, I saw it snake behind me to the established human trail. All the times I thought he'd been charging off just because he wanted to, he'd been following elk trails. How had I missed them? From then on, they were hard to overlook, a network of passageways that webbed the land, carved with ease by hoofed feet that trod through the wild.

Traversing those trails is not for the faint of heart or weak of knee. Elk are ungulates—scientific lingo for mammals with hooves—and they seem to tread anywhere and everywhere a human wouldn't venture. Yet that's precisely where Bryant wanted to go. This sent us up steep, slick hills and into streams bordered with viscous mud. One time, an elk trail led to what I thought was a beautiful waterfall, a riotous cascade some thirty, thirty-five feet high. But then Bryant suggested we scale the hillside that bordered the falls, because he heard a second falls beyond it. I couldn't hear anything over the one in front of us. Still, we climbed—and there was another waterfall, its water rolling over a series of rocks situated in the hillside like stone steps. While the lower trail was raucous, this one was serene, a serenity provided by the steady trailblazing of countless elk.

Yet countless as they may have been, the calves eluded us—and their elusive nature only increased Bryant's desire to find them.

When it comes to humans, the national park requires visitors to move camp every fourteen days. During his weeks-long, even months-long, photographic journeys, Bryant does just this, establishing a photographic basecamp he maintains for less than two weeks before he packs up and stakes down somewhere else. Even though our trip was much shorter, Bryant thought moving camp would increase our chances of seeing more natural spectacles and maybe running into wildlife. Our second camp lay beyond the Bogachiel River ford, in an open meadow, one so charming I nicknamed it Camp Beauty. On our first excursion from this new camp, the nearby human trail, even during the drought, was marked by mud slicks. One spanned the width of the trail. As Bryant approached its leading edge, he paused. "Check this out," he said.

Stamped into the mud were a series of paw prints. Each was about two inches high from top to bottom, the heel pad crowned with four oval toe prints. There weren't any claw marks.

"What kind of animal is that?" I asked.

"Some kind of big cat. Prints look fresh, too." Bryant peered into the under-brush. "Here, kitty, kitty, kitty," he said, giggling. He was the only one laughing.

Along with elk, the park's other big mammals include black bears, mountain lions, bobcats, black-tail deer, and mountain goats, the last a nonnative resident introduced to the Olympic Mountains in the 1920s. Each can impress their own calling card into the soft rain-forest soil, prints a skilled tracker can read. I wasn't that tracker, and after spending the next couple hours wondering—make that worrying—what animal had left its mark, it wasn't until we returned to Camp Beauty I was able to check a guidebook. They were bobcat prints. Thankfully, bobcats didn't count humans as menu fare, though they did dine on mammals. Like baby elk. Not that there was a trace of an animal kill near our camp. Other than elk trails, the most visible animal marking was a line of elk prints in the riverbank, their split-hoof tracks heading into the river.

As we set out on our last full day in the park, Bryant decided our early morning trek should be devoted to finding a baby elk. I countered that if we hadn't seen one yet, our chances were slim.

"It could still happen," he said, "but this might be our last chance."

"Aye, aye, captain. Lead the way."

He remembered, from a past trip, that elk sometimes gathered in a nearby meadow, a half mile or so off trail. To reach it, we stormed through a field of mush. A shaft of sunlight broke through the canopy, a diver's lamp in a terrestrial sea. We found the meadow, but it was the wrong one. Bryant took us to a second meadow, tucked farther into the woods. Other than a swarm of gnats that helicoptered my head and a hidden Pacific wren, who enchanted with its rollicking, rolling mating call, we were out of luck. By that point, I accepted we'd been outfoxed by a baby elk.

Hiking out of the park the next day, I didn't feel cheated. So much of the trek had been astounding. It had also been exhausting and intimidating and even frustrating. But the rain forest, which I'd feared, almost dreaded, had offered immense rewards. True, I been scared out of my wits a few times—that first night in my tent terrified me—but I let those memories, along with any complaints, wash downstream.

At the trailhead, we loaded our gear in the van, and Bryant tossed his camera-mounted tripod on the back seat. I drove along the gravel roadway, a cloud of dust trailing behind us. The roadway ran flat for several dozen yards before entering a slight downhill grade. The grade steepened. As Bryant gabbed next to me, I rode the brake, moderating the speed as I tried to remember, from the drive in, if there was a turn ahead. There was. I slid into it, maintaining a steady grip on the wheel, and as we skidded around the curve, there, blocking the roadway, was a herd of elk. I jammed the brakes. A matriarch stood in front of us trailed by three younger females—and a baby elk. In unison, the elk turned to look at us. Bryant stopped talking midsentence. For a moment, everything held still, the world trapped in suspended animation, until Bryant reached for his camera on the back seat. When he moved, the matriarch flinched. She dashed into the trees. The other females followed. The calf, as dappled and cute as I'd imagined, with big jug ears, brought up the rear. It disappeared into the woods. By the time Bryant looked forward, the herd was gone.

"The one time I don't have my camera, this is what happens?" He cursed.

But I laughed. We'd gone the whole trip without seeing a baby elk, and then one showed up as we drove out of the park? Like any smart performer, this one knew how to make an entrance. That bundle of cute gave the best performance of the trip.

Bravo. ✦

About This Story

Rosette Royale is a Seattle-based writer and storyteller, and writes about being a Black queer person in the woods, which, he admits, "was never far from my mind out there." He's currently working on a book about his wilderness experiences in the temperate rain forests of Olympic National Park.

The generous off-trail access to Olympic's designated wilderness was made possible by the Wilderness Act of 1964. The act describes wilderness as having "outstanding opportunities for solitude or a primitive and unconfined type of recreation." So if a park is designated wilderness, in order to allow unconfined recreation, those visitors should have fewer restrictions. Off-trail hikers should still abide by leave no trace practices, and should know how to navigate using a map and compass, but other than that, the Park Service is eager to let you explore in any direction or path that you wish.

Getting to explore and knowing how to explore are still two different things. Along with Rosette, we are amazed at the knowledge possessed by Bryant—an unhoused individual, often overlooked, who saves his money for photography trips to Olympic. While some of us find ourselves lost on the marked trails, Bryant uses his expertise to see and trace nearly invisible trails left by the magnificent Roosevelt elk.

Whether or not you have a guide, it's important to be prepared for wilderness hiking, which begins with bringing the right clothing and gear. According to the National Park Service, the minimum amount of gear to bring on a wilderness trip (considered to be the "ten essentials"), include extra warm-when-wet clothing, extra food, a topographic map of the area, a compass (and know how to use it!), a flashlight with extra batteries, sunglasses, sunscreen, a pocketknife, matches in a waterproof container, a candle or fire starter, and a first aid kit. It's also important to consider other factors when planning what else to bring—like location, time of year, and length of your trip—so you can safely enjoy your wilderness experience.

Nahkeeta: A Story of Lake Sutherland

AS COLLECTED BY ELLA ELIZABETH CLARK

Many years have passed since Nahkeeta, a beautiful maiden, lived in the northern foothills of what are now known as the Olympic Mountains. Nahkeeta was a gentle girl, greatly loved by her people. She was as pretty and as graceful as the maidenhair ferns which grew in the forest. Her voice was as cheerful and musical as the little stream which flowed from under the waterfall not far from her home.

Her people were canoe Indians. They got most of their food from the salt water, very little from hunting. In the summer, after the salmon had been dried and stored for winter use, the women gathered berries near the edge of the forest. In the autumn, they went to openings in the forest to gather currants and roots and tiger lily bulbs. They almost never went back into the deep woods.

One autumn day, Nahkeeta was gathering roots with her mother and sisters. She wandered back into the woods, enjoying the carpets of ferns, the moss-wrapped logs and moss-draped trees, and the yellow-green light that shimmered through the forest.

After a while she realized that she had wandered far. When she turned round to go back, she found that she was lost. She called to her mother and sisters, but she knew that her voice was lost in the bigness and tallness of the forest. She knew her family would be able to hear only the murmur of the mountain streams. She tried to retrace her steps. Slowly the yellow-green sunlight of the forest faded. Darkness came. Nahkeeta struggled on, often climbing over fallen logs and getting tangled with the vines and ferns and small trees that grew from the old moss-covered trunks. At last, too weary and frightened to go farther, she dropped down on the moss beside a log and fell asleep.

Next morning her people searched for her. "Nahkeeta! Nahkeeta!" they called, again and again and again. There was no answer but the song of the wind in the treetops and the murmur of the mountain streams. For three days her people looked for her. On the fourth day someone stumbled over a moss-covered log. Beside it, in a pool of blood, lay Nahkeeta's body. Some wild beast had torn it.

Grief filled the hearts of Nahkeeta's people as they buried her body in a valley in the forest. For days, mournful chants and the sad wailing of women filled the air. The people's sorrow was so great that the Spirit Chief's heart was touched. One morning when they arose they were surprised to see a beautiful little lake, its blue-green waters surrounded by white-barked alders. The lake covered the place where Nahkeeta was buried.

The Indians called the little lake Nahkeeta. They said that every autumn the birds hovered over the lake and called, "Nahkeeta, Nahkeeta!" The only answer was a ripple over the water.

Today the lake is known as Lake Sutherland, because the first white man to see it was John Sutherland. Nahkeeta has been forgotten, except by a few old grandmothers of her tribe. ✦

About This Story

Lake Sutherland, just east of Lake Crescent and north of Olympic National Park boundaries, is a 350-acre lake created when a landslide separated it from Lake Crescent nearly seven thousand years ago. This version of the Nahkeeta story was collected by Ella Elizabeth Clark for her collection *Indian Legends of the Pacific Northwest*, an origin story that can be traced back to the Lower Elwha Klallam Tribe in the Lower Elwha River Valley and adjacent bluffs on the north coast of the Olympic Peninsula just west of Port Angeles, Washington.

Ella Elizabeth Clark was a white, non-Indigenous American author, educator, and professor who, after working as a fire lookout for the Forest Service in the Cascade Range, went on research trips across North America to interview and capture the oral traditions and stories of Indigenous people beginning in the 1950s. Today, she is sometimes criticized by anthropologists and folklorists for frequently editing the original texts for a more "general readership," while others acknowledge her efforts, as a nontrained folklorist, to preserve and share traditional native stories to a wider audience. In our last collection, "Origin of the Snake and Yellowstone Rivers" was collected by Ella Clark, recounted from Ralph Dixey, a Northern Shoshone man. Because of the lack of reliable documentation on legends, myths, or other native folklore about Yellowstone National Park, Clark's book is one of the few reliable sources of these stories.

This origin story not only paints an illustrative picture of the forests and lakes of the Olympic region, it also acknowledges the history and meaning that is erased when place names are altered to honor white explorers or settlers who claimed to "discover" them.

Still Lifes:
Hoh Rain Forest

GARY MIRANDA

In photographs of it you can hardly tell
which sides are up—a commentary both
on the nature of the place and our compulsive
need to frame things simply, correctly.
The forest is right, I think, in its
refusal—though "forest" is too familiar
a word for what this place with its
hanging, or arching, greenery (like hairy
jump ropes captured at one apogee or
the other) does, or its nurse logs which say
to any come: *Here—take root here!*

It's impossible to guess what—without
these paths, these plaques that assure us
not so much what grows, but that others have
been here—hard to guess what message such
hyperboles of verdure might convey,
Phosphorescent entrails. Spiny rafters.
Green gore of prehistoric spirits
spilt on our behalf (the timorous mind
Insists "on our behalf"). The rain a fact
so close a man could live here for years
and not feel wet, his toes curling like ferns.

As it is, though, curious tourists forage
for photographs beneath the drooping hammocks
of hemlock, fir, spruce, pine, and an occasional
redwood, foreign here itself. Armed against
the wet in forest-green slickers mostly,
in spaced platoons of three or four, this
strange barrage of creatures files past,
pausing the briefest moment at each plaque
or for a snapshot, sensing the forest's
urge to turn us all to moss or lichen, Lot's
wife multiplied in jade, rainy forever. ✦

About This Story

If you've ever wanted to step inside an enchanted forest, the Hoh Rain Forest might be it. Here is a place where you feel the trees are hugging *you*. Reading this piece by Gary Miranda, poet and Pulitzer Prize nominee, we felt it perfectly captured the sense of being in the Hoh Rain Forest. We visited many years ago, and recall feeling its green embrace the moment we stepped onto the trails.

We first joined a guided hike through the forest, led by a ranger on her very first day in Olympic National Park. She was frantically flipping through the notes on her clipboard and answered any and all questions with, "Well, I'm from Alabama *but* . . ." We soon left the hike and instead chose to follow another path through the trees, hoping they wouldn't decide to swallow us up as we strayed from the pack.

Towering coniferous and deciduous trees, dense ferns and vegetation on the forest floor, hundreds of species of mosses covered everything around us. Bright greens, deep greens, fluorescent greens, lime greens, *green* greens—we had never experienced so many shades of green. Everything felt so alive and wet and tangled together, and when you learn it gets nearly fourteen feet of rain a year, it makes sense.

The Hoh River, namesake for the Hoh Rain Forest, forms from glaciers on Mount Olympus, winds through the temperate rain forests, and all the way down toward the Pacific coast. As we approached its banks while exploring what felt like a portal out of a dense forest galaxy, the milky slate blue color of the water caught our attention, which we later learned is caused by glaciers grinding rock into a fine glacial flour. The hue of the forest becomes a filter and a feeling you can't quite capture in a photograph—you just have to visit.

Erasing Legends

LACE LAWRENCE

t took me three highways, one wrong turn, and a potholed county road to finally reach the narrow, winding dirt road I was looking for. It took an entire evening of unpacking before I was able to unwind and crawl into my bed, leaving my cell phone to die in the night. I woke in the morning not to the beeping of an alarm demanding I head to work, but to the scratching of little feet exploring my camper van roof. I lay there in my cozy nest of down trying to identify the name of my alarm clock. Is it a gray jay waiting impatiently to rob my breakfast leftovers? No, too many feet. A squirrel or a chipmunk then. As I pull the first of my limbs out into the cold morning air, I stir the pop-up roof. The scratching ends as my alarm clock leaps into the branches above. A mystery to never be solved.

In the gray predawn light, I brew my coffee in my camp's log shelter, which seems to sag under decades of pocketknife carvings. I read through the carvings on the shelter logs. Dates long faded, poorly etched hearts, and of course carved large is, "The mountains are calling and I must go." John Muir traveled here in the 1890s. I wonder which of his famous words were inspired by the Olympics and if their eloquence convinced President Cleveland to bestow the first national protections for this area in 1897. My kettle whistles, and I am reminded of the elk bugles often heard in these forests. A decade later another president, Teddy Roosevelt, extended these protections to include the habitat of the Roosevelt elk. As an avid hunter and conservationist, he protected these lands so people like him could use them for sport. Drinking my coffee, I think on the fight to designate this area as a national park in the 1930s. The timber industry was dead set against it, so, yet another president, Franklin D. Roosevelt, traveled from one Washington to the other to see this place for himself. When he toured these trails, he said the park needed to be bigger. He believed that we needed to think fifty years ahead and that recreation was more valuable than timber. Standing here in this campground more than eighty years later, I imagine what would have happened if FDR had chosen timber over recreation. In my mind's eye I see nothing but housing developments and strip malls.

The first orange rays of sunrise kiss the treetops, pulling me out of my thoughts and into nature. I make my way to the clearing just behind the shelter. There I watch the light catch the dew on the meadow of scarlet paintbrushes and Olympic violets. I send gratitude up into the branches. Thanks to my furry alarm clock, I have this quiet moment to myself. My neighbors with their impressively large packs and terrifying-looking ice axes set off sometime in the night, this camp just a waypoint on their journey to conquer larger peaks. The campers across the way are still sound asleep in their tents. No doubt sleeping off the many beers they drank and dreaming of the loud, precious memories they retold last night.

In this quiet moment, I see a young buck crossing out of the trees. He can't be more than twenty feet from me. He swings his head my way, showing off his growing rack. It is easy to see he is already used to humans, aware of both the good and the bad we bring. I give him a small bow of my head. He seems to understand that I know I am a visitor in his lands. As he bends his head to tug at the grass, I scan the meadow. My eyes rise up the glades marking the soft rolling shoulder of Blue Mountain. I picture them in their winter dress. I can see the pearly white snow paths cutting brightly through the trees that cast deep navy-blue shadows. I envision my grandfather maneuvering his way down these glades, with giant wooden skis strapped to his feet. I can almost hear his booming laughter on the wind.

That is why I have come here. I grew up on my grandfather's tales of skiing at Deer Park in the Olympic National Park. The ski resort was started in 1936 with a long rope and a motorcycle motor. By the 1940s Deer Park became part of the national park. It had ski jumps, designated runs, and a ski lodge. Being built in a rain shadow, it provided regular bluebird days. After years of war my grandfather and many others flocked here. "Restorative" was always the word he used to describe this place. That restorative feeling is what I have come looking for.

As the sun climbs higher into the sky, I know it's time to get moving, so I clean up and head out of camp. Climbing up Blue Mountain, I look for remnants of the old rope tow that ran a thousand feet up the side of this mountain. I wonder if the forest ranger cabin used to be the ski lodge. It's hard to tell. There isn't really anything left to show that a thousand people a weekend used to come up here for snowy views and ski turns. Looking out, I can see the rain storms brewing over mountain faces still draped in deep snow, and I chuckle at the foolhardiness of putting a ski resort in a rain shadow. It may be storming out there, but here, I am basking in the warmth of the sun surrounded by spring blooms. The ski resort was doomed before it began, but man rarely understands that nature doesn't follow our whims.

Rounding the corner, the expanse of the Olympic Mountains come into view. I scramble onto a rocky outcropping to get my first unobstructed view of the Olympics. Here on this well-trodden path, it is easy to think of nature as bowed to man, but those rugged peaks remind me that nature is truly a wild thing. I shiver in a combination of fear and desire just thinking of being out amongst those peaks. I imagine my grandfather sliding to a stop here and feeling the same awe and desire, before he sluiced his way through the meadows below. I could see this spot seeding my grandfather's love for these mountains. A love that he would spend the rest of his life tending.

I think on the history of these mountains long before my grandfather was tending to them. Back to a time before the forced removal of the Makah, Quileute, Hoh, Quinault, Skokomish, and S'Klallam peoples. I look out on the mountains and visualize what those receding glaciers would look like had this land not been taken. Turning back to the trail I ponder on how different things would be if our relationship to this land had been shaped by Indigenous teachings. Perhaps then our leadership would have formed this park for what it is, not for how it could be used.

I came here to find a connection to the past and the origin of my hand-me-down love for skiing and nature. I came here looking for remnants of the legends my grandfather told of ski racing on bluebird days. It seems all that is left is legend, though, and perhaps that is as it should be. How easily nature can recover from the effects of man's desire to use it for our needs.

I find a sun-warmed boulder at the summit and stop to rest. Up here I can close my eyes and see all the places my grandfather took me in this park over the years. Hundreds of days spent skiing, hiking, and camping, instilling in me a love for adventure and for nature. Suddenly, I hear the *whup-whup-whup* of helicopter blades starting up. I whip my head around, following the sound as it cuts through the air. Rising out of the trees is a mountain goat strapped into a harness and blindfolded. He dangles from the bottom of the helicopter looking for all the world like a tangled trapeze artist.

As I watch the goat rise higher and higher into the sky, I can't help but wish I could pull away his blindfold so he could see this place my grandfather taught me to love. I wish he could look to the west. There he would see the volcanic rock that rose out of the Pacific Ocean a millennia ago, creating an island of mountainous peaks and glacier-carved valleys. An area so unique that species not found anywhere else in the world thrive here. From that height, the dangling goat could see the azurite and emerald lakes strung like jewels across the mountains and valleys. His eyes would certainly rest a little longer on the deep turquoise waters of Lake Crescent, the crown jewel of the Sol Duc valley. I imagine the smell of the damp moss and the decaying giant cedars twitching his nose and turning his head south toward the Hoh Rain Forest. There he could look out on a riot of deep greens that mark the birth and death of giants. As he rose even higher, he could look past the craggy mountains and melting glaciers to follow the rivers and streams on their way to the rocky ocean shore. I like to think he would marvel at the dark coastline created by thousands of basalt, quartz, and jasper stones tumbled smooth by a million years of ice and snow. In his final look, he could gaze down on me standing in the wildflower-strewn high alpine meadows of the only home he has ever known. After taking in all this unique beauty, would he then understand why he cannot stay?

For this goat was born to a place where he never belonged. So many vintage posters and black-and-white photos capture the iconic Olympic mountain goat and the men who hunted it. But it never belonged here. It was introduced not unlike rope tows, ski lodges, and log rain shelters, as a tool for recreation. Another way for man to be restored by nature. The men who shipped the goats to the park revered them for their strength and agility, never thinking on how they would affect the fat and scurrying Olympic marmot or the fragile alpine flowers.

As I watch the goat's skyward journey, I can't help but think of my own impact on this precious place. I have often been the one with the giant pack and terrifying ice axes using a campsite as a waypoint to more famous peaks. I am ashamed of how I used those waypoints, always saving my gratitude for better views. I also think on my own boozy and boisterous campfire stories scaring small creatures in the night. Just this morning I was dry and comfortable under my log shelter, with no thought on how much my comfort cost the forest. I even pumped my camper van full of gallons of gasoline to drive hours, just so I could be restored by nature.

I shoulder my pack and begin my descent wondering if my future grandchildren will ask me about this. If flying goats and glacier-covered peaks will be a legend they hear from me. I am proud that I will get to regale them with stories of my generation's work to erase the marks of the past, but I can't help but wonder what marks from my generation they will have to remove. When I teach them the restorative power of nature, will they ask me what I did to restore the soul of the earth in return? Taking in the last unobstructed views of the Olympics, I wonder if I will have answers worthy of them. ✦

About This Story

Storyteller, adventurer, grant writer, and sometimes beer maven, Lace Lawrence is a writer and First Descendant of the Yakama Nation, whose reservation is today located in southern Washington State. Her story takes place in the high alpine meadows and old-growth trees of the Deer Park area, on the east side of Olympic National Park. Not as classic as the Hoh Rain Forest or Hurricane Ridge, it is home to many bluebird days (a ski term meaning sunny, cloudless weather), and is one of the only places one can spot the Olympic bellflower. A rare plant endemic to this place, the bellflower's floral ancestors were trapped atop the mountain by advancing glacial ice, which allowed it over generations to evolve into its own unique species. That process has occurred many times in Olympic's ecosystems, creating native species such as the Olympic chipmunk, the Olympic snow mole, the Quileute gazelle beetle, the Quinault fawn-lily, the Olympic Mountain ragwort, the Olympic bellflower, and the Olympic marmot.

One species not endemic to Olympic, strangely enough, is the mountain goat—an animal that we had thought of as the mascot of the park when we visited. Sport hunters introduced a dozen goats to the area in the 1920s to have something to hunt. But without any predators, the population would grow as high as one thousand here, presenting a problem as they destroyed fragile native plants and mountain meadows, which in turn killed many of the native species. Even worse, mountain goats have started to present a threat to humans, who they've learned to follow and seek out the tasty salt in their sweat, urine, and food.

In 2019, the National Park Service, the Washington Department of Fish and Wildlife, and the US Forest Service teamed up to capture some of Olympic's mountain goats and transfer them to the Washington Cascades mountains, where overhunting has decimated a native population. This creates the surreal display of seeing a mountain goat, caught and sedated, blindfolded and strapped into a bright orange sling, being lifted two to three at a time by helicopter, over the landscape. By September 2021, 525 mountain goats had been removed from Olympic National Park.

By comparing the removal of the mountain goats with the echoes of the ski resort built for visitors to Olympic National Park, Lace asks us to reconsider our relationship to nature. "How can we as recreationists go from an extractive-based relationship (*what can nature do for me?*)", asks Lace, "to a reciprocal-based relationship (*what can I do for nature?*), while still enjoying outdoor sports and goals?"

A Mountain Blessing

TIM MCNULTY

Across the high basin,
green sloping meadows and bands of rock
drop steeply to a cobalt lake.

Slow, metallic trickles ring
from withering snowbanks;
scraps of cloud dissipate,
and the mountain world is numinous
           with light.

Last night, four bear
—small shadows
        darker than the shadowed cliffs—
emerged and prowled the ledges
and skirts of meadow,
hungry for summer-sweet berries.

We watched as they moved easily
across cliff face and hanging meadow.
The she-bear
and her cub descended a wall
of broken rock
        on invisible steps.
Another stemmed a smooth
water-worn gully

to a hidden pocket meadow
   and disappeared.

We stayed until cold and coming darkness
sent us back over rocks and hummocks
to camp.

Now,
as afternoon shadows cross the slope
and breezes ruffle the lake,
I listen for the ceramic clack
of stone on stone
and watch for those deepest of shadows
to re-emerge
from shrubby cloisters of trees.

I wait attentive and hopeful as a supplicant
for that blessing of the wild
to wash over me
   like a fine north wind,

and deepen my winter dreams. ✦

About This Story

Olympic National Park in the winter is not for the faint of heart. Described as a "never-ending wetness," winter brings a large amount of precipitation to the rain forests and coastline, with snow blanketing the higher elevations. What starts as a sunny day can quickly lead to blizzard-like conditions and hurricane-force winds. As many park amenities and programs wind down for the winter season, so do bears as they prepare for the long nap. Black bears are a common inhabitant of the park and sightings are frequent, as black bears tend to hang out in areas where they are not hunted. Even so, as described in this piece from Tim McNulty, the opportunity to witness these creatures, particularly from a distance, is an incredible experience.

Black bears, which can appear black, brown, or blond, rarely pose harm to visitors in the park, as they tend to be shy and keep to themselves. Much of their time leading up to winter is spent in search of berries on high mountain huckleberry bushes or catching salmon en route to spawn in shallow waters. Bears play a big role in building and rebuilding forests, as the undigested seeds in their droppings (built-in fertilizer!) grow into more giant trees and berry bushes that help to feed other wildlife in the park. Once the winds move in and it starts to snow, bears retreat to a den and hibernate for several months, only to reemerge in the spring once the weather warms and the snowpack begins to melt. Leaving the den with new cubs and hungry bellies, bears go on the hunt for nuts, seeds, tree sapwood or bark, and insect mounds until berries come in season again.

Glukeek Legend

AS TOLD BY HARVEST MOON

Long ago the women and the children had spent most of the day picking the sweet tiny blackberries. As the sun was falling to the west, the women started gathering their baskets of berries and heading back to the village when they heard this rustling in the brush. As this rustling in the brush came closer, the women motioned with just their eyes to the children who could run quickly enough and fast enough to run back to the long house. Now, for the children who were too young, they quickly picked them up, held them underneath their arms, took their heads, and held them close to the mother's heart.

When the small children heard the fast beating of the mother's heart, they knew they had to be very quiet. The women cupped their hands and brought them behind their ears in order to hear as well as a deer. As the rustling of the brush came closer, they knew it wasn't deer because deer has a jumping sound through the brush. They knew it wasn't bear. Oh, bear love those little blackberries as much as we did! But as long as bear had no cub, bear would run away. But as the rustling of the brush came closer, all of a sudden, there was this horrible, horrible stench. Out of the brush came this huge monster. His legs were as big as tree trunks. His skin was covered with hair, and his eyes had a hypnotic red glow to them. This monster started chasing the women all through the berry patch. And as he was chasing them, he took his huge big feet and he started kicking over every basket of berries, wasting them on the ground.

Now, the women managed to escape, and they made it back to their longhouse. The men decided maybe we should go check that berry patch. When they got to the berry patch, they looked for footprints. None to be found. They looked for maybe hair that might have come off, but there was none to be found.

That night when everyone was sound asleep all of a sudden the guard dogs stood up on all fours and they just froze. Now, in the past, those guard dogs would have ran out and chased whatever it was that was coming. But in this case, they didn't make a noise. The hair on the back of the dogs came straight up. And for the first and only time the dogs made a sound that went like this . . . *woooOooOOooOOoooOoOoOOOoo.*

Now some of the people escaped from the secret tunnels we have in our long-houses. Others just froze. That monster came and started throwing pieces of driftwood on the roof, screaming and hollering through the entire night. Just before the sun came up, he disappeared. Now, not having any sleep whatsoever, the salmon fishermen went down to the river and they started to pull up their traps. And as each of them pulled up their traps, lo and behold, there had not been one salmon caught. It was then the salmon fishermen looked up the river, and standing where no man would be able to stand in the Skookums, or the white rapids of the river, stood this monster.

He picked up his smelly, stinky feet and started laughing at the salmon fish-ermen. It was then they realized that as long as this monster was to stand in the river with his dirty, stinky feet . . . that the salmon people, you know, who live at the bottom of the ocean, will never travel up the river again. Women aren't going out to gather food, they're not getting any sleep, and now no salmon. Now, this was happening throughout the entire Pacific Northwest. For the first and only time, all the chiefs gathered together for a meeting. One of the chiefs raised his talking stick and explained: "Let us find the strongest warrior. We'll make a special spear that would be so sharp that it would penetrate that tough leather skin of the monster and we'll be rid of him forever."

As soon as he spoke those words, the Whale Hunter raised his arm and announced, "I should be the one that kills this monster. I kill whales that are ten times as big as this monster!" Then Elk Hunter, he raised his arm and announced he should be the one that kills the monster because he knows the woods better than the Whale Hunter. Well, they argued back and forth until four young men brought forth this huge rock. The rock was as big as your arms could hold around. They dropped this big rock in the middle of the floor of the longhouse. Then a young girl of six seasons came forward with a shell. In this shell was full of bear grease. She took a handful of the bear grease and she started smearing it all over the boulder. For whoever could carry this rock the furthest would be the one that would kill the monster.

Well, it's been said that the warrior who carried that rock the furthest had carried it six and a half miles up the side of a mountain and back without dropping it. After the special spear had been made, as the warrior was leaving, he stopped and asked a very old elder, he said, "By what name shall I call this monster to his death?" And the old elder spoke and said, "His name is Glukeek." So as he was leaving, you could hear "Gluuuuuukeek! Glukeeeeeeek! Gluuuuuuukeeeeeek!"

Weeks passed. The warrior never returned.

The parents who lost their son had a meal in his honor, and it was after the meal that an old, old elder came forward and said, "Let us dig a hole ... dig a deep hole, put some branches on top of the hole and place your prettiest maiden on that very edge of the hole." At that minute, everyone standing side by side started to dig this hole. It took two full moons to dig a hole deep enough that would keep this monster in the bottom of the pit. They just placed the prettiest maiden on the very edge of the hole when they heard the rustling in the brush. Glukeek came out of the brush, ran straight toward the maiden, made it halfway over the hole before he finally fell through. When he hit the bottom of that pit he started screaming and hollering so loud it created avalanches in the Olympics. The people didn't know if they should cover their ears or cover their nose. Days passed. He soon collapsed in the bottom of the pit.

It was then that my ancestors had enough nerve to peer into the pit. And as they gazed into the pit, they thought, "What are we going to do with him now? I don't want to feed him, not after what he's been doing to my tribe!" One of the young men raised his arm and said, "Let us put the dirt we took out and put it back in and we'll bury him alive."

"Well, as we put the dirt back in, he can arrange it at different levels and escape and kill us all!" A young woman raised her arm and announced, "Why don't we just fill the hole with water and we'll drown him?"

"Well, as we fill it up with water, he'd be able to float to the edge and escape and kill us all!"

Well, there were ideas upon ideas until finally came forward the old elder and he said, "Burn him!" The people took a couple steps back. "Burn this monster." Well, his idea of capturing him in the hole worked, so his idea of burning him shall also. So the people quickly got into a line from the edge of the hole all the way to the beach. In this line of people, they started passing up large pieces of driftwood and putting them at each end of the pit.

On the night when there was no moon in the sky, all the people gathered around the pit. The parents who lost their son would be the ones selected to torch the first fire. And as they were bending down to torch the first fire, all of a sudden there was this rustling in the brush. *Are there more than one of these monsters? Are there families of these monsters? Will we be tormented for the rest of our lives with these monsters?*

About then, out of the brush, came their son. His head was bowed low, he didn't want any eye contact, for all that had happened was that he had lost his way. The parents were so happy he was still alive, they quickly handed him the torch and he would torch the last fire. And as he was bending down to torch the last fire, Glukeek reared up from the bottom of the pit and he said, "You can't kill me! Because I am going to get out. And I am going to bite each and every one of you, and suck your blood."

Those people kept those fires burning for four days and three nights. The flames of the fire rose so high into the sky that the people on the other side of the Olympics actually thought Raven, the trickster, was creating a second son from the West. On the fourth night, when there was a small crest of a moon, all the people gathered around the pit. The chief took his walking stick and he started stirring the coals that accumulated at the bottom of the pit. And as he was stirring the coals, sparks from the fire rose high into the sky. And as they got higher, they started to cool and fall as ash. But as the ash touched the earth, it all came to life as fleas, mosquitoes, and ticks.

How many of you have been bitten by Glukeek?

Nahashkah. ✦

About This Story

Perhaps the most widely known lore of the Pacific Northwest is the humanlike, upright, ape-like figure we affectionately know as Bigfoot, Sasquatch, Yeti—or, to the Indigenous people around Olympic National Park, Glukeek. People from all over the world flock to the Pacific Northwest for a chance to get their own glimpse of the beast and partake in the many Bigfoot community happenings—seminars, conferences, festivals, guided hikes, group expeditions, and trainings dedicated to Sasquatch lore. Here, many tales and personal encounters with Bigfoot are shared among true believers, which go beyond the conspiracy theorists and even attract celebrities, politicians, and scientific researchers. Many believers point to the presence of Sasquatch, or Sasquatch-like figures, in legends passed down for many generations in native tribes.

Harvest Moon is a Quinault basket maker, storyteller, and recipient of the Peace and Friendship Award from the Washington State Historical Society in recognition of significant contributions to the understanding of Northwest Indian heritage. As a Quinault Tribal Ambassador, Harvest Moon can be found leading programs and sharing stories of the Quinault people at Lake Quinault Lodge in the park. Her name was given to her by her great-grandfather after she came into the world in the middle of the night under a full moon, following a large harvest of salmon from the Quinault River. As she shared with Wisdom of the Elders, which collects oral history, art, and knowledge from Native elders, storytellers, and scientists, "I went on a vision quest when I was in my teens to find out the meaning of my name, which is 'a light shining forth in the midst of darkness.' It was then that the storyteller started to emerge. Storytelling has always been a part of folklife regardless of nation, race, or creed; in fact, stories and legends have served as the history books of mankind for thousands of years."

We were first introduced to Harvest Moon's brilliant storytelling on YouTube, and soon after making contact with her, we couldn't wait for new emails to arrive. They were always adorned with unprompted vignettes of her day through story, instructions to reach her by phone or "smoke signal," or photographs of handwritten stories to consider. You can see her in action by searching "The Dark Divide - Deleted Scene" on YouTube, an abbreviated version of her Glukeek legend that was filmed for *The Dark Divide*, a film adaptation of the book *Where Bigfoot Walks: Crossing the Dark Divide,* by Robert Michael Pyle, starring David Cross and Debra Messing. Or, if you're lucky, you can catch her live at a Park Service interpretive program at the Lake Quinault Lodge. We are so grateful for Harvest Moon and for her work sharing the legends of her people. "Nothing is stronger," writes Harvest, "than water and the words of women."

One Square Inch

ANJA SEMANCO

Sun glides between hemlocks and cedars while drops of rain condense onto enormous devil's club leaves. Even on a dry morning like today, the Hoh Rain Forest is filled with the sound of water tumbling down the layers of the canopy, searching for the earth. Just standing in the parking lot, the landscape feels thick and muffled—which is precisely what I've come for.

I wouldn't say I'm obsessed with silence so much as desperate for it. Before eight a.m., I hear from my apartment in Bellingham, Washington, a car engine revving so loudly that it sets off someone else's car alarm parked directly beneath my bedroom. I hear an ambulance. A fire truck. A squealing car that needs a new timing belt. A woman on her phone shrieking, "You think you've got it all together, Becky, but you don't!" An oil train that blares its horn exactly eleven times as it crisscrosses downtown. A lawnmower, a leaf blower, and finally a weed whacker—the holy noise trinity. Another train. The drag racers who have settled into a two a.m. circuit that includes, by my best guess, at least three laps down North Forest Street.

These jolts of sound grind like coarse sand through my bones, leaving me hollowed. I tell my therapist the noise is breaking me. She tells me I need to find other ways to ground myself—and to invest in a white noise machine. A friend says to envision the sound of the street like the calming din of a river, and I try, lying on the floor one evening still as a carcass before a dog immediately breaks the spell. It barks for three straight hours. The sound clatters around my empty body.

I am a rattling shell when I stumble across the One Square Inch of Silence project—the fabled quietest place in the Lower 48, deep in Olympic National Park—and I know I have to find it.

· ✦ ·

Olympic National Park is a great big circle. One road runs the perimeter, and, unlike other national parks, there is no way to cross it by machine. More than 95 percent of the park is dedicated wilderness, making it one of the largest wilderness areas in the contiguous United States. The park covers several distinct ecosystems including the Pacific coast, glacier-capped mountains, and old-growth temperate rain forests. It houses creatures from humpback whales to elk, tidepools to tundra. The park hangs off the country like a strip of bark and beckons to those of us in search of something utterly un-urban.

According to the One Square Inch of Silence project's website, I can expect to find this mythical, quiet location 303 feet above sea level about 3.2 miles from the visitor center along the Hoh River Trail at exactly 48.12885°N and 123.68234°W. I will have to pass through an arch created by an old spruce. The spot will be marked by a red square stone placed on a moss-covered log.

Any of this information would have been extremely helpful to write down before leaving for the wilderness with absolutely zero cell phone reception. All I can remember by the time I reach the trailhead with my backpacking gear is that the Square Inch will be about three miles in and marked with a red stone.

My partner, J, is certain someone at the visitor center will be able to help us narrow down the details, so I wait for a line of tourists to wrap around the entrance table before stepping up to the park ranger. He is an older man, in his fifties or sixties, wearing a crisp uniform and seated atop a wooden stool too high for the interactive welcome table. He towers over park pamphlets.

"Could you tell me where to find the One Square Inch of Silence?" I ask sheepishly because technically the One Square Inch is not managed by the National Park Service, but rather by an individual named Gordon Hempton, who has made a life of seeking out the last remaining quiet spaces in the United States.

"I've heard of it," the ranger says and pauses. I think he's about to reprimand me when instead, he leans in. "Honestly we're all pretty new staff here," he says, lowering his voice. "Most of us just started a week ago. I'm not sure about this particular spot, but I bet you someone on the trail will know."

On the way out of the visitor center, I see a chalkboard that informs parkgoers that banana slugs have twenty-seven thousand teeth. I don't know where the One Square Inch is, but I do, at the very least, know this new, horrifying fact.

I am here because I know that exposure to constant noise between 40 and 55 decibels can harm human health, memory, and cognition. A busy city street has noise levels around 70 decibels. Motorcycles and revving engines regularly surpass 95 decibels. Sirens can peak at 120 decibels. Meanwhile, the furthest you can get from a road in the Lower 48 is just 18.76 miles, and removing yourself from the line of roads *and* air traffic is almost impossible. The Hoh Rain Forest—the quietest place in the Lower 48—gets you pretty close. But not close enough to keep some of us from wondering if silence is trickling inattentively into extinction.

The park, the public, and Naval Air Station Whidbey Island have been at odds since 2008 with the arrival of the Growler jet, which roars through the skyline low and fast. More than twenty-three hundred Growlers fly over Olympic every year and by some estimates, a person on a six-hour hike through the park will experience a collective full hour of jet noise. The air station recently put in a request to add another three hundred flights a year.

At the trailhead J and I take a cursory glance at the map, but, of course, the One Square Inch isn't marked there either. The Hoh River Trail will take us straight to the Olympic Guard Station where our campsite is, which is about seven miles from the Square Inch. J asks if I want to try and find some service to look up the coordinates before we start.

"I'm hoping I'll just *know* when we're close to it," I say. I want to believe that my body, so hungry for quiet, will lead me to silence like an animal migrating home. But of course, it never works that way. It only takes a few miles of hiking before I realize there are dozens, if not hundreds, of game trails extending off the main path that all look as though they could lead to the One Square Inch. I hurry down a couple of dirt paths when I think we are about three miles in, but come back empty-handed.

"I'm not going to find it, am I?" I ask J. He smacks through the mud.

"No," he says matter-of-factly. "Probably not."

I tell myself I can come back if I don't find it on this trip, but the annihilation of this sort of silence seems unstoppable. It is possible the quiet of the Hoh Rain Forest will melt like glaciers into the noisy world before I get a chance to return.

Gordon Hempton created the One Square Inch of Silence project on Earth Day in 2005, and it stands to protect large areas of Olympic National Park. In the same way a loud noise—like aircraft—impacts many square miles around it, one square inch, Hempton estimates, could protect a thousand miles of silence. That is the power behind a single square inch.

Once you find the Square Inch, I imagine it's like arriving at some kind of fourth dimension of solitude that extends for a nameless expanse. But of course, that requires you to find the Square Inch in the first place—which I do not.

When we reach Five Mile Island, I know we've gone too far. I contemplate turning back to look for the Square Inch and letting J go ahead without me. I feel a knot tie in my guts.

Then we hear the first *whoomph*, a sound so low and loud, that both of us stop midstride. I feel it through the ground before I hear it. Like a marble dropped onto a tiled floor, the *whoomphs* start slow before quickening into a ricochet. My whole body vibrates. It lasts a few seconds, and then the forest goes quiet.

"What was that?" I whisper to J.

"I have absolutely no idea," he says. We wait a few minutes then hear it again. I can feel it resonating through the soles of my boots, drumming in my chest. It's as though it's coming straight out of the earth. I feel like my heart is beating out of time.

All around us, the enormous Douglas-firs, Sitka spruce, and shaggy red cedars carry the hush of the wind between their branches. Giant pads of dangling moss ripple in the breeze. Two varied thrushes call back and forth in between gusts while the turquoise Hoh River sustains a droning hum. This mystery sound penetrates them all.

With five miles still to go before we reach our campsite, I make the difficult decision to leave the One Square Inch behind and promise myself I'll look harder for it on the way back. I turn my ears instead to this new sound while J and I make wild speculations about its origins. J thinks it might be the sound of tree roots shifting beneath the earth as the wind pulls on the rain forest canopy. I immediately worry that it's something manmade. Despite hearing the sound several more times in the following hours, we don't get any closer to a conclusion.

We reach the Olympic Guard Station in the first wave of evening rain and wait under a low, overhung tree for the storm to slow before racing to set up our tent in between the downpours.

Park maps and pamphlets ensure me that we will see elk on the river. But when I walk out to the stony bank to gather drinking water, I don't see any wildlife at all. The walls of the valley ripple with low clouds sticking in the trees like cotton. The tops of the peaks are dusted with snow, and if I could get just a little higher, I'd see Mount Olympus a few miles away in the distance.

As I walk the water back to camp, and the sun begins to slip down the valley walls, the thumping sound becomes constant. Every few seconds, we hear it. Even when the sun finally dips out of the sky and we're lying in the damp tent warming ourselves around a Nalgene filled with boiling water, we feel it humming through our sleeping pads. "Maybe it's elk?" I say to J. But he shakes his head. We've just moved to Washington from Colorado where we were around elk constantly. "We would have heard it before," he says. And I have to agree that he's probably right. "Maybe it's Bigfoot," I say, and we both laugh. Still, I lie awake for a long time once the tent goes dark knowing something else is out there.

In the morning, we set the tent in a sunny spot to dry while we make our breakfast. I watch the river for elk again, but only spot a deer and her two fawns. We don't hear the thrumming. In fact, we don't hear it again for a long time. We start the hike back in utter silence waiting for the sound. So much rain has fallen in the last forty-eight hours that the trail has become a mess of mud. To hear anything at all over the squelching of our boots, we have to come to a complete stop, which we do over and over again when we think we hear the sound.

After more than two hours, J and I hear the first drumbeat near a thicket of snags and moss-covered logs. He holds up his hand, motioning for me to stop, but I'm already crouching down with my ear toward the ground. *Whoomph, whoomph, whoomph.* Whatever is making the sound has to be less than twenty feet away.

We wait, and just a few moments later, I hear it again, slightly further away. The sound is wandering off. I peer into the woods, but the rain forest is so thick and dark that all I can see is a collection of underbrush and moss. We continue slopping along.

When we're again approaching the area I think the One Square Inch could be, I pause to look out on the river and happen to spot a mottled brown bird drinking at the edge of the water—a female ruffed grouse. She bobs along flicking water and puffing up her feathers. Further up the trail, a hiker laughs loudly, and she scuttles back into the forest, disappearing into the brush. I look down a handful more game trails, but I can't find the Square Inch. Somewhere, just a couple hundred feet from me, is a kind of quiet I've never experienced.

Back at the visitor center, the same park ranger sitting awkwardly over the welcome table says he has no clue what the sound was that we heard. Even his supervisor, who has been around for a couple of seasons, is stumped.

In the truck on the way home, while I navigate I-5 traffic around Seattle, J is deep-diving into internet searches trying to understand what we heard. After twenty minutes, he holds his phone up to his ear and grins.

"I figured it out," he says. He connects his phone to the truck's Bluetooth sound system and turns the volume way up. Even over the roar of the traffic and construction on the busy highway, I immediately recognize the chest-thumping *whoomphs*.

"That's it!" I say. "What is it?"

"It's a ruffed grouse," he says.

· ✦ ·

Finding the Square Inch would have comforted me. In my apartment, the furthest I can get from a noisy road is about twenty feet. The longest I can go without hearing a human-caused sound is a small collection of seconds in the deepest, darkest corners of the night. For me, this is madness. For the ruffed grouse, it would mean death.

The male grouse leans back on his tail, fans his wings, and creates a series of sonic booms. This is the mating ritual I have heard now dozens of times in Olympic National Park, thrumming through my body like a ghost. The little bird finds a log or stump to leave room to fan his wings, risking the attention of predators to attract his mate. If he couldn't hear the surrounding forest because of, say, the rush of modified engines grinding down a busy city street, he'd quickly become someone's lunch.

On the worst nights, when the onslaught of noise from North Forest Street has nearly weathered me through, I slip on my noise-canceling headphones and play a ten-minute track of the ruffed grouse's drumming, like a mantra. This isn't silence. Just an affirmation that silence, somewhere, once existed. And some nights, that's enough to soothe me back to sleep. ✦

About This Story

Anja Semanco is a recipient of one of our travel stipends to visit Olympic National Park. When she applied, Anja had just moved to Washington during the COVID-19 pandemic, after spending the better part of her twenties in the Front Range in Colorado. She had to rent an apartment sight unseen, which landed her in a very noisy spot on a very loud street. As a quiet person, the opportunity to be paid to find solace in Olympic National Park appealed to her.

We were excited about her desire to find the One Square Inch of Silence, and how we relate to our natural environment based on our understanding of ourselves. Anja, who identifies as bisexual or queer, shared she was somebody "who didn't accept or fully understand my own sexuality until my early twenties, and did not see myself reflected in traditional nature and (especially) adventure writing."

Anja's escape from her Bellingham apartment led to a thirty-mile backpacking trip along the coast, navigating maps and tide charts to ensure she wouldn't get stranded when the tides came in. During most of her trip, she thought she'd write about hiking along the coast where the ocean meets the trail, but she could not get Gordon Hempton's One Square Inch of Silence project out of her mind. Ill-prepared, Anja set out to find the One Square Inch. "There are a lot of ecosystems in Olympic and I only saw two," recalls Anja. "I was there for six days and couldn't begin to capture what it encapsulated. There's a wildness that other parks have, but in Olympic it's magical how you pop into one ecosystem and suddenly you're in another. If you're in the rain forest, you wouldn't know there's an ocean twenty miles from you."

Though she ultimately did not find the One Square Inch of Silence, we are glad to have taken the journey with her.

))D0((RENA!

Before Clocks

RENA PRIEST

Before clocks
to keep time meant music;
the steady rhythm of a beat,
the playful plucking of a string,
the full throb of a drum
sounding to the steps of feet.

To keep time meant stillness;
the steady passing of a day
no need for rush or delay
in the fluid timeline
of one's own way.

To keep time meant tides;
the waxing and waning of the moon,
the easy pace of later, and soon,
the warmth of the sun
declaring high noon.

To keep time meant seasons;
the rippling rings of a tree,
the changing disposition of the sea,
the migration of harvests, leading us
to where we need to be.

And it always happened
right on schedule. ✦

Syncing Up at Sol Duc

RENA PRIEST

I have often thought about what life must have been like for my ancestors. I feel closest to them out in the forest or out on the water. I think of how they loved this beautiful place—this majestic landscape, these breathtaking waterways. How could one not have a feeling of affection and reverence for this place?

I feel this reverence most deeply when I take all five of my senses out into the woods or out onto the Salish Sea, and I am removed from the taxing and ever present crush of the evidence of human beings. I feel the pulse of my own timeline slow down. It is the earth, trying to put me back in sync with the rhythm of my own beautiful being. It is healing. It is medicinal.

I have an oral history collection with interviews from my ancestors and other Lummi elders speaking about various aspects of our Indigenous ways of knowing and being. The section on health and medicine begins with my great-great-grandmother, Aurelia Balch Celestine, talking about visiting the Sol Duc hot springs as a little girl. She guesses she was about ten years old at the time, which would mean that the visit was made sometime around 1896.

The family wanted to take Aurelia's aunt to the hot springs to ease her rheumatism. She could hardly walk, but the family made the trek, stopping first at the little village of Jamestown, at Sequim, where an uncle lived. They loaded up a buggy with supplies and took a team of horses to Crescent Lake, where they unloaded the buggy and went across the lake on a scow. When they got to the other side, they loaded what they could of their supplies onto some pack horses. The rest, they carried. Here is her account of that journey:

"It was just a trail, just a trail. We walked and walked and walked. Every once in a while, we'd see a mark there, you know, where it says which way to go to the hot springs. We got to a river. It was nighttime and there was an old house, so we camped there. Every once in a while, you see a little shack where you can camp if you want to camp. Just a shed, that's all. And then next day we walked.

"There were other families that went from Sequim: my uncle and two other families, I guess, went along with us. And we walked along the river. We walked up and down along the river. My dad walked up and down. He got as far as the falls, the big falls, and he come back. And my uncle was sick. He had the TB or something, I guess. So my dad and my aunt's cousin felled a tree across the river, and it didn't go straight; it swung and drifted away. So they had to knock another one down and it reached the other side.

"Then those little horses had to go across with them things by themselves. Then we had to go on a foot log, each one packing little things, holding one another just like monkeys going across the river. Then we got across and continued walking up, following the trail. Took us two days to get up there. We didn't know. Finally, before we reached the place, we met the man that owned the hot springs. He was going to Port Angeles.

"He just told us what to do when we got there, and my dad paid him right away because he was afraid we wouldn't see him when we left. We told him we were going to stay just about a week or so and the man didn't know himself whether he was going to be home or not because he—oh, afterward, we heard that he was a drinking man. When he gets enough money he stays in Port Angeles until he's broke and then goes home. So we paid him there."

She goes on to describe the bathhouse (a little cabin made of fir shakes) and the smell of the hot springs (stink), then she begins to talk about different traditional medicines and their uses. She carried a lot of knowledge about our traditional medicines, all of which were available right there in that forest.

I once had a dream that I was in her house and there was nothing in it at all except for a trunk containing a few old photos of people I didn't recognize, and lots of little glass bottles containing different kinds of plants. They were labeled in our tribal language, so I couldn't read them. There wasn't a person in the house with me, but I heard a voice in my dream. She told me that she wanted me to have these things. That they were a gift.

I woke with a secret hope that the dream meant I would learn her gift of healing, but it hasn't come to pass. Perhaps I will have to wait until my hair turns white, or maybe writing about the beauty of the natural world, encouraging people to allow themselves to be transformed by it—maybe this is a type of healing. I have been healed by time on a trail. I have been healed by time in the trees.

Someday I will have a shower underneath those falls on the Sol Duc River. I will let them wash away all my grief. I know how to get to those falls, but I've never actually been. When I think of this little rheumatic auntie and tubercular uncle making a two-day trek out into the forest to have a medicinal bath in the hot springs, it seems an oversight that I made my first visit to Sol Duc in 2021, though it's only a car ride away from where I've spent most of my life.

My great-great-grandmother, Aurelia, was born in Port Angeles. Her father was born in La Conner. We have ties to Jamestown S'Klallam, but the family settled at Lummi during the allotment period after the signing of the treaties. With the little I know—the little that is given in these oral histories—I am forced to wonder so many things. I have so many questions about their trip from Lummi back to Jamestown, and their journey to Sol Duc.

Sol Duc is a Quileute word meaning "sparkling waters." But it must have been significant to my S'Klallam ancestors as well. For them to have taken such pains to get there, surely the place was regarded as a powerful place of healing. Having been there, I can understand why. I paid my twelve dollars to sit in the pools with strangers as I thought of my ancestors in the little bathhouse made of fir shakes, my great-great-grandmother as a little girl, burdened with supplies, crossing a river on a felled tree.

I only have vague memories of Aurelia. There is a fifth-generation photo of her holding me when I was a baby. When I think about this connection, I think of how I was alive at the same time as this woman who was raised by people who were alive before clocks came ashore and stole their connection to time, before treaties were made to steal their land.

Before the land was given to strangers from far away—strangers like the "drinking man" who then "owned" the hot springs and funded his benders by charging Indians to access their sacred homelands—before the forests were clear cut, rivers dammed, salmon runs ran dry, before invasive mountain goats were tranquilized and helicoptered out. Before this was a park.

If so much can be transformed in eleven short human lifetimes, there is hope for the future. Just as the earth can be transformed for the worse, it can transform itself for the better. It can heal, sync back up with its own radiant, life-giving rhythms. What would happen if the first step toward that healing was to give this glorious land back to its original inhabitants? Yes, it's a bit worse for wear since the mid-1800s, but nothing a few brief centuries of affection and reverence won't fix. ✦

About This Story

Water defines Olympic National Park. Hurricane Ridge traditionally records 30 to 35 feet of snow a year. The coast and western valleys receive 100 to 170 inches of rain annually. From Lake Crescent to the Hoh River, the flow of water powers the glaciated mountains, rugged Pacific coastline, and lush temperate forests of the region.

Enrolled member of the Lhaq'temish (Lummi) Nation and Washington State Poet Laureate, Rena Priest shows us how just one of those bodies of water can carry memories over generations. Rena remembers her great-great-grandmother telling her that if you wash your eyes in the water of this region, you can see clearly. "I'm not sure," recalls Rena, "if she was speaking medically or metaphorically." Rena also told us about the annual Paddle to Lummi event, an intertribal canoe journey that honors the unique cultural heritage of the Coast Salish people. Over one hundred canoe families from tribal nations on the Salish Sea, along the Pacific coast, British Columbia, and Alaska, with invited guests from New Zealand, Japan, Hawaii, and Florida, travel to Lummi shores for this event. This journey honors the rich traditions of the Coast Salish tribes of the Northwest, who gather together to celebrate their relationship with the land and water. The event ends with a potlach protocol celebration, where tribal members share a meal, and each tribe demonstrates their traditional prayers, drumming, songs, and dances.

In looking back, to an era before clocks and a time before we preserved the park, Rena also looks forward. Just "eleven short human lifetimes" have brought about these changes—why couldn't they change back, under the right leadership, in the next eleven? Both practical and radical, Rena challenges our sense of time and change with one profound suggestion.

GLACIER
NATIONAL PARK

Backbone of the World

KNOWN FOR ITS GLACIERS, this place is a
story of melting ice and fire. Visitors scramble
in the summer months to see its turquoise
lakes, old-growth forests, chalets, huckleberries, wildflowers, grizzlies, and mountain
goats just after snowplows clear the infamous
Going-to-the-Sun Road.

illustration by
SARAH GESEK

We first visited Glacier National Park in July 2019. Ilyssa was in her last trimester with our second daughter, Isla, and was kicking off the planning for her organization's third creative sabbatical program in October 2019 with Glacier National Park Conservancy, the park's official nonprofit fundraising partner. We arrived to meet with the team at their headquarters at historic Belton Depot, precisely the same location where, since 1910, travelers exited train cars and got their first glimpse of West Glacier, including John Muir. In his book *Our National Parks*, Muir writes, "Get off the track at Belton Station, and in a few minutes you will find yourself in the midst of what you are sure to say is the best care-killing scenery on the continent—beautiful lakes derived straight from glaciers, lofty mountains steeped in lovely nemophila-blue skies and clad with forests and glaciers, mossy, ferny waterfalls in their hollows, nameless and numberless, and meadowy gardens abounding in the best of everything." Muir goes on to describe what he took away from his time in Glacier: "Give a month at least to this precious reserve. The time will not be taken from the sum of your life. Instead of shortening, it will indefinitely lengthen it and make you truly immortal. Nevermore will time seem short or long, and cares will never again fall heavily on you, but gently and kindly as gifts from heaven."

Belton Depot, which now serves as a retail store, warehouse, and offices for the conservancy, was originally built by the Great Northern Railway as part of their ambitious master plan to turn Glacier into "America's Alps." Competing with other companies who were literally paving the way to new frontiers like Yellowstone National Park, the Great Northern Railway was under pressure to find attractions that would boost tourism. Great Northern played a key role in the founding of Glacier National Park as builders of the railway and the park's now iconic Swiss-style chalets. George Grinnell, whose early advocacy and promotion of the park earned him the title "Father of Glacier," once stated, "Important men in control of the Great Northern Railroad were made to see the possibilities of the region and after nearly twenty years of effort, a bill setting aside the park was passed." Their effort is what ultimately made Glacier's beauty accessible to the masses.

Early advocates for Glacier faced little opposition when urging to preserve this land based on its wilderness character. And when you arrive, it's easy to understand why. Coined the "Crown Jewel of the Continent" by Grinnell, the name characterizes the majestic sharp mountain peaks and ranges sitting atop the northernmost point of Montana, sharing a border with Waterton Lakes National

Park in Alberta, Canada. Together, they form the Waterton-Glacier International Peace Park and World Heritage Site and are both declared Biosphere Reserves by UNESCO. The scenery truly took our breath away—maybe due in part to being pregnant. Below us were the bright blues of the lakes, tinted an unfamiliar emerald green by the glacial dust melting from the snow above. Out of the bright greens of new growth emerging from a long winter's sleep were meadows of wildflowers and beargrass blooms, dropping specks of paint across the landscape. And surrounded by a panorama of blue skies, we felt transported to another kind of wilderness of another time, safely nestled *away from it all.*

After spending time onboard a passenger ferry across Lake McDonald, while our toddler did yoga in the middle of the boat, we decided to hike to Avalanche Lake. Starting from the Trail of the Cedars, we wound our way on the boardwalk through ancient western red cedars and western hemlocks, hoping a grizzly bear wouldn't find our yogi toddler to be a delicious afternoon snack. We finally arrived with the help of two or ten lollipops to get her to power through, and it paid off. With stunning lakeside views of snow-adorned mountains and turquoise water, it's no surprise this is one of the park's most popular destinations. As Lula happily threw rocks and sticks into the lake and ate snacks for nearly an hour, we watched as the sun and clouds put on a spectacular show. Above us was an amphitheater of mountains showing off with a panorama of waterfalls all around us, funnels for the silt of Sperry Glacier. Out of lollipops, we decided it was time to hop in the car and see what the fuss is all about with the Going-to-the-Sun Road, one of the most iconic features of Glacier National Park.

The Going-to-the-Sun Road serves as the park's main artery connecting the east and west sides of the park. It becomes accessible in late June or early July after a months-long effort to clear snow up to eighty feet deep. The name comes from a Native American legend in which the deity Sour Spirit comes down from the sun to teach the Blackfeet the basics of hunting. But the origin of the story is disputed, some attributing it to a nineteenth-century European explorer. Still, it's the kind of winding road with jaw-dropping views that compel you to ponder the last time your brakes were checked. It's also the kind of road where you might not be mad to find yourself inching behind a slow-moving "red jammer" tourist bus, or getting stuck in a "bear jam" or "goat jam," as people slow or stop to gawk and snap photos—the views are really just that good. That is, unless you are traveling with a small passenger who hasn't been on this planet long enough to appreciate this place's beauty, and nothing but one Disney movie soundtrack saved to your device and playing on repeat. Then, you might look out at the cliffs and wonder if you could channel the dexterity and grace of a goat to scale the rock ledges.

Since our visit in 2019, the park has instituted a ticketed entry system to alleviate congestion on Going-to-the-Sun Road, an increasing issue as the park has seen record visitation, exceeding three million in 2021. While this is welcomed by park staff, who have to deal with the consequences of the volume of visitation, it's met with mixed feelings from locals who view the park as their extended backyard. The area's original residents, tribal members from surrounding Indigenous communities, do not need to make reservations to access the road, as they are exempt from paying entry fees—a small consolation for the land and rights that were taken away from them in the founding of this national park.

Glacier is both home to and a place of significance for Blackfeet, Salish, Pend d'Oreille, and Kootenai tribes, and borders the Blackfeet Reservation on its east side. Before European colonization of the continental United States, the Blackfeet Nation relied on bison as a primary food source. But by the end of the nineteenth century, bison had been nearly eradicated, leading the Blackfeet to the point of starvation and forcing them to sell the land to the federal government to survive. In 1895, the federal government agreed to purchase land from the Blackfeet, now the eastern side of Glacier National Park, while permitting the Blackfeet to continue to use the land for hunting, fishing, gathering timber, collecting plants and herbs for food and medicinal purposes, and ceremonial use. In 1897, this land was deemed a forest reserve and the agreement was honored for fifteen years until the region was designated as the country's tenth national park in 1910, at which point the courts ruled the terms of the agreement obsolete. To this day, the terms of the 1895 agreement are not recognized, though in 1973 a judge ruled in favor of the Blackfeet's right to visit the park without paying an entrance fee.

While the park is largely referred to as the "Crown Jewel of the Continent," the Blackfeet have historically referred to this region as the "backbone of the world." This spirit is embodied in their strength, defiance, and refusal to be used or taken for granted today. According to the Glacier-Two Medicine Alliance, a nonprofit dedicated to the protection, stewardship, and shared enjoyment of the wild lands of Badger-Two Medicine, a "threat of oil and gas development has loomed over the Badger-Two Medicine area of the Helena-Lewis and Clark National Forest since the early 1980s when the Reagan administration illegally issued forty-seven leases in the area. Ever since, the Glacier-Two Medicine Alliance, the Blackfeet Nation, and other tribal and conservation partners have worked diligently to prevent any energy development from occurring in this area long considered sacred by the Blackfeet Nation." In June 2020, the US Circuit Court of Appeals resoundingly rejected the lower court decision and reinstated the cancellation of the leases.

To some, Glacier is nature's "playground"—a landscape that offers excellent boating, horse riding, hiking, and fishing. A place where frozen mountaintops feed more than 130 pristine turquoise lakes and grow nearly a thousand species of flowering plants, serving as a backdrop for millions of people recreating there every year. For the native people, this is the backbone of the world—their physical and spiritual home, and a vital ecosystem that provides all the resources needed to sustain their way of life.

We applaud the continued advocacy of Indigenous communities and organizations like the Glacier-Two Medicine Alliance, as the park faces the new threats of climate change. The park has been seeing record temperatures, warming at a pace nearly two times the global average. The park's remaining namesake glaciers are melting at a record pace—going from between 80 and 150 glaciers in 1850, to 26 in 2015, and still dwindling. Wildfires, though natural and an essential part of this landscape, have become more common and even more devastating. Scientists estimate that climate change has doubled the acres burned in western US wildfires since the 1980s. With names like Going-to-the-Sun or Trail of the Cedars, Glacier seems like a place calling on an ancient sort of wisdom. We hope that wisdom will come across in these stories, and inspire a relationship of care and respect, as the tribes have always shown.

The Crown of the Continent

GEORGE BIRD GRINNELL

Far away in northwestern Montana, hidden from view by clustering mountain-peaks, lies an unmapped corner—the Crown of the Continent. The water from the crusted snowdrift which caps the peak of a lofty mountain there trickles into tiny rills, which hurry along north, south, east, and west, and growing to rivers, at last pour their currents into three seas. From this mountain-peak the Pacific and the Arctic oceans and the Gulf of Mexico receive each its tribute.

Here is a land of striking scenery. From some bold headland that rises abruptly from the plain, one looks eastward over naked yellow prairie. Near at hand, the ground is undulating, rising and falling like the swell of a troubled sea, but smooth and quiet in the far distance. Away to the east rise from the level land the three sharp pinnacles of the Sweet Grass Hills. On a clear day the dark column of smoke from the coal-mines of Lethbridge is seen seventy miles to the northeast. Here and there the yellow of the plain is broken by winding green watercourses, along which grow fringes of cottonwoods and willows, and at intervals little prairie lakes gleam like silver in the sun.

If one turns his back upon the prairie and looks west and south, the view is barred by a confused series of unknown mountains. Here are cañons deeper and narrower than those of the Yellowstone, mountains higher than those of the Yosemite. Some are rounded and some square-topped, some are slender pinnacles, and others knife-edged and with jagged crests, each one a true sierra. Many are patched with snow, and the highest wear their white covering from year's end to year's end. Along their verdureless slopes slow-moving ice rivers still plow their deliberate way, relics of mightier glaciers, the stiffened streams of which in a past age fashioned the majestic scenery of to-day. These old glaciers dug out for

156

themselves channels between the mountains, and, when the ice melted, left deep cañons, the walls of which sometimes rise vertically from three to four thousand feet above the course of the stream flowing through the valley; or, again, they stand farther back, and are faced by long steep slopes of rock fragments fallen from the heights above. Often this talus is bare, or it may be covered with a dense growth of sturdy pines up to the limit—here less than eight thousand feet—where trees will no longer grow.

The rock which composes the mass of the mountain is very ancient, probably Cambrian. It consists of some thousands of feet of heavily bedded slates and shales capped by limestone. These rocks yield easily to the weather, which has carved out the mountain peaks in fantastic shapes, which lend strange interest to their profiles.

It was once a great game country. Over the far-stretching prairie roamed count-less thousands of buffalo, and their advancing hosts creeping up along the mountain-sides covered the foot-hills and surged up the narrow valleys, as the swelling tide overflows the reefs and fills up the estuaries on some rocky shore. Far and near the prairie was black with them, and then again, in obedience to some mysterious impulse, the mighty herds receded and left it bare. In those days deer and elk without number fed in the river bottoms. Antelope dotted the plain. Moose, elk, and mountain bison had their homes in the thick timber, and wore deep trails through it from park to park, and down to the water, and again up to the high naked buttes, where they liked to lie in the sun. Still higher, along the faces of rock slides and cliffs, are the hard-trodden paths worn by the mountain-sheep and the white goats, which dwell above the timber-line, and only now and then pass through the forest.

The game is almost all gone now from mountain and plain. Buffalo and bison are extinct everywhere, but in the dense forest a few moose, elk, and deer still exist, and, as of old, bears prowl through the timber, tearing to pieces the rotten logs for worms, or turning over great stones to find the ants and beetles on which they prey. On the high lands game is more abundant. The cliffs are still climbed by the nimble sheep and the sure-footed white goats, and there is no reason why the hunter should starve. During the migrations there are swans, geese, and ducks in great numbers; five species of grouse are found on the mountains; the streams and lakes swarm with trout and whitefish; and in early autumn the hillsides are covered with huckleberries.

The region is one of great precipitation. The warm west winds, which bring their freight of vapor from the distant Pacific, are chilled when they strike the cold high peaks of the main range, and their moisture is condensed, and much of it falls as rain or snow. Looking from the summit of Mount Allen, at an elevation of about eleven thousand feet, I have seen half a dozen tall peaks which lay west of my station, all apparently smoking like so many factory chimneys. A fresh wind was blowing, and not a cloud was to be seen in all the blue arch, yet from each of these cold pinnacles of rock a long streamer of heavy mist swung off to the southeast, hanging level in the air as the smoke of a passing steamer hangs over the sea, hiding the view; and in the shadow of each streamer of cloud more or less rain and snow was falling. It is this precipitation that maintains the glaciers which still lie on the north sides of all the higher mountains of this region.

No words can describe the grandeur and majesty of these mountains, and even photographs seem hopelessly to dwarf and belittle the most impressive peaks. The fact that it is altogether unknown, the beauty of its scenery, its varied and unusual fauna, and the opportunities it offers for hunting and fishing and for mountain climbing, give the region a wonderful attraction for the lover of nature. ✦

About This Story

Known as the father of the movement that led to the establishment of Glacier National Park, George Bird Grinnell is lesser known as a pioneer whose efforts launched American conservation. Grinnell is the founder of the first Audubon Society, created in response to the loss of bird species, and his work is widely acclaimed to have contributed to early federal legislation to protect migratory birds, setting the precedent for the Endangered Species Act. Grinnell was also an avid hunter and founder of the Boone and Crockett Club with Theodore Roosevelt, to promote "fair chase" of big game. Conservation was different then.

Growing up on the estate of John James Audubon, Grinnell longed to be a naturalist and explorer of the wilderness. But upon graduating from Yale, he found much of the United States had already been "discovered" by other pioneers. Many of his expeditions were centered around naturalist surveys, fossil collecting, fishing, and hunting. In 1885, after a strenuous journey by railroad, stage, wagon, and saddle horse, he arrived in Montana near what is now known as Glacier National Park—having learned about the area at his time as editor of leading natural history magazine *Forest and Stream*. Much to his delight, the region appeared to be relatively "undiscovered" (ahem, white man), and he went on to not only visit yearly (primarily for surveying the land, fishing, and hunting), but wrote about it extensively in publications like *Forest and Stream* and *The Century Magazine*, which featured this piece in 1901.

Glacial Flow

ANN MANSOLINO

ell me how the glacier moves, while looking like it doesn't. How many years ago, scientists put boulders in a line as markers across the surface of the ice, returning later to find evidence of downhill flow, to find that things that look solid had moved and weren't where they had left them.

Tell me how your life is like that glacier, and the markers of movement in your own life are two visits to Glacier National Park, four years apart. How you stood in the same place and looked at the same glacier, which is not the same ice as before, and realize that you are not the same you who stood here four years ago, yearning to return before even having left.

Tell me how the layers of ice move over one another, how the depths remain solid while the brittle surface cracks and fractures, implying a false sense of deep instability. How you've remained unwaveringly true to yourself, but mistake the brittle fissured surface of your life for the condition of the core. The solid core flows. The fractured surface flows. Life flows. The glacier flows. Time flows. Downward, ineluctably yet imperceptibly downward, under its own weight, impelled by gravity. You can't see it move. You can't stop it from moving.

Tell me what the view is like from the edges, of your life and of the glacier. How you stood at the edge of the ice and watched and watched and thought that nothing had happened, not knowing yet that the movement is too slow to see, that the center moves faster than the edges, not knowing that watching is not enough, that change is change, even if it cannot be seen. From the edge of your own life, no shift is visible either. The shifts happened too deeply and slowly for you to notice.

Tell me about the surface of the glacier, the one you walked so far to reach. How deep striations in the ice mirror those in the rocks above, how the undulating upper edges of glacial ice cling to the steep cirque walls in small pointed peaks, forever straining toward the mountain summit, toward the distant sky. You see each echoing landform creating a sense of unity within the shifting, impermanent features of the earth and sky and ice and snow and cloud and atmosphere and your life.

The ice of the glacier is a rock. Geology books tell me this, tell me that the glacier is not just frozen water in the ordinary sense, tell me this to my surprise. It is metamorphic rock, beginning as snow, and being transformed through pressure, stress, flow, and recrystallization into glacial ice. Tiny snow crystals become large glacier ice crystals. What did I start as? What have extensive pressure and stress done to me? I have undergone my own metamorphosis, as improbable as snow into rock, and hopefully into something as solid as disparate elements that I've tried to assemble into a self.

Tell me about the debris that you've carried along with you as you've advanced across the landscape of your life. When can you set it down? Even glaciers cast off what they can no longer carry, depositing their burdens of rock and silt upon the land when they melt. But you: you need not wait until the terminus of your life to set your burdens down. For you are not a glacier.

Tell me about going to the toe of the glacier and dipping your own toes in the meltwater at the base, then stretching them out while looking long along your legs and beyond, toward the edge of the ice, extending the end of yourself toward the end of the glacier, yet it is not the end. And you know this.

The glacier is about the glacier, but also about me and you and time and life and everything we think is permanent but is flowing, changing, moving, melting.

Tell me how the glacier is receding, melting, not just flowing but disappearing. As you are, as I am, as life is, a bit at a time, despite looking as solid and enduring and unmoving as ever. It flows, it moves, it dissipates. And this is why you need those markers—to know what has moved and how and when, to be able to tell me how two trips to Glacier allowed you to see the flow of your own life: where you have been, where you are, where you are going.

In the end, you had to return to the glacier in order to understand that you didn't need to, in order to learn that what you thought you could find here and only here is what you already are and already have. You stand at the toe of the glacier, at the edge of the water that used to be ice, at the edge of the stillness that used to be movement, where the glacier ends and the rest of your life begins. Coming back was thus less important and more necessary than you could have known. ✦

About This Story

For a park named after its glaciers, you'd think you'd be able to get to them. Many of this park's glaciers are hidden high along the Continental Divide, obscured by shadows and semipermanent snowfields.

But these unseen forces have defined the park. Around 1850, at the end of the Little Ice Age, there were between 80 and 150 glaciers here. Glaciers are made of fallen snow that becomes packed over many years into a thick mass of ice. Unlike ice, glaciers are so heavy that they flow, even if very, very slowly. The glaciers of the Pleistocene Ice Age, the ones that melted ten thousand years ago, carved out these valleys, filled these lakes, and cut these mountains into what we see today. The glaciers continue to melt, contributing to irrigation for agriculture, cold streams for wildlife, and lakes for recreation. In 2015, the park counted just twenty-six named glaciers remaining.

There are a few glaciers that can be viewed easily in Glacier National Park, most on the less visited eastern side of the park. The Jackson Glacier is the easiest, spotted from an overlook off the Going-to-the-Sun Road. Piegan Glacier views come after a challenging 3.5 mile hike one way from the Siyeh Bend Trailhead, and 1,350 feet of elevation gain. Or, if you want to see the most famous glacier of the park, Grinnell Glacier is 5.1 miles one way from the Grinnell Glacier Trailhead, or 4.5 miles one way by boat from Many Glacier Hotel.

Ann pondered these glaciers as an artist in residence during the early days of the coronavirus pandemic. Just as unseen forces have shaped the park and all the features within it, Ann invites us to consider the unseen forces that keep us flowing, changing, and moving.

What Makes the Grizzlies Dance

SANDRA ALCOSSER

June and finally snow peas
sweeten the valley.
High behind numinous meadows
ladybugs swarm, like huge
lacquered fans from Hong Kong,
like the serrated skirts
of blown poppies,
whole mountains turn red,
and in the blue penstemon
grizzly bears swirl
as they bat snags of color
against their ragged mouths.
Have you never wanted
to spin like that
on hairy, leathered feet,
amid the swelling berries
as you tasted a language
of early summer—shaping
lazy operatic vowels,
cracking hard-shelled
consonants like speckled
insects between your teeth,
have you never wanted
to waltz the hills
like a beast? ✦

About This Story

Sandra's love story with Glacier began when she and her husband were newlywed artists in the park teaching workshops on that year's National Park Service theme: sustainability. They taught forest ecology and park preservation, made paper upon which campers wrote poems, and constructed pinhole cameras from discarded mini cereal boxes. They built a four-foot-tall bifold storybook painted with mountains, birds, and glacial lakes to exhibit the myriad poems, photographs, and paper creations.

Sandra says the park was "under the spell of grizzlies" that year. She and her new husband spent the first night in Apgar campground near the park's West Entrance, and it was not long before their own grizzly encounter. "As we balanced on rocks tucked into tall grasses above McDonald Creek, sharing hot coffee and peanut butter sandwiches while we prepared to meet the naturalists with whom we would spend our honeymoon, a giant rolling figure crossed the creek diagonally in front of us. My eyes saw a costumed dancer, reddish fur moving in waves with each extension. High, worried forehead—check. Back hump—check. Dish face—check. It was the closest we'd ever come to a grizzly in our lives, and it had cut silently behind us as we sat watching the water and brainstorming about the month ahead."

Wolf Trail

AS TOLD BY MARIAH GLADSTONE

In the long-ago time, the place now called Many Glacier was filled with deep ice. These were the ancient glaciers that shaped the landscape, carving away stone to form the valleys we see today. It was along this ice that Old Man Naapi was exploring. Naapi is known by many as a trickster, though it is said that he also helped create much of the land and animals that we see today. However, his motivations are not always altruistic; he can be boastful, lazy, and filled with pride.

Naapi was drawn to a beautiful crystal stream that flowed from one of the valleys. He followed it upward. He passed two elk running down toward the prairie, then later, two antelope. Before long, he heard singing. As he came over the next rise, he found a group of wolves dancing along the banks of the ice river. They sang, "Iinniiks, poō" sapoōk'" and two bison jumped out of the river and ran down to the valley below.

Naapi saw that the wolves had a great power and he wanted it for himself. However, knowing that these animals were also delicious, he saw this as a way to find himself an easy meal. Naapi approached the wolves and asked them to teach him the song and dance so that he may help with this work.

The wolf chief was hesitant. Naapi was not known for trying to be helpful. However, he eventually gave in and agreed to teach Old Man. He told Naapi that he could only use this medicine on the river of ice they stood upon. Naapi gave his word and the wolf chief taught him. Together, the wolves and Naapi sang and danced and called animals into the world together.

Finally, Naapi decided to part ways with the wolves and continued exploring. By now, the sun was sinking lower toward the mountains into the late afternoon. It wasn't long before he found a different stream away from the wolves. He thought this would be the perfect place to summon a rabbit for supper and make camp.

He started to sing the wolves' song and dance along the banks of the new river. "Aattsisstaiks, poō"sapoōk'," he sang, asking rabbits to jump out of the water.

Nothing happened. The water gurgled away, surface undisturbed. Again, he repeated the song and dance, this time becoming more frantic. "Awakaasiiks, poō"sapoōk'," he sang, this time calling for white-tails. Again, the water remained uninterrupted. Naapi began to panic, grabbed his belongings, and ran back to the original river, slipping along the ice. He quickly found the place where the wolves had been dancing. They were nowhere in sight.

Still out of breath from his run, he began to dance and sing, the sun sinking behind the mountains. Before he was able to summon anything, he heard the click click of toenails against the ice. Naapi turned around and came nose to snout with the wolf chief, the rest of his pack close behind. The wolf chief spoke.

"Naapi, you gave us your word and then broke the promise you made to us," he said. "One of our scouts followed you and saw you trying to use this gift upon another river." Naapi glanced around himself anxiously, unsure of what would happen next. "Now, we must take this river away; no one will be able to abuse this power."

In the next moment, Naapi was flung backward and blacked out. He awoke to the sound of his own teeth chattering from the cold. As he came to, his eyes adjusted to the dark. He found himself between two low walls of ice, body sprawled along the dry riverbed. Old Man climbed out of the streambed to the banks where he had danced with the wolves. The river was gone, leaving only the crack in the ice where it had run. However, as he looked around, he realized that he could still see the crystal river, though it was far out of his reach. If you are lucky enough to see the night sky from the Blackfeet Territory known as Glacier National Park, you too can see the Wolf Trail. What Piikuni people call Makoyohsokoyi, you may know better as the Milky Way. ✦

About This Story

Mariah Gladstone, who is both Cherokee and Blackfeet, grew up in northwest Montana. Her ancestors have been in the area known as Glacier National Park for the past fourteen thousand years, which is documented archaeologically. Mariah's mother has served as an interpretive ranger for the park, and her father, Jack Gladstone, is a musician and storyteller hailed as "Montana's Troubadour." Mariah calls upon this lineage as a Glacier park ranger, and continues to share campfire stories like this one at Apgar or Many Glacier campgrounds through the Native America Speaks program.

"These stories," Mariah told us, "provide an understanding of the world, our relationship to the ecosystem, care of the ecosystem, and . . . guide us in our own values and morality, how things came to be." Trickster stories in particular are lessons on morals and how we should treat one another. Mariah told us that the "history of Glacier is older than the national park, and Indigenous context takes us to a place where we can dive into Naapi's eyes embedded in the aspen trees."

Mariah goes on to share that "the Blackfeet people consider the Wolf Trail to be the last stop on the spirit's journey after death. The first is the Sweetgrass Hills, which is both a physical location in north central Montana but also a metaphor for choosing a balanced life. The second place the spirit travels is the Sand Hills in southern Alberta. The physical place has sandy dunes that symbolize our inability to take anything with us after death. Finally, the spirit joins the Wolf Trail where it can travel among the stars.

This story in particular tells us of how the Makoyohsokoyi (the Milky Way), or the Wolf Trail, came to be and how it serves as a last stop on the soul's journey after death. Glacier and its sister park, Waterton Lakes National Park of Canada, are certified International Dark Sky Parks. This certification shows a long-term commitment to decreasing light pollution to preserve or restore dark skies. We appreciate this promise and hope these parks will not break it, as Naapi did.

When We Visit

SARA ARANDA

Above, short hoots led to a wail. The hollow warmth was sudden. I'd gotten used to the occasional rattling of creatures: rodent, restless human, beetle falling from a place that might as well have been another world. I softened in my sleep, the thin bodies of sound landing as they did, here, there, upon me. A twig, a leaf. I shifted and dozed. The owl bloomed again, a song I'd never heard. The notes were deep, I could almost feel them in my own throat.

There were two phrases. The short hoots and then the wail, a drooping tremolo followed by an eerie silence. Perhaps the whole forest had become an air-filled breast, the reverberation so penetrating, the moments of waiting so heavy. I finally lifted my head to peer through the mesh of my tent. The dome of night was embossed with tree after tree. *Hoo hoot hoohoo, hoo hoot hoohoooo*—I imagined the owl's throat expanding, and I even held my own lungs. Finally, a faint response fell from the north, closer to the lake. Then, nothing, or I suppose, a filled return of the sounds the owl had briefly displaced.

I lay there and tried to recall the series of hoots and trills I'd heard, but the potency seemed to quietly dissipate from my brain, which soon itself drifted off to sleep.

The morning I was to meet with Alger Swingley of Blackfeet Outfitters, an Indigenous-owned guiding company, I sat in my Jeep outside park boundaries and watched two crows rise from the east. Sharp dive, upward grace, rolling coasters of wind. I was at a trailhead off the highway down the hill from Marias Pass facing the Badger-Two Medicine wilderness. It had rained the night before and into the dawn, deepening the dense expanse of lodgepole pine and spring foliage. Lingering clouds held the sky in pieces.

A young man showed up to assure me Alger wasn't too far behind. Ryan Hawk Plume Loring recently served in the US Marine Corps and was ready to begin another season with the outfitter, a job he's enjoyed since he was a teen. Tall, polite, talkative. I told him my little brother had also served, so we discussed the similar places they had been stationed. But I don't know very many details about my brother's life, so I took solace in the fact that Ryan did and could understand. My brother still has an aversion to the idea that hiking can be fun, so I was honored by Ryan's very presence and motive that day: to hike with me, a stranger, albeit a paying one.

Two weeks prior, I was sitting in a room eight hundred crow miles away listening to a podcast by Black Mountain Radio. In episode five, host Erica Vital-Lazare briefly touched on the idea that people have to suspend comfort in order to truly meet. The risk, as Vital-Lazare put it, is one of "knowing too much and getting too close. That means we will in some way be accountable—that we will have to accept the failure or the victory—or that ultimately we have to think differently and therefore do differently. Or, goddess forbid, suspend our judgment."

This is all to say that when we listen, we are obliged to change, and when we talk, we are asking this of others. Alger arrived with fellow tribal members Katherine Mary Meier and Tony Calf Boss Ribs, and several horses. Alger had long hair, graying wisps, kind eyes. He asked what my expectations were. I didn't really have any beyond asking myself to be as present as possible.

Tony was the eldest, traditional in the Blackfeet ways, and he shared stories of his lineage and connection to the sacred Beaver Medicine. Tony animated his hands and arms while speaking as if the sky was an extension of himself. He comes from an oral culture, and I felt very much like a child entranced by the power of words, the power of baring one's soul, like singing, like a *hooo* on a branch in the cavern of night.

Kathy told me about the personal hiking she's done across the imaginary border that is Glacier National Park, a place the outfitter isn't allowed to guide. The rocky passes, the wildflowers, the lakes. This is the land their people are from, and I wonder all the time what that must feel like, to truly know land like a relative.

I hiked the most with Ryan while the others rode their horses. He told me that a common rite of passage in hunting is to take a bite of raw liver from your first successful hunt. "Almost as if to confront what you've done?" I asked. Ryan agreed but there was also humor in the task, he said, but undoubtedly the acknowledgment is the same, that life is certainly sacred. I am not a hunter, but my dad comes from a lineage of hunters. So, again, I took comfort in hearing about things I've never known myself. Inevitably, Ryan and I found a place our lives could directly intersect: losing a parent at a relatively young age.

What Alger and his team really showed me was a new way of thinking about the word *visit*. I was used to thinking of the word superficially. One is often a visitor, like me being here in northern Montana; one visits a friend or family member, but the word seems to dissipate at the door, as if it describes transition more than anything else, that there is something temporary about it. Awareness often shrinks to *having a conversation* or becomes vague like *spending time*. My perception of the English language didn't extend *visiting* to encompass all that takes place beneath, because of, in tandem with its canopy. *Should we have lunch while we visit?* Kathy had asked as we sat by the river. *Since we're visiting, I think we'll be fine,* Ryan had said during our hike about the chances of us surprising a bear.

Perhaps visiting is acknowledging the many ways in which listening can be embodied, an exchange between the senses of all those involved. Like hunters, who know all the nuances between elk, moose, black or grizzly bear tracks and bodies. Ryan promptly identified the grizzly in the mud, within minutes of us starting the day, not fresh but not particularly old either. Later, wolf prints. He knew which direction the elk had gone and how rushed they were by the elongation of the tracks themselves, their momentum painting different strokes.

Listening had become an apparition granted by the recent rains, hearing as seeing. Like how smell can become taste, taste a feeling, all senses branching to the same point, a long story in the brain. We heard birds, the river, each other. Flowers burst in the afternoon sunlight. Dead trees cooed liked ghosts in the wind or mimicked the bugles of an elk. We talked and talked, both as a means to visit our humanness and to announce our presence in the forest, for others to hear us, perhaps paw a different course, share in the context of the ecosystem—so many homes, where visiting never ends.

The owl appeared my first night at Apgar campground. The following day, I rode my bike to the Apgar Lookout trailhead and hiked alone. I played music from my phone and slowed my pace for blind turns, bear spray at hand. June had just begun, and I was north enough for sunsets to happen after nine p.m., at the foot of mountains that can house snowdrifts one hundred feet deep in the winter, and yet, there I was, overdressed and hoping the eighty-six-degree forecast was a mistake (according to the Park Service website, this area has an average high of seventy-two in June). Snow could only be seen far off in the distance, mere lingering drapes at higher altitudes. The rivers and lakes brimmed.

From the lookout, I glimpsed the mountains that are home to what the Blackfeet call *Niuoxkai-itahtai*, or the Triple Divide, the hydrological apex of North America, where water eventually makes its way to the Pacific Ocean, the Arctic Ocean, and the Atlantic at the Gulf of Mexico. Of course, the reality that a single place can impact or have relations to distant lands and even oceans is as old as the earth itself. The lines we draw on maps and the fences we build are part of a dangerous myth, for both mountains and inhabitants alike.

Perhaps listening beyond the self is also an act of remembering how everything bends or blurs or bleeds. Like the way a random man whispered to me as I jogged down. He expressed how proud he was of his wife for being out there given her recent survival of breast cancer. "Are you training for something?" she had asked me first. "Life?" I replied. "I knew it," the man laughed, then he leaned in to tell me. "My mom died from breast cancer," I told him. His face filled with both awe and dread, and I peered at his wife up the trail. She was looking out over the river corridor. What vast refractions of light caught in the shapes of joy or grief she must see. It was my turn to lean in. "She's amazing. Give her all the love," I said. "You've got to," I heard him say.

Boundaries burned as I ran down. I had no intention of writing about my mom this trip, but this is my momentum, and now I must contemplate the serendipitous nature of this couple's life, of them and me arriving there, of him giving in to impulse to entrust a passing stranger with his story. I suppose, at the very least, this is what storytellers do all the time. Did he find solace in knowing that I could understand her miracle? Did he feel the cloak of loneliness evaporate with the heat?

The following day, I went to another fire lookout on a mountain the Kootenai named Wolf Hat and was met with a band of mountain goats. I passed them as they grazed below snow line. Their thin bodies appeared beneath half-shed, knotted winter coats. They drooped their heads to eat, kept me in soft focus. Two goats slept beyond the wooden lookout. They were tucked into themselves, backs bowed south, horns resting north, facing the deepness of the glacier-cut mountains.

Later, as I began my way down, the other goats appeared in their eerie silence at the other end of the snowy ridge. I watched them rub head and throat against the tip of a buried pine, one after the other. I moved upslope to allow the traversing band to drift toward the sleeping ones, quickness only in their necks or in their willingness to lock eyes with me. I pondered all the more how in tune to home we all once were, their hooves and my steps singing reminders in short, shifting notes. What does it take to suspend the self in order to meet the homes of others? To heed their sacred songs? *Hoo hoot hoohoo, hoo hoot hoohoo* . . . What does it mean, what does it mean to visit the world? ✦

About This Story

To write this story, Sara Aranda received one of six travel stipends awarded to writers selected through our call for submissions. In her application, Sara wrote about her preference to research the Indigenous life and stories of the areas in which she bases her essays—an approach that fell right into line with our project to uncover and tell more diverse tales of and from our national parks.

Sara hired Blackfeet Outfitters, an Indigenous-owned guiding service near Glacier. Her conversations with Alger, with Ryan, with Tony, and with Kathy provided profound insight, allowing her to create a picture of this place not by examining the history or the imaginary borders, but lyrically weaving together moments spent in the presence of its people and animals. Practically, Sara was able to directly support the Indigenous people of the area, and find a group to hike with in grizzly country, where solo hiking is discouraged.

Going-to-the-Sun

CASSIDY RANDALL

We're straddling our bikes in a canyon of snow. Some of us are on mountain bikes, some on road bikes, with a menagerie of steeds covering every type in between. I'm on my ten-year-old hardtail with outdated rim brakes, high on endorphins from the relentless climb and blissfully oblivious to the fact that the impending brake-burning descent would be the end of those particular brakes.

Every spring, an underground movement of cyclists journeys to the sublimely beautiful Going-to-the-Sun Road in Glacier, Montana's northernmost park. They ride the tails of plows run by an elite force of Glacier National Park employees tasked with clearing snow from the steep, narrow ribbon of pavement that, after deep winters, can rise eighty feet above the asphalt.

Once the road is clear to Logan Pass in early June (at the most optimistic), Going-to-the-Sun opens to the millions of cars that travel its length. As the only road that traverses the whole of the park, it runs east–west and climbs 3,300 feet over the Continental Divide, offering staggering views of glacier-carved peaks and walls, thundering falls, and hanging gardens. The road is famously slender with a drop-off into space, making for something of a death-defying journey. It's barely wide enough for two sports cars abreast, let alone motorhomes and F-350s squeezing past each other on its tight ledges. Which is why the park's signature vintage red buses are similarly slender. These tour buses from the 1930s—said to be the oldest touring fleet of vehicles in the world—sport roll-back tops to maximize tourists' vertical views of the park's ramparts. Locals call them "jammer buses" for their slow progress on the narrow road.

All that to say: when it's open, Going-to-the-Sun is suboptimal for biking unless there's a death wish involved. But for now, while the pass still hibernates under the weight of snow, the road in all its ferocious beauty belongs to the human-powered pilgrims.

This Memorial Day, a dozen of us caravanned the three hours north with bikes mostly strapped haphazardly to racks on hatchbacks. We set up camp at Sprague Creek, one of the few campgrounds open in the early season and the closest one to the hallowed road. The folding camp table was quickly laden with whiskey bottles, and we cracked local IPAs with sandbagged alcohol content as we began elaborate dinner preparations—always a protracted event when the sun doesn't set until ten p.m. In a state where it regularly snows in June (or used to, anyway), the warm season becomes a phenomenon to be celebrated in full glory.

The everlasting daylight of northern summers also allows for lazy mornings. After several cups of coffee, we slowly rallied to begin our sixty-four-mile round-trip pedal for this classic Montana adventure, where the challenge and scenery are rivaled only by the road's rugged history and intrigue.

Before Glacier was established in 1910 as the country's tenth national park, only a few wagon roads existed aside from the Great Northern Railroad tracks that transported people to chalets tucked into the interior of the great mountains. The first survey to map out the road's route, in 1924, required workers to hike three thousand feet up to the work site on a daily basis, walk nauseatingly thin ledges, and hang on ropes over the sheer walls and cliffs that define Glacier's extreme landscape—conditions that spurred a staggering 300 percent turnover in the workforce in the first few months alone. As we start the unforgiving climb out of the cedar forest from Lake McDonald, I can sympathize with that attrition rate.

Biking the road—with no windshield boundaries and the benefit of a slower pace—offers a window into the true magnitude of what went into the road's construction. We pedal through West Side Tunnel, where the road starts to rise out of the forest from Lake McDonald. Like most of the features on the Going-to-the-Sun, including the retaining walls built on sheer cliffs, the tunnel is made with native materials excavated from other parts of the road's construction as part of national park landscape architects' master plan in the 1920s for the road to blend into the environment. The directive was so strict that contractors were allowed to use only small blasts to cut out the spectacular Garden Wall to avoid scarring the landscape, and some features were even painstakingly excavated by hand.

The Loop comes next, the only switchback on the entire road. The original planned route called for fifteen switchbacks until the revolutionary mind of NPS landscape architect Tom Vint stepped in. Now, the Loop affords the first views that make Going-to-the-Sun one of the most fiercely beautiful roads in the country.

To distract from burning legs and lower backs aching from the consistent climb, we gaze at the views; our slow passage allows plenty of time for ogling. We pedal past the lookout to Bird Woman Falls hurtling down Mount Oberlin in the distance and stop to douse ourselves at the Weeping Wall that's gushing full bore, running in and out of the frigid waterfalls like kids in a glaciated sprinkler. Our bike-by of the Garden Wall with its spectacular hanging gardens has us exclaiming over countless flowers we can't name. We shout a hundred variations of "it's so beautiful!" through our burning lungs as the Big Bend rounds out to reveal Heavens Peak.

Finally, we're halted by the wall of snow and a plow at rest just a half mile before the apex of Logan Pass. A trio of mountain goats scatters at our approach, fading into invisibility on the overhanging snowfield above, which we eye warily as we catch our breath and prepare to descend. In 2019, a late-afternoon avalanche in the Triple Arches area left thirteen cyclists marooned on the Logan Pass side of the road for eight hours before plows could break through to rescue them. It's only lucky they weren't the latest sacrifice to Going-to-the-Sun.

The building of the road, which took thirty-five years to complete and required backbreaking work in excavating features by hand and small explosives to preserve the landscape, claimed the lives of three men. The road has claimed many more lives since then, including tourists falling over retaining walls and slipping into creeks that plunge hundreds of feet, and the grisly 2013 incident of a woman pushing her newlywed husband to his death just off the Loop.

I'm well aware of the road's savage nature, which is why I ride the brakes on my hardtail for most of the descent. I'm glad to be on a mountain bike for this; the pavement is pockmarked in wounds left from the plows, strewn with tiny concentration-breaking pebbles and day-ruiner boulders shed from the steep walls, and its snowmelt-slick curves offer the terrifying opportunity to test flight patterns into space.

Finally turning back into Sprague at the bottom with an ecstatic grin (far behind the road bikers in our crew who boast way more guts) and brake pads just this side of long gone, I come to a halt to stretch before heading to our campsite. I want the solitude to bask in this moment. With Glacier becoming ever more popular and crowded, requiring lotteries to drive Going-to-the-Sun and snag backcountry camping permits, it's becoming much rarer to be able to enjoy the park at all. We're lucky to have had such an experience, made all the more extraordinary for it being the result of the power of our own legs. ✦

About This Story

When we first traveled to Glacier National Park in July 2019, we were extraordinarily lucky. Our trip landed just after Going-to-the-Sun Road had reopened to car traffic, following its winter hibernation under dozens of feet of snow. With a name like that, we already knew this road was sure to offer something more than a means to an end. But we weren't quite prepared for the stunning postcard-worthy views in every direction. The road feels dangerous not just for its constant curving up and down and around the mountains, but for the narrow single lanes and sheer cliffs that leave zero margin for error when the driver is in an awe-inspired daze while sharing the roads with red buses and tourists trying to take pictures out the window.

Our friends at Glacier Conservancy shared the locals' tip about Going-to-the-Sun being open to bikers and those on foot in the spring. From here is an unobstructed view at your own pace, as the plows slowly make their way to the other end of the park to reveal the majesty of what lies just beyond the snowpack. We knew we wanted to include a story about this breathtaking road, but most stories we could find gushed over the engineering feat of building it—not the experience of being on it. We were thrilled to stumble across this piece by Cassidy Randall, an outdoor journalist who has also written about the Blackfeet Nation's bid to defend their sacred land, who so beautifully captures the experience of bicycling down the road, for the many of us who may not be able to make this journey by pedal.

Hiking Up the Dry Fork
in the Two Medicine Valley

BOB MUTH

Silence is somehow the foundation of all reality.

—RICHARD ROHR

It doesn't take long climbing
Over downfall, mud, and the
Dry Fork's lingering snow to
Realize that the power of the
World never depended on who
Won yesterday's war or who is
Ahead in the never ending
Polls. It doesn't take long to
Realize that we need a story
Larger than our isolation to
Carry us through: a story of
The silence and this-ness of
Everything, a story of the
Excellence of the avalanches
Calving from the last cornice
On Rising Wolf and of the
Bighorns bedded down in the
Wildflower meadows below Red
Mountain. It doesn't take long to
Realize that the mountains are
Always searching for a silence
That can be heard above the
Noise of the world's success. ✦

Earth Prayer from the McDonald Valley

BOB MUTH

I was standing on the highest mountain
of them all, and round about me was
the whole hoop of the world.
                                    —BLACK ELK

Land of lichened rock
And enlightened heart,
Cedar, hemlock,
And mossy thought.

Place of airy promise
And house of hidden roots,
Dancing creek, blue lake,
All gift and ageless grace.

Preparer of the way
And tenderness unseen,
Come trillium, violet,
And the patient green.

Valley of verdant verse
And cascading loss,
Varied thrush, moose,
And our lost harmony.

Voice of suffering
And beauty abused,
Nations, tribes,
All life's Sacred Hoop.

Mitakuye oyas' in
(all my relations)
We have strayed
From earth's mind.

Restore us.
Reteach us
The old ways.
Create us
One more time. ✦

About This Story

Bob Muth is an admired local junior high English teacher from Columbia Falls. Now in his eighties and retired, he draws his muse for poetry from the landscape where he hikes several times a week as a volunteer backcountry ranger for the Park Service.

When we first read Bob's piece about hiking in the Two Medicine Valley, we swore it was written during the pandemic as a reflection of these times, and it resonated deeply. When everything around us felt like it would bring certain disease, and the politics and the protests kept getting louder, the thought of mountain goats munching on shrubs on top of Logan Pass and the sun disappearing behind mountains and lakes brough calm and certainty to our present lives.

It was only in the process of pulling this collection together that we learned it had been written years prior. Bob's ability to capture the rich beauty of Glacier in "Earth Prayer" recalled images of the region's stunning landscape and served as a reminder that we not only have a lot to learn from nature, but can use it as an example for how to heal.

Glacier National Park, Montana

Excerpt from *The Hour of Land*

TERRY TEMPEST WILLIAMS

For my family, Glacier National Park is a landscape of fire, not ice.

The summer of 2003 is known as "the pinnacle year of fire," in the history of Glacier National Park breaking all records; twenty-six fires were burning in the park, consuming more than 145,000 acres in three months. It was also the summer the Tempests decided to take a family vacation to celebrate our father's seventieth birthday.

On July 23, 2003, we had reservations for twelve at the Granite Park Chalet for one night, and the Sperry Chalet for another, with campsites reserved in between. My father wanted to duplicate the backpacking trip we made in 1982 (the same trip where I met Doug Peacock on the trail), hiking sixty-six miles in six days from the Sperry Chalet to the Granite Park Chalet, over Swiftcurrent Pass, culminating at Many Glacier. This time we were hiking the route in reverse, beginning with the Highline Trail.

More than any other park I know, Glacier embodies the majesty of alpine landscapes, surrounded by rock castles and slow-moving rivers of ice with secret lakes the color of turquoise. The hike into Granite Park Chalet, beginning at Logan Pass, is a glory of wildflowers: red paintbrush, sticky geranium, larkspur, and the flowering stalks of bear's grass appearing as white globes lighting up the meadows. Our family spaced themselves evenly along the narrow trail beneath the Garden Wall, with the strongest hikers in front led by my brother Steve and his wife, Ann, followed by their family, Callie and Andrew (newly married), Sara, and Diane. My father and his companion, Jan, walked with them; my brother Dan and his wife, Thalo, followed behind. And Brooke, perhaps the strongest among us, stayed in the rear with me, gathering bones.

There is something soul-satisfying about carrying what you need on your back: water; food; a cook stove; a sleeping bag, pad, and tent; rain gear; a down vest or parka; hat; gloves; a change of clothes; camp shoes; sunglasses; sunscreen; bug dope; a first aid kit; a good book and headlamp to read by; a journal; pens; binoculars; camera. And then, with a topo map in hand, you chart your course and walk.

Some of the miles you may talk to your hiking partner, some of the miles you remain quiet, observant to the world embracing you. And there are other miles when your mind not only wanders through a labyrinth of thoughts but climbs the steep hills of obsession, be it love or loss or laments. "Walking it off" is not just a phrase but a form of reverie in the religion of self-reliance, where every mile is registered in the strength of calf muscles.

Eight miles later, Granite Park Chalet greeted us with an opaque view of Heavens Peak. Visibility is obscured due to the smoke. The Robert fire was raging in a far-off drainage that we could see with our binoculars; and the Trapper fire, with plumes of smoke visible to our naked eyes, had begun earlier in the week. But we had been assured by rangers at Lake McDonald, who carefully checked our itinerary, that the current fires would pose no threat to us.

The Granite Park Chalet is full of alpine charm, a largely stone building that sits at the base of Swiftcurrent Pass with the Grinnell Glacier Overlook just a short, steep hike above. The chalet was built by the Great Northern Railroad between 1914 and 1915 to attract more American tourists with a hut-to-hut trail system like those found in Europe. Of the nine alpine chalets that were built in that era, two remain.

Each of us settled into our designated cabins, furnished with a set of bunk beds that we completed with our sleeping bags. Half the party stayed at the chalet, while the other half hiked up Ahern Pass for a wider view.

My brother Dan and I sat at the picnic table on the chalet's porch and talked about Jim Harrison's novella *Legends of the Fall*, set in Montana.

"Do you think fathers and sons are fated to destroy each other?" Dan asked.

"I can't answer that—" I said. "But I remember hearing a psychologist talk at a conference on boys. He said, 'If you want to see a man cry, ask him about his father.'"

Our conversation changed to our mother.

"Do you think we'd all be different if Mother had lived?" Dan asked.

"No question."

"How?"

And that conversation carried us into the late afternoon.

We all cooked dinner together inside the chalet, having been warned by a large handwritten sign not to touch the shrimp in the freezer. Rumor had it the shrimp had been flown in as a special surprise for First Lady Laura Bush, who, with some of her girlfriends, was arriving at the Granite Park Chalet toward the end of the week.

We watched the sun burn through the smoke and stare at us like the red eye of a demon. And then a blue haze settled on the valley.

That night, I dreamed a spiral of bats flew out of the forest followed by flames. I woke up anxious.

The next morning, we all noticed the smoke had thickened. As we ate breakfast on the porch of the chalet, fire was on everyone's mind. Chris Burke, a Park Service employee, appeared anxious as well, his worry heightened by the discovery that the water pump at the chalet was broken. He hiked out to meet a maintenance worker on the trail to get a new part as a safety measure.

About midday on July 24, the flames from the Robert fire appeared to be coming closer. Dad walked down to the edge of the chasm, a sizable rock-faced cliff that separated us from the forest, to calculate the distance from the fires to the Granite Park Chalet.

"It's a fair distance," he said. "But if the winds change, we could be in trouble."

Just then, a helicopter hovered above us and landed on flat ground. To our surprise, a captain from the smoke jumpers, stationed out of Los Angeles, stepped out of the chopper looking like Cool Hand Luke. He had been instructed to stay with us in case the fires escalated. He found a canvas director's chair, carried it to the top of the knoll, sat down, and crossed his legs as he gazed toward the burning horizon, offering us a relaxed image, the epitome of calm.

The other guests at the chalet began to gather, also alarmed by the smoke and the fires that seemed to be advancing. Chris was back with the new part needed for the water pump and installed it, and quickly, with the help of Brooke and D. began wetting down the roof of the chalet.

Suddenly a spiral of bats flew out of the forest just like I had seen in my dream. They rose in a black column of wings against the gray sky and just as quickly disappeared. My heart began to race. I looked at my watch: 4:30 p.m. The smoke was increasing. The fire was escalating, with spot fires gaining momentum ahead of the blaze, igniting all around us. The captain stood up from his chair. Several deer emerged from the trees and ran behind the chalet. Chris was on his cell phone, talking to the fire lookout. What we didn't hear from the woman on the other end of his conversation was this: "We can't calm the beast of Trapper fire . . . it looks like it's making a run for the Granite Park Chalet!"

Chris and the fire captain called us together.

"We seem to be at the center of a perfect storm," the fire captain said. "The Robert fire, the Trapper fire, and a new fire unnamed seem to have merged into one crown fire they're calling the 'Mountain Man Complex.' It's all blown up in the last four hours—and it appears to be heading our direction."

"We must prepare ourselves," Chris added. "Keeping the chalet wet will help, and we need to get rid of whatever could burn on the porch. I could use some help."

Brooke, Steve, and Andrew worked with Chris, throwing the picnic tables and chairs off the porch down the hillside so there would be nothing burnable next to the stone walls of the historic chalet.

The propane tank nearby was a concern. The winds were picking up dramatically; it was increasingly hard to hear. Chris and the captain passed out particle masks. We stood on the porch bathed in an eerie orange glow, watching in disbelief as firs and pines exploded into flames with pieces of charred bark raining down on us. We could feel the waves of heat as the flames roared from all directions.

Thalo and Dan ran down to their cabin and returned with their backpacks strapped on. "We're leaving," Dan said. "Does anyone want to come with us?"

"I'm gettin' the hell out of here, before we burn up!" Thalo said, her blue eyes bloodshot and frantic. "I saw what happened to the people who listened to the authorities inside the World Trade Center on September eleventh and thought they'd be rescued."

"You're better off staying here with the rest of us," Chris said. "Don't panic—I don't think you'll make it up to Grinnell, the fire's moving too fast."

Thalo was already gone.

"I'm going with Thalo," Dan said. And we watched them disappear into the smoke—the Grinnell Glacier Overlook, still a steep mile and a half away.

"Do something, John," the captain said to my father.

"He's a grown man, he's going to do what he's going to do," Dad said. "I can't stop him."

"The next person who leaves is under arrest," the fire captain said. "Everyone needs to put on their hiking boots and make sure you have your personal ID with you. Go—now—hurry! I want to see everyone inside the chalet as fast as you can get there."

Flocks of birds were flying helter-skelter into the chaos of the crosswinds. More deer were running out of the woods ahead of the burn. Heat singed my eyelashes. Our eyes were red and our faces were flushed. Everyone wore masks. I had two extra and put one on each breast for comic relief. Sara and Diane laughed.

Dad, Jan, and I rushed down to our cabin to get our necessary gear, fear accelerating with the advancing fire. Chris had run down to the campground and brought other hikers back to the chalet for safety. He mentioned that two former Bureau of Land Management employees from Alaska who had registered at the chalet earlier in the day had disappeared.

Walking briskly back to the chalet with the heat chasing us, I kept looking up the mountain to see whether I could see Dan and Thalo, but it was consumed in black smoke. The spot fires increased as flames jumped over trees like banshees; the wind howled like a speeding train. I turned to see the blaze, now an inferno, racing up the mountain toward us.

Ann was inside the chalet with the girls. Callie and Andrew were standing on the side porch, watching the flames behind us. Brooke and Steve were still working with Chris, getting rid of more flammables, including trying to move the propane tank farther away from the building, and then, with longer white canvas hoses screwed together, they continued spraying down the roof and porch of the chalet until the very last minute.

"Everybody inside, now!" the fire captain yelled.

A couple had been playing Scrabble. They quickly put away their game. Two women held each other's hands, crying. A young man, crouched in the corner, seeming a bit dazed or drugged, continued playing his guitar, quietly singing, "Come on, baby, light my fire," until Chris put his hand on his shoulder to get him to stop. I stared out the windows. All I could think of was my brother and his wife in the middle of the firestorm.

Chris made a quick count and turned to the captain. "Two others besides the two that left are unaccounted for. Everyone else is here?"

Thirty-five of us stood in the center of the chalet, most of us coughing.

"Okay, everybody, listen up: I want the children sitting in the center. Everyone else sits in a circle around them. The fire is going to reach us in minutes. Stay calm—low to the floor. You're going to hear a loud roar coming closer and closer. It's going to get hot, real hot. The windows will shatter. The oxygen's going to be sucked out of the room—temporarily—and then, hopefully, the fire will quickly move over us, and shoot up Swiftcurrent Pass and we'll all be just fine. The Park Service knows we're here. Any questions?"

No one said a word, we just sat on the floor, children in the center, holding each other, waiting . . . some with their eyes closed, praying.

We would later learn that we had been taken for dead by the Park Service. Miraculously, we survived—as did Dan and Thalo, who watched the fire come within two hundred feet of the historic Granite Park Chalet, split around us, and rejoin its force as it roared up Swiftcurrent Pass. The windows didn't blow out, nor did the oxygen get sucked out of the room. The fire missed us. We were alive.

In Christopher Burke's words: "We could see that the crown fire that had been coming our way had arced around and above us, burning through Swiftcurrent Pass with two-to-three-hundred-foot flame lengths and seventy-mile-per-hour winds . . . At sunset the flames surrounding us lit up the chalet with an orange-pink glow and spot fires continued to burn above and around."

The two former employees of the BLM who had disappeared reemerged from the latrines before dark, where they had positioned themselves next to the pit toilets, ready to jump in the dark, nasty holes if necessary.

Our family stayed up all night and, from the porch of the Granite Park Chalet, we watched the fires burn. The intensity of our focus must have been tied to a delusional belief that if we just kept our eyes on the flames, we could keep them at bay. This kind of magical thinking soothed us, even though we all knew it was only the luck of the winds changing direction that had allowed the flames to split and burn around us instead of through us—leaving behind a charred heap of bodies, a circle of ash.

Early the next morning we "escaped" the continuing fires by hiking out the way we had hiked in—single file on the Highline Trail. Only this time, we were led by Christopher Burke, with the fire captain bringing up the rear. Three grizzlies walked out with us, slightly below the Garden Wall ledge, having also survived the historic Trapper fire of 2003.

On February 5, 2005, Secretary of the Interior Gale Norton presented the sixty-second annual awards for outstanding service and valor to government employees. Chris Burke, having just completed his twentieth season with the National Park Service, was among those honored:

> Christopher J. Burke—In recognition of his willingness to place himself at great personal risk in order to save the lives of 39 others.
>
> At 3:30 p.m. on July 23, 2003, while Mr. Burke was working at the Granite Park Chalet, a historic high mountain chalet in Glacier National Park, he noticed heavy smoke coming toward them from the Flattop Mountain area of the Trapper Fire. He radioed the Swiftcurrent Lookout for an update on the fire and was told that the wind had shifted. The lookout had been smoked out and was unable to see the fire activity. Mr. Burke and another co-worker scrambled to get pumps running and suppression sprinklers and nozzles charged and ready. Mr. Burke noticed that the drive belt had broken on the main water supply pump. With some very quick and resourceful modifications, he was able to switch to a different pump to supply water to the chalet fire suppression system. The wind was blowing approximately 70 miles per hour, knocking Mr. Burke and his co-worker to the ground. Mr. Burke ran for tools he needed to make emergency repairs to the pumps and water system. Returning, he was caught by thick hot clouds of smoke and had to feel his way back to the chalet. After hearing radio traffic talking about a running crown fire heading in their direction, he and his co-worker opened up all of their charged lines and began the defense of their lives and the historic chalet. Mr. Burke marshaled assistance of seven volunteers and assigned tasks to defend their position. They were being struck hard by burning bark, embers and ash as they wetted down the front of the chalet. Most of the chalet occupants huddled in

the dark and smoke-filled room of the chalet, some praying and some crying. One of the men declared he was going to escape by hiking ahead of the fire over Swiftcurrent Pass. Mr. Burke quickly recognized that he had to establish firm control over the group. Mr. Burke explained that the safest place to stay was in the chalet and that their defense was strong and holding. Over the next several hours, the fire continued to rage around and past the chalet, finally dying down around 9:00 p.m. Mr. Burke and his co-worker had successfully defended the chalet and the lives of everyone in it. In the morning, Mr. Burke and his co-worker organized the group for the hike out to Logan Pass to safety. Before leaving, however, they received a standing ovation and personal thanks for their heroic efforts from each of the grateful survivors. For his heroic actions, courage, and professionalism, Christopher J. Burke is awarded the Valor Award of the Department of the Interior.

Glacier National Park is a landscape of change. Today if you hike into the Granite Park Chalet on the Highline Trail, you will see evidence of the Trapper fire in the standing forests of black-burnt trees now in a state of regeneration, marked by the magenta flares of fireweed. Hike up to the Grinnell Glacier and you will see more change from a different kind of heat.

In 1850, 150 glaciers were recorded within the boundaries of Glacier National Park. In 2015, only 25 active glaciers remain. After decades of research, scientists have concluded that the glaciers for which the park was named could be gone within fifteen years as a consequence of the burn of global warming.

Climate change is not an abstraction here, but real change in real time: the rapid retreat of glaciers. Rock once covered now lies bare. To touch warm granite beds once blanketed by glaciers is both a hard fact and a perversion. No longer do you see the chiseled high peaks defined by fields of snow. In the twenty years our family had been visiting Glacier National Park, from our first visit in 1982 to the fires of 2003, the absence of ice was disorienting and unnerving. A vital characteristic of the terrain is being erased by global warming. The geographic relief of the mountains was rendered monochromatic and bland. The "Crown of the Continent" is slipping. I wonder what the mountain goats are thinking, these "beasts the color of winter." In this part of the world, predicting the future is a foolish proposition.

No one knows this better than the Blackfeet Nation. They are the true witnesses of change. The Blackfeet Reservation borders Canada to the north and Glacier National Park to the west, what the elders call "the backbone of Mother Earth." The Blackfeet have been living in this landscape for generations, spanning hundreds of years and thousands more before that. With the knowledge of their ancestors still present through ceremonies and stories shared, contemporary Blackfeet are able to reach back through time and reclaim traditional wisdom, just as they are in the process of reclaiming the land that was once theirs.

When Glacier National Park was established in 1910, the Blackfeet were displaced and physically removed from their home ground where the men hunted bison on horseback and women gathered berries and roots for their families. It wasn't just their food that was derived from the land, but all their medicine, as well. Not only were they removed from their sources of subsistence, but they lost access to much of the land where their spiritual life took place. They were not only ripped from the land where they lived, but torn from their spiritual traditions, inhibiting songs, dreams, prayers, and ceremonies, especially those ceremonies and vision quests practiced within sight of Chief Mountain, a geologic formation central and sacred to the tribe. By the laws of another nation, foreign and disconnected from their own, the Blackfeet were not only displaced but deceived by the U.S. government, disregarded and dismissed as a sovereign nation with rights.

The first superintendent of Glacier National Park, William Richard Logan, was no friend to the tribes even though he was an Indian agent to the Assiniboine and Gros Ventre at the Fort Belknap Reservation. He wanted Blackfeet land for the minerals believed to be in the mountains and for the future economic value of tourism.

In 1895, the U.S. government initiated a deal with the Blackfeet Nation to trade the western mountains on their reservation rumored to be filled with gold in exchange for cash and the continued nonmineral rights to hunt and fish on their land as they had always done.

White Calf, one of the Blackfeet leaders, said, "I would like to have the right to hunt game and fish in the mountains. We will sell you the mountain lands from Birch Creek to the boundary, reserving the timber and grazing land."

Pressured to sign the agreement, the Blackfeet asked for $3 million. They were paid half that by the federal government. George Bird Grinnell was one of the government negotiators and an early advocate for Glacier National Park. He gave his word to the Blackfeet that they could retain their hunting and fishing rights as long as these lands remained public. But upon the opening of Glacier National Park in 1910, their native rights were revoked on the technicality that these were no longer public lands but park lands. It made no sense other than Indian removal. The Blackfeet were denied (with some Indians even being arrested) the previous access they had been promised.

Where is the valor in these actions taken by the U.S. federal government?

Much of the enduring valor of the Blackfeet Nation is drawn from fire. Between the glaciers that continue to hang in the high peaks above their homes and the slow rivers of ice that have carved the landscape around them, it is fire that helps to maintain their traditions and strength. Whether it is smoking the sacred pipe in ceremony or participating in sweat lodges with steaming stones and smoldering sage to purify the body and spirit, fire is a truth teller among the Blackfeet people. Even the Sun Dance, once practiced secretly for fear of government reprisal, imprisonment, or death, is now practiced openly in the name of prayer, sacrifice, and renewal, honoring the Sun that lights up the world, a force that both gives life and destroys it.

It is said that the Blackfeet get their name from their characteristic moccasins darkened by the ashes of fire.

Fire is akin to many tribes.

There is a long history of Indians as fire preventers and firefighters within the United States. In 1933, with the creation of the Civilian Conservation Corps under President Franklin D. Roosevelt, more than eighty-eight thousand Native Americans were employed in the Indian CCC Division to build fire lookout towers, fire cabins, and hundreds of miles of trails within remote forested terrain that provided access to firefighters should the trees ignite.

In 1948, the famed Mescalero Red Hats organized themselves to become the first Native American fire crew to fight fires in the Southwest. Most of them were World War II veterans. They were also the ones who rescued an orphaned bear cub after a large burn in New Mexico that later fostered the legend of Smokey the Bear, dressed in a ranger suit and advocating for fire safety in our national forests.

During that same period, David H. DeJong of the Native American Research and Training Center writes, "The Hopi Indians organized a trained firefighting crew; two years later, the Zuni Indians did the same. In 1954, the Red Hats and the Zuni Thunderbirds received meritorious service citations for firefighting from the U.S. Department of Agriculture. During 1953–55, Native American crews were formed in Montana from the Crow, Northern Cheyenne, Blackfeet, Flathead, Rocky Boys, and Forts Belknap, Peck and Hall reservations. In the mid-1950s, the Bureau of Land Management (BLM) also organized crews from among Alaska Natives."

According to the Bureau of Indian Affairs National Interagency Fire Center, close to 25 percent of all firefighters working today on wildfires on our public lands in the United States are Indians. In Montana, many are Blackfeet. The distinguished "Chief Mountain Hot Shots" are comprised of highly skilled Blackfeet crews who are dropped into dangerous fire zones to tame the flames. They are known as the "Fire Warriors."

I can't help but wonder how many Fire Warriors were fighting the "Mountain Man Complex" we witnessed in the summer of 2003.

Fire has been a traditional tool of warfare among the Blackfeet Nation for centuries, creating fire walls against enemies as well as using fire as a tool of restoration to rejuvenate land through intentional burns and fire management essential to the regenerative health of the prairies. It makes sense that the work of the "Fire Warriors" would be heightened in the twenty-first century as global warming is causing bigger and hotter fires due to the ravages of the pine bark beetle in western forests. Freezing temperatures during long, cold winters killed the beetles. Now, no longer. Now, due to higher temperatures in both summer and winter, pine bark beetles go through multiple breeding cycles that kill more trees.

The same climate changes that are creating more wildfires in the American West are creating the retreat of glaciers. Fire and ice are harbingers of change and both are found in the dynamic landscape of Glacier National Park.

A political fire is also burning in Glacier National Park. After more than a century of promises made and treaties broken by the federal government, the Blackfeet are challenging the status quo. They are demanding reinstatement of their reserved treaty rights to hunt, fish, and gather medicinal plants inside the national park boundaries. They are also asking for the voluntary closure of cultural sites essential to their spiritual practices. And their final ask is for joint management of Glacier National Park itself.

Here is one prediction that can be made: Soon, the Blackfeet will stand shoulder to shoulder in shared governance of these parklands with the National Park Service. After more than a century of being forced to retreat, the Blackfeet Nation is advancing like fire. The Blackfeet identity is rising from the ashes of national park history. Two-thirds of the Blackfeet live in Canada. Like the ecosystem of Waterton-Glacier, they have been divided by an international border. Today, their sky-blue flag flies high at the Lake McDonald Visitor's Center—flanked by the American flag on one side and the Canadian flag on the other—inside America's tenth national park. Three sovereign nations merge in an International Peace Park where Glacier National Park and the Waterton Lakes National Park create a contiguous boundary of faith.

It was at this intersection of nations that we celebrated John Tempest's birthday in Canada on July 26, 2003, across the border in Waterton Lakes National Park, a country away from the fires of northern Montana, but still within sight of melting glaciers.

In 1990, the writers Bill Kittredge and Annick Smith edited a thousand page anthology of Montana literature including Native storytelling, the journals of trappers, poems, short stories, and essays from close to 150 writers, offering a mosaic of some of the finest writing past and present that had ever been written in the American West. The collection was called *The Last Best Place* and it became a regional phenomenon that both jump-started a western literary renaissance and captured a hard truth in one poignant phrase—the disappearing landscapes within the Rocky Mountains.

Darnell Davis, a Blackfeet elder, said recently, "The last best place is our first place." ✦

About This Story

Double our maximum word count, and already featured in our last anthology—if we're going to break the rules for anyone, it's going to be for Terry Tempest Williams. This chapter would not be complete without her masterful voice on place and our national parks. To us, this piece tells one complete story, in two chapters—the Williamses' own survival story, which we can only imagine has been shared around a campfire in all subsequent family trips, and the park's history dealing with the increasing threat of wildfire in the region. Connecting to the lessons learned in George Bird Grinnell's piece and Blackfeet Nation member Mariah Gladstone's Naapi story, we love how Terry's essay returns to the idea that Indigenous communities are the best stewards of the land.

Since the release of her 2016 book, *The Hour of Land*, Glacier National Park has experienced additional major wildfires and heat waves, reaching record-setting temperatures during 2021. In a typical year, the park has a narrow July-to-September season. Visitors flock to the park to traverse the Going-to-the-Sun Road, just now clear of snow to connect east and west ends of the park, and providing access to Logan Pass and other iconic trails. But if a wildfire strikes during peak season, it can be catastrophic to the landscape and the people who depend on it. The park and local economy rely heavily on this high volume of visitors to stay, recreate, and explore in the parks. Wildfires limit visitors' ability to see and experience the park. Worse, visitors may change or cancel plans completely, and the fires even threaten to wipe out iconic features of the park, like the Sperry Chalet.

Listed on the National Register of Historic Places, the Swiss-style Sperry Chalet sits on a rock ledge at an elevation of 6,550 feet and is one of Glacier National Park's most iconic buildings. It offers incredible views of striking waterfalls and mountain peaks and can only be accessed by foot or horse.

In August 2017, a thunderstorm moving through the park produced more than 150 strikes, which ignited the Sprague Fire—just three miles from the Lake McDonald Lodge. This area had not experienced fire since the 1700s, and the entire western United States was unusually hot and dry—eighty-three active fires were already threatening structures and lives. Firefighting personnel were spread thin, making it difficult to combat the growing Sprague Fire, which was soon headed toward Sperry Chalet.

In total, the fire burned over two months and burned nearly seventeen thousand acres. Despite best efforts, the Sperry Chalet dormitory was consumed by fire, but the four other buildings on the complex were saved. The dormitory has since been restored and reopened in 2020, in large part due to the efforts of Glacier National Park Conservancy, who quickly got to work and created the Sperry Action Fund to help pay for the restoration.

JOSHUA TREE NATIONAL PARK

Where Two Deserts Meet

JOSHUA TREE'S EXPANSIVE barren landscape has long inspired dreamers, musicians, writers, and artists alike, and its rather odd namesake—Joshua trees—are emblematic of the outcasts that find themselves drawn here. This fragile yet resilient desert is seen by some as a wasteland and a playground of rocks to others. A barren desert to many and a bountiful supermarket to those with ancestral ties here.

illustration by
PAVONIS GIRON

ur first time visiting the desert was for volume one of *Campfire Stories*, when we stayed in Zion National Park for two weeks. It was hotter and drier than any climate we've known, and we were slow to drink it in. Only through reading others' perspectives on the desert, their love and their inspiration, like Terry Tempest Williams, did we find our own ways to appreciate it. When we began to research Joshua Tree for the book in 2020, we learned it was the tenth most visited national park and how terribly uncool we were to not already love it.

Joshua Tree has been cool since rock 'n' roll put this region on the map in the 1970s and 1980s. Maybe the most iconic album connected to this place is Irish rock band U2's *The Joshua Tree*, which was released in 1987 and has sold over 25 million copies worldwide. This album planted memorable images and music videos into the American psyche of a lone Joshua tree in a desert landscape, which was captured along a highway while the band and photographer were exploring the deserts of Coachella and Death Valley.

The Rolling Stones' Keith Richards and American rocker Gram Parsons would often visit Joshua Tree with friends and bandmates, disappearing into the desert for days at a time while under the influence of psychedelics and looking for UFOs. Gram Parsons notoriously overdosed and died in 1973 at age twenty-six in his hotel room at the Joshua Tree Inn before the extent of his fame was even realized. His remains were later stolen by his road manager, on a mission to fulfill Parsons' alleged funeral wish to be cremated at Cap Rock in Joshua Tree, the place he loved.

In addition to those who might see themselves as outcasts from traditional society, like those hoping for alien encounters, Joshua Tree continues to be a mecca and inspiration for creatives, serving as a destination for many artist residencies. So many people have flocked to the region, triggered in part by a great urban escape from the COVID-19 pandemic, that a 2022 *New York Times* article estimated 2,043 Airbnb and VRBO properties are listed for short-term rental here. Southern Californian deserts also have a reputation as a magnet for criminals and convicts, perhaps because of the rough, jagged terrain and oftentimes harsh, inhospitable weather that leads people to wonder why anyone would *choose* to live here. They must be trying to remain unseen and escaping *something* for good reason.

Take the legendary Willie Boy story, for example. A new audio-visual art installation at the Oasis Visitor Center in Joshua Tree National Park retells this story, a tragic tale of love, murder, and a manhunt across the desert wilderness that ended in a shootout and the demise of Willie Boy. This version of the story is written by Cahuilla artist and author Lewis deSoto from the perspective of Carlota, the woman at the center of the story. *"A young man has come to the oasis. His name is Will. They say he is family, but I do not know him. He is strange and powerful. I am drawn to him. He stares right into my spirit. He is a Ghost Runner."*

Underneath the park's storied human history is a fragile ecosystem of flora and fauna prone to abuse. The Joshua trees thrive in the cooler Mojave desert climate on the west side of the park, while ocotillo and cholla have adapted to the lower elevation and hotter temperatures of the Colorado desert in the eastern side. This dry and seemingly barren landscape is often deemed wasteland, except by those who love it. Charles Augustus Keeler—a naturalist, poet, and adventurer who was director of the California Academy of Sciences' natural history museum in the 1890s—described the desert as "a region of arid plains and barren mountains. The soil is of sand encrusted with alkali, and the mountains are bold, rocky and inhospitable, frequently in the shape of abrupt, sharply pointed cones with miles of disintegrated rock, known as talus, sloping away from their bases. Again, great boulders are piled in chaotic heaps, wrenched and wracked by the elements, worn by the action of waves upon this prehistoric ocean shore, and now standing as silent witnesses of the vast work of ages. Indeed, there is always something cosmic and elemental about the desert. We seem to be transported into some earlier geologic time, when the heart of nature lay bare to the action of the elements, and the bleak barren world knew not the songs of birds nor the glory of flowers. And herein lies the wonder of it! There is a fascination in its very sterility in its boundless expanse and its haughty disdain of all that is tender and lovely. It is terrible and grand."

Also drawn to the beauty and bounty of the desert was Minerva Hoyt—a wealthy socialite and activist who fell in love with Southern California's desert plants through a passion for gardening in the 1920s. On one of her many trips to the desert, she was quoted as saying, "I stood and looked. Everything was peaceful, and it rested me." She was appalled by the widespread destruction of native desert plants like cacti and Joshua trees that she witnessed. In addition to organizing exhibitions that put desert plants on display across major cities in the United States and England, she went on to create the International Deserts Conservation

League to preserve these beautiful habitats. She worked with famed landscape architect Frederick Law Olmsted Jr., to prepare a report that recommended preserving these unique landscapes and their threatened plants. Large parks should be created, they said, in Death Valley, Anza-Borrego Desert, and Palm Springs. Over time they became convinced a larger national park was the best way to protect these desert habitats. The biggest threats at the time included plant collectors and vandals, including one who set fire and destroyed an eighty-foot Joshua tree in Antelope Valley in 1930. Hoyt's goal was to prevent these criminal acts from occurring in the first place, because these desert ecosystems survive in a delicate balance, and once harmed, are much slower to heal.

President Franklin D. Roosevelt established the region as a national monument on August 10, 1936, protecting 825,000 acres of desert land. Many suggested the park be named after Minerva Hoyt, but policy at the time prevented parks being named after living people. So Joshua Tree National Monument was selected to acknowledge the region's most whimsical mascot, the Joshua tree. Although not recognized as widely as early male advocates of national parks, you can find Hoyt's efforts honored within the park by visiting Minerva Hoyt Trail and looking off at Mount Minerva Hoyt, which was designated in 2012.

Human history here dates back anywhere from four thousand to eight thousand years ago. The native people of what we now know of as Joshua Tree National Park and its surrounding regions include Pinto culture—the people who predated today's tribal groups—followed by Indigenous tribes like the Serrano, the Chemehuevi, and Cahuilla. While some see the Southern California deserts as desolate, Indigenous peoples did not. To them, this region was essentially a supermarket. Known to the Chemehuevi people as the Oasis of Mara, the place of little springs and much grass, this land was used for hunting and gathering, as it was rich with resources. Early tribal territories existed near reliable water sources, which also attracted abundant life in the form of bighorn sheep, deer, amphibians, reptiles, rabbits, and birds. Indigenous tribes used at least 121 plant species for food, medicine, or making baskets, hunting and agricultural tools, and cordage. They subsisted on foods and medicinal ingredients like berries, seeds, cactus fruits, pinyon nuts, and acorns.

Today, the Serrano and Cahuilla people are still here, serving as stewards to the land as they always have, and continuing to preserve and share their history and culture. This includes the Dorothy Ramon Learning Center, named after a Serrano elder recognized as the last primary speaker of the Serrano language, and knowledgeable about the traditional way of life of the Serrano people. The book *Wayta' Yawa' (Always Believe)* was created over twelve years by linguist Eric Elliot and Ramon, who was well into her eighties then, in an effort to save the region's cultural knowledge and language. Her nephew, Ernest Siva, now an elder himself, helps run the learning center as more of a learning and cultural center than museum. Through the center, they share memories, songs, stories, and readings. Still alive today are Bird Songs performances, an ancient tradition from some Southern California and Arizona tribes, where bird singers of varying generations sing and dance to a steady beat of gourd rattles. These local tribes sing bird songs as a way to keep their history, stories, and lessons alive.

We find ourselves today repeating a vicious cycle of destruction in the Joshua Tree region that Minerva Hoyt and early park advocates worked so hard to prevent. During the 2019 government shutdown, the longest in US history at thirty-five days, Joshua Tree remained open with limited staff despite many other parks closing to the public. But tending to the essentials—handling trash or cleaning bathrooms—and monitoring the fragile landscape became impossible. While most visitors were on good behavior, too many broke park rules and went wild: camping illegally, driving onto delicate natural areas, and even intentionally destroying several of the park's century-old Joshua trees by running them over or chopping them down. This stark lack of respect for the land that our Indigenous ancestors stewarded for centuries has major consequences. The damage during this period was so significant that we won't see recovery in our lifetime. According to former Joshua Tree National Park Superintendent Curt Sauer, "What's happened to our park in the last thirty-four days is irreparable for the next two to three hundred years."

The park and its Joshua trees also face the threat of increased heat and droughts due to human-induced global warming. According to the National Park Service, on a worst-case scenario emissions trajectory, temperatures will increase by eight degrees Fahrenheit (five degrees Celsius) by 2099, and "under these conditions, it could eliminate nearly all suitable habitat for Joshua trees in the park and reduce habitat in the Southwest by 90 percent." And the lower emissions scenarios don't look much better. As Hoyt discovered nearly a century ago, these fragile landscapes depend on a delicate balance. Rising temperatures will have dire consequences for the many birds, animals, and plants that depend on that balance, including habitat loss and declining populations.

The Joshua tree has inspired everyone from Mormon settlers, who saw their prophet reaching out hands in prayer, to Gram Parsons, who looked to reach another plane of existence. Preservation here is made harder by the fragility of the landscape. But this is the place where two deserts meet and create a unique ecosystem that exists nowhere else, with plants and animals that make those who feel they have no place anywhere else feel seen and heard. This collection of stories shows us the strange paths that one can take when in Joshua Tree. It's up to us to walk those paths and decide the legacy we want to leave for future generations, to the steady beat of the birdsong.

Joshua Tree Imprimatur

RUTH NOLAN

"The great Creator told us, 'I'm going to teach you these songs,
but before I teach you these songs, I'm going to break your heart.'"
—LARRY EDDY (CHEMEHUEVI SALT SONG SINGER)

I

In Joshua Tree
In the land that crowns its needled glories with sand
In the desert made of pavement fallen from the Milky Way
In the desert made of deep holes carved by grinding stones
In the desert made of canyons cut through geologic zones
In the desert made of walking rain that eyes can far-off see
In the desert made of fan tree palms

II

In the desert made of cold
In the desert made of blinding mirage
In the desert made of light so old
it whispers like grooved bones
Where the woolly mammoth and rattlesnake
cross through time and home
Oceans of time rising and receding
land quaking in their tidal paths
Where the granite batholiths arch their backs
Where the red-tailed hawks vault their hunting songs

III

Oh, desert night lizard!
With your comet tail, sparking eternities of stars
With your rustling dance amongst
Washingtonia filifera fan palm families,
Your invisible sipping at these faint green oases
With your instinct for scuttling sideways up sharp rock hills
With your narrow paths in native grasses
With your nest inside fallen Joshua trees
With your burrowed body penetrating sand dunes
With your zigzag shape, you whip your way into abandoned mines, old
    gut wounds of the world
The way it was, whole and un-deserted then

IV

In Joshua Tree
In the land that prophets barren land
with shouldered trees
that are not trees
but members of the asparagus family
they call you by many names
In the desert, where flash floods chorus and howl in summer's long
    suffocation crawl
In the desert
where footsteps penetrate the night
In the desert
where bobcats and mountain lions prowl
In the desert
where bighorn sheep scuttle at sunset
across the highest rocks
In the desert
where shade rests in deep and narrow space
In the desert
early Pinto people carved their words into eternity
In the desert

Chemehuevi and Serrano people
call Oasis of Mara home
In the desert
where small cemeteries mark empty land

V

Oh, desert homestead!
With your early people hunting big game
With your ancient glaciers carving the land to bone
With inland waters now faded into long ago
With your old men and women anxious for gold
With your young lovers, Willie and Carlota
who shared their love in silence in this frowning land
With your reliance on creosote for medicine and tea
With your vast wisdom, your quaking downfalls
With your cemented reservoir at Barker Dam
Fighting over water, drowning in flash floods
With your earth-gouged wounds, gutted for their jewels
With your millions of tourists and rock climbers.
Musicians, ravers, thrilled children, city refugees
all feeling they have found a home
here
where
the sky stands still
and the wind
blows shotgun shacks down

VI

In Joshua Tree
In the land where rattlesnake meets highway
With your ancient trails snaking their way
from the Colorado River
to the ocean at Malibu
The California Hiking Trail
Highway 62 following the old routes

With your hidden palm oases
shouldering timeless stands
from the age of the dinosaur
With your visiting vloggers and influencers
With your nearby cities
fighting to swallow the last
of your rare resources
With golf courses from the other side of the hills
blowing invasive species of mustard grass
With a Marine base exploding into
your sacred sister mountains
With high desert towns
competing for your northern love
With your sloped drop on your southern edge
into the land we call hot and low
In the desert raging with wildfires
Torching buckwheat and Joshua trees
Until they are dissolved

VII

In the desert where people wander off and get lost
In the desert where coyotes and tarantulas
shoulder a slow, desert tortoise crawl
In the desert
where Minerva Hoyt came to your rescue
and turned you into a National Park
In the desert, where Eagle Mountain dump
nibbles at your eastern fringe
In the desert
where orange and ruby sherbet sunsets are your dessert
In the desert
where your shallow-rooted makeshift trees
Gnarl their arms skyward in a massive prayer
In the desert
where wind shreds your needled skin into pulp

In the desert
where snowstorms powder the barren ground
into a lonely, deserted delicacy

VIII

In Joshua Tree
Where canyons spill into nowhere lands
Where Dayglo bright colors paint the sand
in spring's melodic flower verse
Where the June sun
tarnishes the artist's canvas brown
Where boulders become pillows
for society's aching back
Where lovers fight and surrender
into the long sweep of Key's View
Where the Wall Street Mill offers empty promises
of long-ago fortunes earned and gone
Where families camp and come to explore
Where tourist hordes sometimes come to destroy
Not knowing where they stand
How fragile and irreplaceable
This forsaken land

IX

In the desert
where the crush of Los Angeles melts away
In the desert, where off-road vehicles scream and grind
In the desert
where Ryan Mountain imposes its stoic handhold
In the desert
where the Little Mountains rise with pinyon pine
In the desert
where transition zones abound
In the desert
where rain may not nourish this thirsty land

for weeks and months, sometimes a year
In the desert, where water comes too hard
Then sinks into the sand too fast
In the desert
your name is scratched into the stars
In the desert, you survive, you survive
Respect the sun and heat
You will survive

                              X

In Joshua Tree
Oh, Joshua trees
populating this arid land
where prophets turn for words
when colors bloom and fade
When lovers come and do not stay
When the last footprints have quickly blown away
When the first impressions of human hands
have been imprinted for us to find
When there is nothing left to take
When visionaries drop to their knees and pray
You will find your true name
In Joshua Tree
Where the sand filters through your hands
In the desert
you are lost
and
In the desert
you are found. ✦

About This Story

Ruth Nolan grew up in the Mojave Desert before it was "cool." As a young girl in the 1970s, her family moved across the country from Brooklyn, New York, to Apple Valley, California, just a stone's throw from Joshua Tree National Park. Ruth immediately took to the desert and its clear air, and it became a place for nurturing, transformation, inspiration, and healing. She says it looked a lot like Joshua Tree does now, but it's evolved into an unrecognizable suburban and developed landscape far from the rocky terrain she remembers.

She shares that it's strange to see her hometown become a hip, desirable place to live. But she gets it, too. "What I think people are drawn to is that there's nothing like it. Everything is exposed. There's a continuity and flow that doesn't happen in more urban, colonized places."

We first learned about Ruth through her essay "Memorial Burn," which follows her search for evidence of wildfires in Joshua Tree National Park and how they transform the landscape. Ruth worked as a seasonal wildland firefighter for the Bureau of Land Management's California Desert District and several seasons for the US Forest Service's Mojave Greens wildland fire crew. She was often one of the few women, sometimes the only woman, on the engine and helicopter crews.

After we learned about her anthology, *No Place for a Puritan: The Literature of the California Deserts*, and her professorship at the College of the Desert teaching English and creative writing, we knew Ruth was the perfect person to capture the essence of Joshua Tree.

"Joshua Tree Imprimatur" was initially written and narrated on commission for a short experimental film produced by UCR/California Museum of Photography called *Escape to Reality: 24 hrs @ 24 fps*. The piece was inspired by Edmund C. Jaeger—an important figure in Mojave desert science, ecology, and literature—who wrote a desert book called *The Magic Circle*. Ruth wanted to take a 360-degree view of desert plant and animal life and write about it. So she sat herself in one of her "cosmic spots" and took in the landscape. She also wanted the piece to evoke the idea that there is so much life—past, present, and future—in this landscape and invite others to experience it. Her hope is that the piece demonstrates that Joshua Tree is not a wasteland to trample or quickly drive through. It's a place to sit, drink it all in, and allow it to envelop and heal you.

The First New Plants

Excerpt from *Stories and Legends of the Palm Springs Indians*

FRANCISCO PATENCIO

N ow, when everything burned was cold, they filled the grave and smoothed it, and went back and burned the house because Mo-Cot before he died told them to do this thing—not to live in the old house where he had lived. Someone might get sickness.

In three days they went to look at the grave, and they saw some plants sprouting up where they had burned their father Mo-Cot, and they did not know what it was.

They said to each another, "Our father never said anything about that, so how can we find out."

Now one man among them was smart and intelligent, and he asked, "Did our father not leave someone with the power of knowing about this?"

But no one knew, and then he said, "I am going to chase him until I find him, and then I am going to find out."

So the people said that was right; that he should go and ask him about it, and find out. The man who was going to chase our father, his name was *Pal mech cho wit*, meaning "water not believing." He went over to the grave where they had burned the body, and he stood waiting there, looking at the plants.

Soon a very small whirlwind started going around, and he watched it until it went away from the plants, and he followed it as it went to the east. The whirlwind was getting larger and larger. He followed it until dark came, and in the darkness the whirlwind became light, so that he could see, and he still followed on. He found after a time that the whirlwind was not a whirlwind, but a person.

He followed him, but could not get near to him; but anyway he could see all right until the daylight came. He saw tracks, and he followed the tracks. But the great red ant walked over the tracks till he could not see them any more. Then he used the tracks of the red ant to follow.

Pal mech me wit said, "It is yourself, my father, using the tracks of the ants, and so I am going to follow you."

Then the tracks of the great red ants were covered by the tracks of the *Cev la bet em*, the big black beetle, the bug that stands on its head, but not the small bug of today. So *Pal mech me wit* used that track, and said, "I know that it is you yourself, my father, using this track." And he kept following until darkness came.

After the dark came he kept going toward the East. Then he came to the grease-wood tree, and seeing the bunches of mistletoe in the trees, thought it was some person, but found it was only mistletoe, such as grew in his own country.

Pal mech me wit said, "It is your own self doing this to frighten me, my father."

He kept on going till he came to the desert willow tree. He thought it was a person till he came close to it. He thought perhaps it was Mo-Cot, but it was only desert willow. He kept on going till he saw a palo verde tree, and the bunches of mistletoe again. He was very much afraid, so far away from his people, but he was brave, and would not be frightened by a palo verde tree covered with bunches of mistletoe. Now this was palo verde (*ow ow wit*) with the flat seed; the other kind is *taw how cut* with the round seed, and he saw this kind also with the bunches of mistletoe. Still he kept going, and all things small looked large to him till he came to them, when he found they were all small.

He was seeing the mirage across the sand. He kept going on till he came to the sand country, sand and sand hills, which in the Indian language is called *na che wit*, a country with nothing but sand.

After passing through the sand country he came to prairie country. There he heard an owl howling, and he knew he was getting near to the place he was looking for. When the night came, he could see the light shooting straight up to the sky. He kept on going, and then he came close to Mo-Cot. As he came nearer, a wave of heat came across his face, and he knew he was coming closer to Mo-Cot's spirit.

He was filled with fear. He was not quite up to him, but he was nervous, and trembled so much that he could not go farther. Mo-Cot's spirit was asking him to come closer if he could. He tried, but could not. He had no strength left to stand up. He could not walk any more.

And because *Pal mech me wit*'s strength turned weak when he saw the Spirit, so have all people since become weak when they see a spirit.

He could see Mo-Cot's spirit. The body was like crystal at night time, with pale colors glowing over it. He could see the face, but not the features, and the spirit was beautiful.

Mo-Cot's spirit knew who he was, and what he had come after, too, but anyway he asked, "Who are you?"

Pal mech me wit answered, "I am of *No cot em*, the people, who gave me authority to come and ask you something. In our grave something is sprouting up. We don't know what that is. I and *No cot em* want to know."

Then Mo-Cot's spirit answered and said, "I was going to explain all these things to you people. I did not know what you people were thinking about when you bewitched me, but that is all right. Now I will tell you.

"These plants are all my body; all kinds: my bones, my skin, my head, my eyes, my ears, my nose, my arms, my fingers, my legs, my feet, my liver, my guts, my heart, my hair.

"Everything is what you will use for your living. You are going to eat that.

"My teeth will be your corn; the melons are my heart; my eyes are your fruit; your grass is my hair.

"Everything that you have, that you will eat, that will be some part of my body.

"You have to go back to the people and tell them that I will be there in one day, two days, or three days."

So *Pal mech me wit* went back, and when he got there he called them every one together, and he told them everything that Mo-Cot's spirit had told him—all about the plants which were to be ours to use. The people did not know one plant from another, so *Pal mech me wit* told them all of the names of everything, even those we see today.

The first name that they had was the beans, which were the fingers of Mo-Cot. These were named *Ta va my lum*. The corn was named *Pa ha vosh lum* and the wheat was named *Pach che sal* and the pumpkins were *neh wit em*, the watermelon was *Is to chen*. At the same time *Pal mech me wit* told them that Mo-Cot's spirit would be with them in one day, two days, or three days.

They were all glad and satisfied to have Mo-Cot's spirit come again. They waited those three days, but the night of the third day they all fell asleep.

Then one of them, a man named *Chip chip wit*, he awoke and saw coming the spirit of Mo-Cot. He saw very plainly the spirit of his father, so he jumped up and he yelled to all the people, "All my brothers and sisters, our father is here now!"

They jumped up, every one of them, and they looked and asked each another, but they could see nothing. They asked each another, "Who is it that says our father is here?"

Then *Chip chip wit* became nervous at what he saw, and fell down unconscious. He spit blood from his mouth.

When he got better, he told them that he saw his father's spirit. "Maybe I am mistaken, but I saw it." he said.

And so it was that some, but not all, could see the spirits. ✦

About This Story

Francisco Patencio, chief of the Cahuilla Indians, saw a problem. The elders of the tribe were passing away. The children were being taught by American churches and schools, and the beliefs of the Indian people, he mourned, were being forgotten. And so, Chief Patencio, with the help of Margaret Boynton of the Palm Springs Desert Museum, wrote down the stories of the Palm Springs Indians. The real audience for these stories, Patencio clarifies, is "our children and our children's children, and those yet to come, that when the Indian customs are forgotten, they may read and know and remember in their hearts the ways and thoughts of their own people."

The lands that comprise Joshua Tree National Park were once homelands to the Pinto, Serrano, Chemehuevi, and Cahuilla tribes. It is thanks to Chief Patencio and Margaret Boynton that many of the values and lessons of the Cahuilla are preserved in *Stories and Legends of the Palm Springs Indians*. This story is just one part of a fascinating, dynamic, and complex tale of the origin of the Cahuilla people by the god Mo-Cot, who is killed by the people he creates, but leaves behind many of the unique desert plants for his people to continue to thrive. It is a difficult and nuanced story for non-Cahuilla people to tell authentically, and we are grateful to Chief Patencio for leaving this legacy.

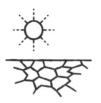

The Land of
Little Rain

Excerpt from *The Land of Little Rain*

MARY AUSTIN

East away from the Sierras, south from Panamint and Amargosa, east and south many an uncounted mile, is the Country of Lost Borders.

Ute, Paiute, Mojave, and Shoshone inhabit its frontiers, and as far into the heart of it as a man dare go. Not the law, but the land sets the limit. Desert is the name it wears upon the maps, but the Indian's is the better word. Desert is a loose term to indicate land that supports no man; whether the land can be bitted and broken to that purpose is not proven. Void of life it never is, however dry the air and villainous the soil.

This is the nature of that country. There are hills, rounded, blunt, burned, squeezed up out of chaos, chrome and vermilion painted, aspiring to the snowline. Between the hills lie high level-looking plains full of intolerable sun glare, or narrow valleys drowned in a blue haze. The hill surface is streaked with ash drift and black, unweathered lava flows. After rains water accumulates in the hollows of small closed valleys, and, evaporating, leaves hard dry levels of pure desertness that get the local name of dry lakes. Where the mountains are steep and the rains heavy, the pool is never quite dry, but dark and bitter, rimmed about with the efflorescence of alkaline deposits. A thin crust of it lies along the marsh over the vegetating area, which has neither beauty nor freshness. In the broad wastes open to the wind the sand drifts in hummocks about the stubby shrubs, and between them the soil shows saline traces. The sculpture of the hills here is more wind than water work, though the quick storms do sometimes scar them past many a year's redeeming. In all the Western desert edges there are essays in miniature at the famed, terrible Grand Cañon, to which, if you keep on long enough in this country, you will come at last.

Since this is a hill country one expects to find springs, but not to depend upon them; for when found they are often brackish and unwholesome, or maddening, slow dribbles in a thirsty soil. Here you find the hot sink of Death Valley, or high rolling districts where the air has always a tang of frost. Here are the long heavy winds and breathless calms on the tilted mesas where dust devils dance, whirling up into a wide, pale sky. Here you have no rain when all the earth cries for it, or quick downpours called cloud-bursts for violence. A land of lost rivers, with little in it to love; yet a land that once visited must be come back to inevitably. If it were not so there would be little told of it.

This is the country of three seasons. From June on to November it lies hot, still, and unbearable, sick with violent unrelieving storms; then on until April, chill, quiescent, drinking its scant rain and scanter snows; from April to the hot season again, blossoming, radiant, and seductive. These months are only approximate; later or earlier the rain-laden wind may drift up the water gate of the Colorado from the Gulf, and the land sets its seasons by the rain.

The desert floras shame us with their cheerful adaptations to the seasonal limitations. Their whole duty is to flower and fruit, and they do it hardly, or with tropical luxuriance, as the rain admits. It is recorded in the report of the Death Valley expedition that after a year of abundant rains, on the Colorado desert was found a specimen of Amaranthus ten feet high. A year later the same species in the same place matured in the drought at four inches. One hopes the land may breed like qualities in her human offspring, not tritely to "try," but to do. Seldom does the desert herb attain the full stature of the type. Extreme aridity and extreme altitude have the same dwarfing effect, so that we find in the high Sierras and in Death Valley related species in miniature that reach a comely growth in mean temperatures. Very fertile are the desert plants in expedients to prevent evaporation, turning their foliage edgewise toward the sun, growing silky hairs, exuding viscid gum. The wind, which has a long sweep, harries and helps them. It rolls up dunes about the stocky stems, encompassing and protective, and above the dunes, which may be, as with the mesquite, three times as high as a man, the blossoming twigs flourish and bear fruit.

There are many areas in the desert where drinkable water lies within a few feet of the surface, indicated by the mesquite and the bunch grass (*Sporobolus airoides*). It is this nearness of unimagined help that makes the tragedy of desert deaths. It is related that the final breakdown of that hapless party that gave Death Valley its forbidding name occurred in a locality where shallow wells would have saved them. But how were they to know that? Properly equipped it is possible to go safely across that ghastly sink, yet every year it takes its toll of death, and yet men find there sun-dried mummies, of whom no trace or recollection is preserved. To underestimate one's thirst, to pass a given landmark to the right or left, to find a dry spring where one looked for running water—there is no help for any of these things.

Along springs and sunken watercourses one is surprised to find such water-loving plants as grow widely in moist ground, but the true desert breeds its own kind, each in its particular habitat. The angle of the slope, the frontage of a hill, the structure of the soil determines the plant. South-looking hills are nearly bare, and the lower tree-line higher here by a thousand feet. Cañons running east and west will have one wall naked and one clothed. Around dry lakes and marshes the herbage preserves a set and orderly arrangement. Most species have well-defined areas of growth, the best index the voiceless land can give the traveler of his whereabouts.

If you have any doubt about it, know that the desert begins with the creosote. This immortal shrub spreads down into Death Valley and up to the lower timberline, odorous and medicinal as you might guess from the name, wandlike, with shining fretted foliage. Its vivid green is grateful to the eye in a wilderness of gray and greenish white shrubs. In the spring it exudes a resinous gum which the Indians of those parts know how to use with pulverized rock for cementing arrow points to shafts. Trust Indians not to miss any virtues of the plant world!

Nothing the desert produces expresses it better than the unhappy growth of the tree yuccas. Tormented, thin forests of it stalk drearily in the high mesas, particularly in that triangular slip that fans out eastward from the meeting of the Sierras and coastwise hills where the first swings across the southern end of the San Joaquin Valley. The yucca bristles with bayonet-pointed leaves, dull green, growing shaggy with age, tipped with panicles of fetid, greenish bloom. After death, which is slow, the ghostly hollow network of its woody skeleton, with hardly power to rot, makes the moonlight fearful. Before the yucca has come to flower, while yet its bloom is a creamy cone-shaped bud of the size of a small cabbage, full of sugary sap, the Indians twist it deftly out of its fence of daggers and roast it for their own delectation. So it is that in those parts where man inhabits one sees young plants of *Yucca arborensis* infrequently. Other yuccas, cacti, low herbs, a thousand sorts, one finds journeying east from the coastwise hills. There is neither poverty of soil nor species to account for the sparseness of desert growth, but simply that each plant requires more room. So much earth must be preëmpted to extract so much moisture. The real struggle for existence, the real brain of the plant, is underground; above there is room for a rounded perfect growth. In Death Valley, reputed the very core of desolation, are nearly two hundred identified species.

Above the lower tree-line, which is also the snow-line, mapped out abruptly by the sun, one finds spreading growth of piñon, juniper, branched nearly to the ground, lilac and sage, and scattering white pines.

There is no special preponderance of self-fertilized or wind-fertilized plants, but everywhere the demand for and evidence of insect life. Now where there are seeds and insects there will be birds and small mammals, and where these are, will come the slinking, sharp-toothed kind that prey on them. Go as far as you dare in the heart of a lonely land, you cannot go so far that life and death are not before you. Painted lizards slip in and out of rock crevices, and pant on the white hot sands. Birds, hummingbirds even, nest in the cactus scrub; woodpeckers befriend the demoniac yuccas; out of the stark, treeless waste rings the music of the night-singing mockingbird. If it be summer and the sun well down, there will be a burrowing owl to call. Strange, furry, tricksy things dart across the open places, or sit motionless in the conning towers of the creosote. The poet may have "named all the birds without a gun," but not the fairy-footed, ground-inhabiting, furtive, small folk of the rainless regions. They are too many and too swift; how many you would not believe without seeing the footprint tracings in the sand. They are nearly all night workers, finding the days too hot and white. In mid-desert where there are no cattle, there are no birds of carrion, but if you go far in that direction the chances are that you will find yourself shadowed by their tilted wings. Nothing so large as a man can move unspied upon in that country, and they know well how the land deals with strangers. There are hints to be had here of the way in which a land forces new habits on its dwellers. The quick increase of suns at the end of spring sometimes overtakes birds in their nesting and effects a reversal of the ordinary manner of incubation. It becomes necessary to keep eggs cool rather than warm. One hot, stifling spring in the Little Antelope I had occasion to pass and repass frequently the nest of a pair of meadowlarks, located unhappily in the shelter of a very slender weed. I never caught them sitting except near night, but at midday they stood, or drooped above it, half fainting with pitifully parted bills, between their treasure and the sun. Sometimes both of them together with wings spread and half lifted continued a spot of shade in a temperature that constrained me at last in a fellow feeling to spare them a bit of canvas for permanent shelter. There was a fence in that country shutting in a cattle range, and along its fifteen miles of posts one could be sure of finding a bird or two in every strip of shadow; sometimes the sparrow and the hawk, with wings trailed and beaks parted, drooping in the white truce of noon.

If one is inclined to wonder at first how so many dwellers came to be in the loneliest land that ever came out of God's hands, what they do there and why stay, one does not wonder so much after having lived there. None other than this long brown land lays such a hold on the affections. The rainbow hills, the tender bluish mists, the luminous radiance of the spring, have the lotus charm. They trick the sense of time, so that once inhabiting there you always mean to go away without quite realizing that you have not done it. Men who have lived there, miners and cattle-men, will tell you this, not so fluently, but emphatically, cursing the land and going back to it. For one thing there is the divinest, cleanest air to be breathed anywhere in God's world. Some day the world will understand that, and the little oases on the windy tops of hills will harbor for healing its ailing, house-weary broods. There is promise there of great wealth in ores and earths, which is no wealth by reason of being so far removed from water and workable conditions, but men are bewitched by it and tempted to try the impossible.

For all the toll the desert takes of a man it gives compensations, deep breaths, deep sleep, and the communion of the stars. It comes upon one with new force in the pauses of the night that the Chaldeans were a desert-bred people. It is hard to escape the sense of mastery as the stars move in the wide clear heavens to risings and settings unobscured. They look large and near and palpitant; as if they moved on some stately service not needful to declare. Wheeling to their stations in the sky, they make the poor world-fret [sic] of no account. Of no account you who lie out there watching, nor the lean coyote that stands off in the scrub from you and howls and howls. ✦

About This Story

Part travelogue, part memoir, part ethnography, Mary Austin's 1903 *The Land of Little Rain* is considered a seminal work of environmental writing, influencing authors from Terry Tempest Williams to Gary Snyder. And all written by a woman wandering alone, which at the time was unheard of in the desert. Austin's writing has never been as celebrated as contemporaries John Muir or Aldo Leopold, and we think it's time to fix that.

Wearing flowing dresses popular at the time, Austin often traveled alone through the Mojave desert, and befriended the Mexican and Chinese immigrants and Shoshone and Paiute people she met along the way. For women, traveling in general was frowned upon, but here was Mary, hitchhiking with strangers to unknown destinations. Her writing through her life would continue to advocate for the rights of Native peoples and women. For twelve years, Austin wandered these deserts, observing its animals and people until the desert was so in her bones that writing *The Land of Little Rain* took only one month.

Austin herself spoke about how this work was intended to evoke the mysticism and spirituality of this place, and admits to "mythologizing" the people she depicts, which, especially for the Indigenous community, is now seen as condescending. So instead, we focus on Austin's keenly observed details about the landscape.

Pinto Basin

CYNTHIA ANDERSON

> Beside the dry wash
> wind in my ears
> blows me backwards—

I make my home in the desert, and the ancient camels draw closer. Their breath ripples the sheer fabric of reality. As my eyes adjust to the prodigal light, I can see farther. Scraps of evidence—a lecture here, a book or article there—lead to meeting places, urge me deeper.

> Small waves lap the shore
> ringed by a lip of mud
> bruised and torn
> where camels come to drink

The basin tells a succession of tales. Climbing a rocky hill, looking east, I picture the ebb and flow: a primeval lake, then a winding river, then creosote flats cut by a wide wash, banks lined with vanished campsites.

> I sit inside the circle
> watching the Old Ones
> as they watch me
> from the safety
> of their own time

Scattered on the surface, crumbling camel bones mingle with relics of Pinto culture—metates and manos, scrapers and knives, hammerstones and dart-points. A meeting of eons.

Nothing is certain
but the deathless current—
where we come from
where we are going ✦

Split Rock Loop

CYNTHIA ANDERSON

The forces that made
this maze of rock
let me walk

through the midst
of upheaval—

past the Indian shelter
at a riven boulder
marred by graffiti,

down a narrow trail
toward the wild—

thick mineral veins
roll east to west
across the convoluted

landscape—a chronicle
of chaos I trace
with my eyes—

three times I step over
fresh, black scat—
but Coyote hangs back,

silent, screened by
pines and scrub
and piled granite—

late, a pewter sky
breaks to blue-streaked
clouds and contrails—

and me, standing
among magenta
pencil cholla

wrapped in
my skin, breath,
aspirations—

coming to know
my place
by placing myself here— ✦

About This Story

Cynthia Anderson has lived in the Mojave Desert near Joshua Tree since 2008. She's the author of eleven poetry books, of both long and short form poetry, including haiku, senryu, cherita, and tanka, and five books about the region. Through her work and own curiosity, she has delved extensively into Joshua Tree's ancient past, drawn to the layers of time and history that are no longer visible: like primeval lakes and fossils of creatures that roamed these deserts eons ago. While "Split Rock Loop" captures her favorite trail in Joshua Tree National Park, "Pinto Basin" takes us back to prehistoric times where ancient camels roamed this region.

Wonderland of Rocks

SHEREE WINSLOW

After a few days in Palm Desert and a warning on local news announcing the last days to hike before it was too hot, I left the resort where I was staying and headed west along I-10 to the south entrance of Joshua Tree National Park. Road signs warned drivers to turn off air conditioning to avoid overheating, creating an interesting conundrum: The car or me? If I turned off the A/C, I might get too hot. If not, I put the car at risk. I settled on a compromise. I turned down the fan, turned off the radio, and drove while monitoring the temperature gauge as lights moved between the *C* and the *H*.

Beyond the gates, I stopped at the welcome center and studied the map before heading into the interior. Then, I began the drive that winds through the park, stopping at a roadside plaque to read history of the Pinto people. The arid breeze dried my skin as I scanned the vast landscape of varying grays and browns—tumbleweed, dirt, barren hills, and yucca—a monochrome sea where, in the distance, low mountains of similar heights seemed to hide behind one another. Looking at the terrain, I felt like I was lost in either time or space. Turning one direction, I waited to see dinosaurs stomping around, their big bodies lumbering through an open environment scaled to their size. Faced another way, I expected alien lifeforms to approach with questions made of sounds I couldn't translate even if I knew they were demanding to know how I landed on their planet. I hadn't stepped inside a time machine, yet I already felt like I was moving into another dimension.

I returned to what was not a spaceship but a hybrid sedan, a sure sign that I was still on Earth, and drove until I reached the Ocotillo Patch. The ocotillos' spindly branches reached toward the sky like dry, white arms stretching to the heavens. The small green leaves that fill the bush after rainfall were gone. This wasn't the season for blooms either. To see the bush filled with inflorescences of red tubes and stamens dripping bright yellow pollen, a feast for bees and hummingbirds, I would need to visit another time.

Further down the road, the Cholla Cactus Garden greeted me with two unique signs. One warned me that the cactus was hazardous. Another warned of bees. My journey had just begun, yet I had encountered several signs that I had never seen anywhere else. Has it always been like this? Were there warnings on the paths I traveled gaining less of my attention? But now, after so much time indoors, isolated with unhealthy parents, mandates and changing rules, nightly death counts, and a year of COVID-19 news overconsumption—was my eye hypersensitive, trained to notice every alert?

Before I could fully consider this possibility—a worsening propensity for fear—I walked straight into hope. If the giant saguaro in the Sonoran desert are the dignified statesmen of the cactus world, then the chollas are the toddlers. Low to the ground with thick appendages, the fuzzy teddy bear cholla were dry. In some, portions of the plants had turned from pale yellow to dark brown to black. But everywhere new branches sprouted, pinch-pleated yellow buds shaped like opening flower heads. Even in extreme conditions, the cholla not only survived but found new ways to grow. I walked the looping trail that wound through the garden, returning to my car unscathed. No stings. No cactus attacks. No needles stuck in my skin or clothes. As long as I didn't go off the trail and attempt cart-wheels through the cactus or chase the pollinators, I was safe.

I followed Pinto Basin Road, passing fields of boulders as I turned west to follow Park Boulevard. Although I didn't venture into the area identified on a map as the Wonderland of Rocks, it seemed the name could describe the entire park. Before me, a geologic playground emerged. Giant rocks dotted the landscape. Hikers dotted the rocks. Advanced climbers scaled steep walls. Smaller rock clusters provided places to hop from one to the next for casual climbers. Visitors crouched and stretched, moving higher until they could claim position as if playing king of the mountain. At Skull Rock, which looked exactly like the name suggested, the adventure became a sedimentary Rorschach test. Now tell me, when you look at the rocks, what do you see? Park visitors positioned themselves behind other groups waiting their turn in front of the rock with the sunken eyes and hollow nose.

As I neared the West Entrance Station, I began to see more Joshua trees, some that stood high and others that bent over like a gnarled witch in a children's fairy tale. I was expecting a forest, endless rows of trees, but I saw only the ones left standing after drought and fire. Their branches twisted in all directions. Some had leaves in a pattern that looked like a clenched fist. Others had dying stubs that played tricks on my eyes. I thought I saw a seated owl, but it was just a broken branch.

Near the exit, I found another kind of rock formation. Towering "piles" looked like totems or row houses pressed together, blocks stacked one on top of another. But a park sign explained these were not stacks but the result of magma below the surface cooling to granite before it was pushed upward by tectonic movement and sculpted over millions of years by wind and water.

Here, as I was preparing to leave the park, I realized that Joshua Tree isn't really about trees. That might be one piece. And in different seasons, the flora and fauna may offer a more colorful visit. But year-round, the park's defining feature is the chance to understand our relationship to terra firma. Even at night when dark skies fill with a thousand stars, the look up sizes our position in the universe and reminds us we are grounded, supported by one big rock.

Before heading into the park, my mom had handed me the Sunday *Los Angeles Times*. On the front page above the fold, in an article titled, "Imagine no Joshua trees in Joshua Tree National Park," writer Steve Lopez described his time in the desert with ecologist Jim Cornett. Cornett had tagged forty trees in the park in 1988 and only four remained. Meanwhile, dry conditions limited new growth. Lopez began the article with an anecdote about stumbling across a rat's nest built into the base of an ocotillo bush. After examining the nest then noticing dead cacti nearby, Cornett concludes that the unusual behavior is the result of thirst. Unable to find water in other places, the rats dug into the plant's roots. Throughout the story, the writer and interviewee discussed the delicate balance of desert life. When plants die, the rats die. When rats die, the snakes don't have food. When there are no snakes, hawks starve.

In the desert I glimpse what might become our reality as Earth continues to get hotter. Cholla shows us that life can grow in spite of conditions. The rock piles teach me that we are not fully formed, yet continue to evolve. In the desert, the bright sun illuminates all these things, teaching us where to exercise caution, or how to survive. Teaching us to keep climbing. Teaching us to move forward. ✦

About This Story

Sheree Winslow received one of six travel stipends awarded to writers, to visit these parks and write new stories about their experience. Although Sheree had lived most of her adult life in Southern California and Los Angeles, she had never been to Joshua Tree National Park. Maybe it's that her light complexion burned easily. Or that she found the desert heat stifling. Or that the desert carried the aura of a dangerous place. Upon seeing our call for submissions, Sheree, stressed and tired while working through the pandemic, saw a great excuse to visit the nearby park that had always been just out of reach.

What Sheree was expecting to see was what she already loved about desert landscapes—cholla and other cactus plants that look like they can't survive, yet are thriving. But Sheree discovered that Joshua Tree is not just about trees, but is also a celebration of geology, and a hopeful sign of how we might evolve.

Having grown up on the Northern Cheyenne reservation in eastern Montana, Sheree is familiar with extremely hot, and extremely cold weather. Reservations, she tells us, are often on remote lands, and are subject to extreme conditions. Her experience teaches her that the land you expect may not be the land that you get. But as Sheree comes to learn the true essence of Joshua Tree National Park, she is renewed by the need to appreciate and protect the land she discovers.

Salvation Canyon

Excerpt from *Salvation Canyon*

ED ROSENTHAL

Day One
Friday, September 24

The air was stale and hot with a small breeze. The heat was excessive, heading towards Warren View. The trail steepened and ramped up a green hillside, where the grass hunched close to the ground, woven into sparse patches alongside white boulders, fir trees and junipers. At the top, I arrived at a plateau under a large sky with a row of trees at its extreme edge. My heart raced, it felt so good to be closing in on my cherished view of San Jacinto. But I also felt some time pressure. I rushed along what was left of the trail, an indistinct footpath twirling through the foot-high windblown grasses of the plateau.

Never having mounted this particular cone before to see Warren View, the steep incline surprised me. Loose stones and dirt rolled out from under the pressure of my boots. Then my cell phone rang. A co-worker. I watched my step and let the call go to voicemail. Treading with care on the unstable ground, I reached a spot where two grey rocks stuck from the hillside, making a chair. The last few steps made me feel the mid-day heat more than the previous two miles. I took the pack from my back and squeezed my hips into the one-foot-wide "chair," caught my breath, and sat to admire the Palm Desert expanse, snow-capped San Jacinto Peak, and the jade-green Coachella Valley.

A rock tumbled down the cone, ending my reverie. Awake to the heat, I stood up and shuffled around, settling the orange pack on my back as pebbles slipped from under my feet. After a hundred yards or so, I found myself amidst multiple short paths circling the grass, but I couldn't see a clear trail weaving through. I scanned the ground for a trail but found nothing. I needed a marker in the landscape. My throat was itchy; the air had heated up. The sweatband on my hat was damp and dripped on my forehead. I needed to find the shade of the woods and then down and out of Black Rock Canyon, but there were no footprints of any kind, not even my own.

I thought that if I found the West Trail sign, I would retrace my steps to the water bottles in my trunk, and head to the motel, but between the rocky conical hill and inside the row of green firs that lined the edge of the plateau, there was no sign. The sun continued to burn. Grasses, prickly pear cactus, and creosote bushes, nothing else. My mouth itched, and I was now desperate to find my way back.

Through an opening in the dense underbrush, a channel a foot high and a few feet wide cut the edge of the plateau in one spot. I craned my neck for a view and saw a pebbled trail on a landing ten feet down. I disentangled myself from the spines of a prickly pear cactus, which had attached itself to my backpack, its purple fruit swung back into place, and I stepped out to the ledge of the ditch to peer at the trail below. A turkey buzzard chanced an air current into the distant desert, and I stopped squirming inside the ditch. I found my resolve and took off my pack, then threw it over the edge onto the dirt, sent my hiking stick out ahead of it, and jumped.

Day Two
Saturday, September 25

I woke in the faint light of dawn. The sun was not yet visible, but the moon was a white circle in the pale blue sky. Gorgeous Vega and her companions Altair and Deneb were gone. With the silver veins of earth no longer glowing and the surrounding desert visible, I saw cute little Baby Canyon for what it was, a slight dip in an endless stretch of hills. I looked along my elongated shadow to where I had entered this tunnel the night before and saw weathered grey and white sandstone ridges extending below the moon. Turning around to look in the direction I intended to take, I saw that the forty-foot wall which blocked me was surrounded by the very same sandstone formations, and these extended above the walls and beyond to where the steaming sun sat.

The pit of mingling trails was a barbeque, and I was the meat. Even a Bedouin would drop dead in the spot where I stood. Everything was a mass of white until I turned and saw a brown and green hillside. A sloppy surface of creosote bushes, gravel, sand, large rocks, and low tight bunch grass clung to a steep hill, and the miserable, forty-five-degree hillside had one remarkable feature: an isolated single needle pine with broad green branches stood midway up the hill.

A deep gulley filled with broken rocks snaked from my boots to just below the solitary pine. I had only to get there. I would not escape the desert, but I had to escape the heat. Each time I lifted my legs in the dirt and rock trench, the weight of my boots resisted. I seemed slower with every step. At points along the way, the gulley was shoulder height, and I worried that I might not be able to pull myself out when I reached the evergreen, but I was lucky. Where the tree was, the trench was only a few feet high. I pulled myself out and collapsed in the dirt at the foot of the pine.

The single needle pine threw a lace pattern over my back. Downhill in the snaking gully, white-hot rocks glared. I took the limp bladder from my pack and placed it on the ground. I tried to suck water from the flat camelback. A sound came out. With a turn of the bottom seal, it emitted a pop. I stuck my fingers inside and licked off two solitary drops.

Day Three
Sunday, September 26

I woke in the canyon. The white heat was gone. I tried to get up, but my right leg buckled, so I held my stick and pushed down, using my left leg to stand, dragging my right alongside. Limping, but grateful that I had not lost my legs on an open arroyo, I went in my stocking feet to a flat rock twenty yards away in the middle of the enclosure and sat on the two-foot-high perch. From there, I could see the wide basin.

Again, I surveyed my situation. I'd be found one day, dead or alive. Out of the elements I could survive several days. My phone was long dead. The clip of a ballpoint hung on the pocket of my short sleeve shirt. I searched for paper in my pack. I took off my hat and tested my pen on the inner lid, and it worked, so I began a letter to my wife and daughter.

"Dear Hilary and Nicole, I love both of you, not sure if I can make it out of here. I made a wrong turn and didn't take enough water. Call Andrew for my commission. Collect the life insurance." Encouraged by my ability to communicate, expanded my instructions: "Give my love to Gary, Jerry, John Kaji, Harold, Mark Moniz, Tyson, Rabbi Debra, My Brother, Sister, Chris Cooney, Steren and Felisa."

Writing the names of my friends, I felt better. As each name brought a different memory, my mind separated from the loneliness of my body on the rock. Many of my friends never had met each other, and I began to plan.

"My funeral will be a wake. Have the Downtown poet Richard McDowell recite a poem."

Now, I became encouraged there might be a tomorrow.

Day Four
Monday, September 27

I filled in the Monday section on my hat's chart. "Slept in the same spots as Sunday." I started a space for the Tuesday section, but I wasn't sure I'd make it to morning. I placed my pen back in the pocket of my sandy white shirt. I shoved my pack inside my circle of possessions.

After four dehydrated days on the Mojave, the sight of Blue Vega and giant Altair rising above the canyon had no pizzazz. I bent like an empty can by the scarred trunk of the acacia and recited the prayer for Jews who may not live until dawn. *Shema Yisrael Adonai Eloheinu Adonai Ekhad* Hear O Israel: the Lord is our God, the Lord is One.

A wispy funnel of clouds around me. Everything inside and outside was black and pervaded with illuminated objects, a gigantic Chumash sky painting. I floated upward inside with my hands extended towards the top. The white funnel was also moving as it stretched to the top of the black sky. But I was moving faster than the funnel itself. I was accelerating towards the extremely bright aperture at the very top. Effortless, accelerating bliss. I was eager to reach whatever was generating the brightness at the opening above.

A spectator, I was almost entering the light when an open palm with white cuffs on a black sleeve appeared. It blocked the opening. The bearded face of Moshe Greenwald, the young Chabad rabbi of Downtown Los Angeles, appeared. He smiled, then asked with his palm still held out, "Ed, are you really ready for this?"

I answered, "No" and woke up inside my body, on my pack alongside the half-burned acacia in Salvation Canyon.

Day Six
Wednesday, September 29

I opened my eyes. I was in my spineless situation under an undecided sky. The fly buzzed off my chest and circled my ring of possessions like a security guard on his rounds. I followed his flight, without lifting my body. From the corner of my eyes, I saw something extraordinary by the dull copper cliffs of the northern wall, thirty yards from last night's signal fire. Propped on my elbow, I turned my body toward the place. It was a spot where I'd never slept or walked.

I lifted my stick in my right hand, stuck it in the ground and leaned on it to raise myself to my knees. In a staccato motion of stick, knees, palm, torso, knees, I crawled by the acacia and left the circle of possessions. The horsefly rode on my shoulder beneath the cloudy sky.

We crossed the burrows and lines that my body and stick had left in the sand on my sleepwalking slides from the acacia to the southern wall. I felt no bigger than one insect carrying another. We got to the cliffs. We were on a threshold of smooth sand and stared up at a rock alcove that seemed to be growing as my perception of it sharpened. It took on a faint yellow color, and then lifted a few feet above the floor of the canyon. The walls it grew were smooth. It occupied a space apart from the northern cliff that it pushed back. Glowing inside was a light, which was not anywhere else in the canyon.

I leaned on my elbows and stared. A fully-formed, fifteen-foot-high figure appeared. At the moment he materialized in his alcove, I was sure he came from the cliffs behind him, but I didn't see him come in. Unlike the alcove itself, he showed all at once. It was as if there was a portal that allowed him to enter from another dimension. His sudden appearance and calm demeanor suggested a messenger. My companion and I stayed on the desert floor looking up. His eyes desired to help me, to assist me. His pleated skirt was well pressed and held close to his slim waist by a simple leather belt. He emanated peace. Speaking the first words I had spoken in six days, I asked him, "What should I do?" I waited for something, and the desert responded. A ray of light lit his face. The sky turned blue.

The cliffs turned rusty copper as their metal shone. The sky darkened and stirred, and my question disappeared in the brewing sky as drops of precious water fell. The earth dimpled with brown pools. I took off my hat and felt water stream down my face into my mouth and swallowed the first drops of water in five days. The white sands dimpled with brown spots. But the drizzle stopped as quickly as it had begun. The holy messenger evaporated as the blessings of the rain ended. His canyon alcove became a vacant rupture in the rocky cliffs.

Day Seven
Thursday, September 30

On all previous days on the Mojave, I woke before the desert lit. Thursday morning, I didn't wake of my own accord and wouldn't have woken at all, but late in the morning, I heard a sound. It disturbed me from the deepest sleep. I was dazed and couldn't make out my own location in the canyon. I was face down and propped myself up on my right elbow, straining my ears toward the source. It was outside the canyon past the northern wall. I saw the wall, but I couldn't see anything else. Without the strength to stay up or energy to lift myself, I lay down again, and seeing my possessions in the sand, remembered where my body was. My chin stayed propped up on the sand, my eyes directed at the sound.

A black metal object came into view. It hovered a hundred feet in the air, about fifty yards past the wall. A real live helicopter was outside Salvation Canyon. All the other copters I'd seen, or thought I'd seen, in Baby Canyon long ago, had no relation to me. They were just red and blue lights in a distant sky. But this one was so close I was able to make out the finish and color. Real metal, I remember saying to myself. A new element had come into being, not only in my life, but in the universe.

The thing disappeared momentarily and then popped up, over the lip of the supernatural northern wall. I squirmed around on my stomach, trying to raise my arms, and noticed my friend the horsefly was gone. The air stirred wildly, and I heard a sentence boom, "Are you that Rosenthal that's out here?"

When I remembered that question afterwards, it seemed intensely funny, as if I would answer, "No, I'm not," or, "No, he's in the next canyon." But it was not funny at all. I screamed out to the best of my ability, "Yes, I am!"

"Can you stand up?" asked the voice.

"Yes, I can," I answered.

It took so very long, but soon I heard vibrations closing in. They had turned and headed my way. I told myself that the pilot was looking for a place to land. The sound lit up my insides. I told myself, "I am going to survive." My heart filled with joy. I would leave this wonderful canyon alive. Nobody would have to find my hat. ✦

About This Story

"When I was finally rescued by helicopter, I saw myself as something other, a buried seed. I was something tiny, dredged from something gigantic, a mathematical miracle; a feeling that has not completely left me."

It was September 2010, and the weather was in the triple digits. Ed Rosenthal—a real estate broker and poet affectionately known around town as the "poet broker"—set out to celebrate his biggest sale yet by hiking one of his favorite trails in Joshua Tree National Park. But soon, he was inexplicably lost, without food or water. He was reported missing after his car was found at the Black Rock campground, which set off a search by foot and by helicopter, lasting six days until he was rescued.

Because of the frequency and complexity of incidents in the park, Joshua Tree National Park Search and Rescue (JOSAR) was established in the 1990s to perform searches, evacuations, and treatment on site for lost and injured parkgoers. JOSAR team members are highly trained to handle the unique challenges and risks that the desert can bring year-round, but the volume of incidents increases exponentially during the summer months when temperatures soar to 120 degrees.

The intense sunlight and unforgiving heat of the desert bring risk of dehydration, heat exhaustion, heat stroke, and hyponatremia—an illness caused by drinking too much water and losing too much salt through sweating, causing low sodium in the blood. Experts advise drinking at least one gallon (four liters) of water to replace loss from sweat and having a cache of salty snacks to provide your body with the calories and electrolytes it needs. If you plan to be active during the hot months, you'll want two gallons (eight liters) per person, per day, and when you notice your water is half gone, it's time to head back. Always be sure to carry extra water in your vehicle in the event of an emergency, and if you experience car trouble, stay with your vehicle. This makes it easier for you to be spotted. Your risk increases the longer you're exposed to the elements, where you will quickly deplete your limited resources (drinking water) and could get even more lost. While you don't want to sit in a hot car, it offers better chances of survival by providing options: a suitcase or removable seats elevate you off the hot ground, or an open door or hood might give you some shade.

Desert weather can change suddenly and significantly, so it's important to be prepared. Other risks come with the territory, too. Storms form in an instant and can bring powerful rainstorms that cause flash floods. If you're caught in a storm, avoid canyons and washes and seek high ground. If driving, take caution and avoid driving through dips in the road where you see water running across: "Turn around, don't drown."

Iconic Mojave desert flora can be rather unfriendly when observed *too* closely, and it's advised to travel with a first aid kit, comb, tape, and tweezers to help remove cholla and cacti spines from skin. Joshua Tree is home to venomous scorpions, black widow spiders, and snakes—including six species of rattlesnakes. Be mindful of where you place your hands or feet while hiking and climbing. Swarms of bees are natural to the park, and in the summer months can get particularly thirsty and aggressive. In fact, swarms of thirsty honeybees have led to closures in certain areas of the park due to their frantic search for water from sources that roll into the park from visitors like water bottles or car air conditioning units.

Like Truman Everts before him, who spent thirty-seven perilous days lost in Yellowstone, Ed Rosenthal also experienced the unfriendly parts of the landscape. But as Everts did, Ed survived to tell the tale. His experience was harrowing but uniquely attuned to the landscape—at once cautionary, but inspirational in what the human body is capable of.

Asleep in an Old Ranger Station in Joshua Tree, CA

ED BOK LEE

Past midnight, the way-

ward arms of a thousand banished angels
await the Kingdom's return.

The desert is a time machine.

In lined pockets, the teeth
of a billion creatures are recorded
upon each spiked tendril of ocotillo crown.

The time machine is alive and breathing.

Take all these silvery ideograms outside,
under the moon's curved fang.
In total these trees spell: Welcome
to the Garden's long-forgotten instructions.

Of course, the wind doesn't care.
Nor the wood rats; not even
the coyotes or the lizard sharpening

a stone beneath the floorboards;
nor that mountain
lion surveying these rattling windows like an adumbrated skull.

Eventually, even the desert stars
livid with hunger
once again begin to retreat into their holes

though it won't be for yet another hour,
when that squirrel prays
to its newest seeds
on your porch

and a tiny finch of war
alights onto a cholla
to fussily entreat the mammal to share—
that you yourself will rise

to see
through the blood of coffee
a time when every word
was an animal—
every sunrise, as this one,
a grave of rainbows. ✦

About This Story

Poet Ed Bok Lee was raised in South Korea, North Dakota, and Minnesota. For four weeks, he stayed in an old ranger station in the middle of Joshua Tree National Park after being selected for their artist-in-residence program. "No internet or cell phone reception. It was wild," recounts Ed.

Artists are invited for a one-month stay in fall or spring. They are housed in the Black Rock area in the northwest corner of the park, where it's cooler than other areas. Still, artists are warned of extreme conditions, like high winds and temperatures that can range from one hundred degrees Fahrenheit during the day to thirty degrees at night. If you're in Joshua Tree, check out the Black Rock Nature Center for exhibitions and contemporary interpretations of park themes.

After reading Ed's poem, we wondered, "What do we learn about Joshua Tree?" Ed wrote back, "The desert is, among many things, a kind of mystical, mysterious, dreamlike place, that in some ways is more alive at night than during the day (while we humans are dreaming)." He asked us to challenge our readers, to invite you into an unfamiliar experience of looking. Quoting the poem "Ars Poetica" by Archibald MacLeish, Ed told us that "a poem should not mean / But be."

Precise, beautiful, and dreamy, we invite you into Ed's time at Joshua Tree.

Coyotes

RAE DELBIANCO

2019 was the year of the super bloom, with valleys filled with flowering cacti, and I heard again and again from desert dwellers that spring that the desert hadn't looked like this for twenty years. The rock and ground were blanched brown and eggshell and cream; the new blooms spread across it in the lurid brights of spray paint and drugstore makeup. The name of the spectacle was apt but fell short of the full moment—nature is a constantly moving scale, and life begets life. The flourishing plants were the base of an ecological chain that led to the flourishing of the beetles, the lizards, the solpugid, the hummingbird and Gambel's quail and black-tailed jackrabbit, and the coyotes.

I drove into Joshua Tree in a secondhand Mustang convertible I'd bought in Texas. My route from Pennsylvania had tracked I-40 through Amarillo and Cadillac Ranch (and its lesser known Combine City, an assortment of upended tractors), an off-the-grid cabin in the Painted Desert with a lock on the spigot to keep the feral cattle from helping themselves to a drink, and a mud-and-cedar dwelling in Monument Valley where I spent a day riding a rangy saddle-broke mustang stallion all the way up a mesa with a Navajo guide and steered my horse along the top of the world through the untouched remains of WWII camps from when the rock behemoth had been a uranium mine.

When I was two miles from the Joshua Tree Highlands Artist Residency cabin that was to be mine for a time, the road disappeared and turned into sand. I took this as a sign that I was where I was meant to be. It was almost a year since my debut novel was published, I had about ten new pages of writing to show for it, and it was safe to say that I was fully sat in the saddle of my sophomore slump. I grew up raising cattle, was stunned by the myriad kinds of people I met at university and finally traveling the world, and had been seared by the very particular pain and pleasure of being momentarily celebrated in New York. I knew that what I needed most was to learn to be a good animal again. And because of their tenacity and their elusiveness, and their scrappiness mixed with just enough danger and wolfish grandeur, I wanted to see a coyote.

I met my first coyote four hours later, lit up in my headlights on my drive back from the residency welcome party. I emailed the residency founders, ecstatic. The next afternoon, I breathlessly watched two slip through my yard from ten feet away behind my glass porch doors. It was the year of the super bloom; the coyotes were everywhere.

Soon, I was catching every sunrise I could to go watch the coyotes come in from their hunting grounds back toward their den. Spring is the gentlest time in Joshua Tree, but one morning when my alarm went off in the dark I could hear the audible swell of high winds hitting the walls of my cabin. I packed my bag with a thermos of hot coffee, a pair of binoculars, a satellite GPS with an SOS button, a flashlight, two liters of water, a pocketknife, and a little writing notebook and pen. I set my hiking boots in front of me and sat on the bed and picked yesterday's burrs from the lining of my boots and pulled the cholla spines out of their soles with a knife, then laced on the boots and strapped gaiters over the tops of them like little tents. I put on my headlamp and wrapped a blanket around me and my backpack, and went out.

I walked about a mile along dirt sand roads stamped with a mosaic of tracks from the night before, from the tiny three-pronged Y's of quail to the elongated dog's foot of coyote to the arroyos in miniature left by snakes. Off the road I took the narrow paths that wind across the desert floor of Joshua Tree. They are animal made and shared, tiny highways of cleared sandy dirt that weave around the scrub brush and yucca and cacti. My watching place was a boulder at the base of a craggy cliff that was crowded with lizards and birds when I'd climbed it. I knew from my guidebooks and tracking research that animals are less active in windy weather; the wind makes it harder to hear and harder to smell, and therefore so much less safe when every venture out from your burrow or rock hiding place risks death.

I climbed my boulder still in the dark, a safe and comfortable eight feet up at its top, and listened to the wind for a few loud minutes, until I found the cold was too much for me. I shifted down a bit further hoping it would abate but it didn't, and finally slid down into the crevice between that boulder and the next, a concealed space out of the wind on the desert floor that was just big enough to fit me. My field of vision was a narrow V, but I had my eyes trained on the paths I had learned the coyotes normally took, without fail, twenty minutes after sunrise. The sun rose to my left, setting the park sky alight before spreading outward to town. Still no coyotes. It would be the first day in a month they'd failed to appear.

I kept checking my phone for the time. It was well past the expected moment. The sun was up but the light was diffused by the cloud cover. I decided I would give it another twenty minutes in the cold. I had been starting my days by watching the coyotes then returning home to my writing desk, feeling strengthened by their mere survival in that environment. Every moment of thriving in the desert feels dearly earned. It took courage to hit the blank page and they gave it to me.

Then, crouched there among the loose spines of old dead cholla and papery seeds left by kangaroo rats, a flash of brown went past my face, an arm's length away. The closest I have ever gotten to a coyote, and the closest I ever will.

It was a split second at best, too fast for me to even see its face, and it never knew I was there. The only glimpse I got, an image still clear in my mind today, was of its stomach—a female with new pups. She passed to the east, toward hunting grounds, away from the safety of the den. The conditions were poor, the hour was late, but she had a need.

I hiked home a half hour later. I don't know all of the fates that befall coyotes, but they had their reasons for hunkering down that day, and I don't know whether she made it back or not. But that doesn't matter as much as it matters that, in conditions that kept the others underground and hungry, she still went out.

In the wild, we get to see the very best of what we can be reflected back at us. When we sit down from our hike and are silent, and let the world open up and watch the wilderness roar alive again after it hushed for our passage. Stop being, just observe, so that you can become. And go find your coyotes. ✦

About This Story

In our research we noticed an unusual number of writing and artist residency opportunities based in and around Joshua Tree. To better understand why, we reached out to Caryn Davidson, another contributor to this chapter, who served as the program manager for the park's artist-in-residence program until she retired in 2017. Caryn shared with us that "the solitude allows [artists] to focus with a rare intensity on their work, and to spend time thinking through their project free of the usual distractions present in their normal routines. The silence of the desert allows them to listen to their internal dialogue, and ask and answer questions that arose without interference from the usual background noise." While there is universally a period of adjustment to being unplugged, she describes, the absence of disruption and cell service proved to be a source of enhanced concentration. She went on to share, "the freedom from the usual demands of contemporary life, coupled with the beauty of the surrounding landscape, draws artists working in many disciplines to the southeastern deserts of California."

Described as a "redneck kid" and called "a revelation" by *Rolling Stone* and a "rara avis" by *Vogue,* Rae DelBianco grew up in Bucks County, Pennsylvania, raising livestock and founding a beef cattle operation at age fourteen. Following her own experience in residency in Joshua Tree National Park, Rae went to work on her second novel. It feels like a special privilege to have this glimpse into her writing process and to imagine the ways she may be finding the inspiration and courage to put pen to paper for her next novel.

Tales of Desert Symbiosis

MIKE CIPRA AND CARYN DAVIDSON

On a Pacific Crest Trail hike to Big Bear this spring, we watched the land transform into something it was not supposed to be. Joshua trees grew in robust bunches beneath pinyon pines and rose out of recently burned scrub forest like spiky green phoenixes. We were at nearly 7,000 feet, rarefied air for these sentinels of the Mojave Desert. The elevation ceiling of *Yucca brevifolia* (a.k.a. the Joshua tree) is considered to be a thousand feet lower than where we ate our lunch—surrounded by these perfectly weird and beautiful plants.

Walking the PCT is an invitation to reflect on how poorly the natural world conforms to our definitions. The changes in elevation and topography create transitions in ecological communities, and these changes over the space and time of a PCT journey challenge us to continually re-examine and appreciate the unpredictable earth, the blue-bellied fence lizards that have never seen a fence, the red-tailed hawks with tail feathers that are less rufous than sun-bleached, and yes, the Joshua trees that are technically not trees, and moreover, are not supposed to be here.

We're all refugees from another world up here, including the hikers that share this intersection of dirt and sky, all of us becoming something we never knew we could become. And—this is an important difference from the last 2 billion years or so of the DNA-defined critters—we're taking the planet along on our particular journey.

· ✦ ·

Mike:
I was 17 years old—an angry, awkward kid. Pretty creepy around girls. A constant tide of hormones made me want to crawl out of my own skin. On a sunny day in

May, I ditched school and drove a beat-up 1965 Ford from inner-city Los Angeles to the Mojave Desert, emerging from the smog of the L.A. Basin to clear skies and withering heat. I had a battery-operated cassette player strapped in the shotgun seat, pumping this awesome new album by U2 called *The Joshua Tree*.

My near-worship of that album was only part of why I wanted to see a Joshua tree so damn bad. Honestly, I wanted to see another living thing that looked as awkward as I felt. I wanted to see branches sprawling in every direction and caress those sharp daggers that were its leaves.

Inside Joshua Tree National Monument, I parked the car and walked into a whole forest of *Yucca brevifolia*, more than a million of those awkward-looking plants. It was not a religious experience. I was just a lonely human being on the Earth, surrounded by trees that looked like people but kept blessedly silent. I found a path in the desert, and I walked for miles.

Mormon pioneers came up with the name we use for this member of the agave family, because they saw the prophet Joshua in the anthropomorphic form of the plant, reaching his hands toward God. I've never believed in anything as grand as what the prophet Joshua saw, but I do believe that my experiences in the desert wilderness led me to a path working in conservation. What else could lead a dopey urban kid to become a park ranger at Joshua Tree National Park? What drives me today to strap on a backpack and walk hundreds of miles on the Pacific Crest Trail?

For an answer, I look to the Joshua tree, a species that has a symbiotic relationship with a particular insect that is crucial to the survival of both species. Joshua trees rely on the female *Pronuba*, or yucca moth, for pollination. As far as scientists can determine, no other animal visiting Joshua tree flowers is able to transfer the pollen from one flower to another. In fact, the female Yucca Moth has evolved special organs to collect and distribute the pollen onto the surface of the flower. She lays her eggs in the flowers' ovaries, and when the larvae hatch, they feed on the Joshua tree seeds. Without the moth's pollination, the Joshua tree could not reproduce, nor could the moth, whose larvae would have no seeds to eat.

Symbiosis is nature's feel-good story. It gives us hope, as we walk upon this earth, that there is a way for us to live in balance with other living things.

· ✦ ·

Caryn:

I saw my first Joshua trees when I was 16. I noticed them through the passenger-side window of my boyfriend's blue surfer-chic VW bus, and soon got a closer look when we broke down along the highway on our way to Arizona. While he reattached a valve cover with a length of coat hanger wire, I wandered and took a mood reading of the landscape. Its unexpected openness put me slightly ill at ease; its unfamiliar vegetation was disorienting. But I was seduced, and felt drawn into its idiosyncratic beauty.

Eighteen years later I moved to the Mojave Desert and began working at Joshua Tree National Monument. That improbable development allowed me to become far more intimate with the landscape that I, too, first glimpsed as a teenager; and it has engendered a visceral relationship that continues to sustain me.

Like the Moebius strip of causes and effects, the Joshua tree expresses the complex interplay of the desert's harsh conditions. Less than ten inches of rain per year, often half that amount. One-hundred-seven degrees in the depths of summer. Twenty-seven degrees mid-winter. Few plants can tolerate the bipolar point spread of the Mojave Desert's temperature range. But without the desert's extreme temperatures, the Joshua tree's meristems, or growing tips, would not undergo the damage required to produce a flower. Without flowers, Joshua trees would be incapable of attracting the female Yucca Moth, whose singular agenda—finding food for its larvae—ensures that the flowers' pollen is distributed so that, after fertilization, the fruit appears. The sacrificial fruit nurture the larvae, and although many more seeds are produced than are eaten by the emerging moths, the vast majority of those seeds are eaten by hungry desert animals.

The improbability of a Joshua tree seed falling on the ground, germinating, and surviving into treehood is enormous. In fact, it is estimated that around half of the young Joshua trees in the National Park owe their existence to "nurse plants." In this not-so-symbiotic relationship, seeds that have fortuitously landed in a perennial plant, such as a blackbrush, receive protection from foraging rabbits, ground squirrels, mule deer, and woodrats. Once the young tree is established, at around four years old, its leaf blades are fibrous and tough enough to withstand the assault of the herbivores. The Joshua tree grows up through the nurse plant and kills it.

And adolescence does not always preclude animals from gnawing on the Joshua trees. In drought years, one can see widespread evidence of animal desperation: blunt leaf blades have been chewed off at their base; pseudo-bark is stripped away from trunks and branches; and holes have been burrowed to gain access into the Joshua tree's roots.

In the continuous quest for food, termites bore into the soft wood of dead Joshua trees, while opportunistic Yucca Night Lizards—North America's smallest reptile—devour the termites. In the unending concatenation of appetites, night snakes eat the lizards, hawks swoop down on the snakes, and many are fed. It has been said that nature is a conjugation of the verb "to eat," in both the passive and active voices.

· ✦ ·

The Joshua tree doesn't merely tolerate the Mojave Desert's seeming inhospitality— it has thrived in this harsh place. It depends on the intense mood swings of this vast ecosystem. But take it from two former teenagers who now live in the desert and walk in its mountains: Those Mojave mood swings are changing. Climate change is driving desert temperatures up, and some researchers are predicting that the additional few degrees of stress will cause the Joshua tree as a species to disappear from great swaths of its southern range. How this may affect the ecological web connected to those forests of Joshua trees is anyone's guess.

So do we continue to consume without sentiment or regret, as nature some- times teaches us? Or do we attempt to live in a symbiotic balance with the world, as nature sometimes teaches us?

It is initially painful for us as organisms to consume less. But as anyone who has walked the PCT knows, it is also very freeing to make do with less, to distill our possessions to a level of supreme efficiency, and to do all this while connecting with the natural world. There is no "silver bullet" to addressing climate change, but reducing our consumption is a great start. And so is walking the earth, for that matter.

And when you find yourself walking on the PCT, take a moment in the cold of morning or the heat of noon to stop among the Joshua trees. Maybe you will be lucky enough to see a Joshua tree in bloom, its massive cluster of lily-like flowers looking like an absurd growth of popcorn perched on a branch of sharp green leaves. Maybe you will be able to look inside the wet bloom and see the wings of the Yucca Moth glowing with pollen.

There is an awkward hope in the natural world, improbable sources of strength that sustain us on the trail, beauty that haunts us importantly throughout our lives.

Sometimes these moments suggest new ways of interacting with other creatures. And sometimes, when we witness the world undressing itself, that experience has enough power to alter the fundamental path of our lives. It is not naïve to believe we can change. This is simply what walking on the earth teaches us. ✦

About This Story

Caryn Davidson worked in the education branch of Joshua Tree National Park for twenty years. Mike Cipra has worked as a park ranger at Joshua Tree, Mesa Verde, and Death Valley National Parks, and Craters of the Moon National Monument. As with all superheroes, they too have origin stories.

Here we not only get to see Mike and Caryn's first encounters with the *Yucca brevifolia*, we also see what would lead to their careers in conservation—how their curiosity and intellect helped them learn and describe in great detail how the Joshua tree is an ecosystem unto itself. Mike directs our attention to the yucca moth and its symbiotic relationship with the tree, while Caryn shows us the cycle of termites who eat its wood and are eaten by yucca night lizards, who are eaten by night snakes, who are eaten by hawks. These authors show us that even in the desert, which we think of as spare, there is an abundance of life, if one knows how to find it.

A whole host of animals and plants are adapted to the Mojave Desert's seeming inhospitality. Cacti have evolved to have sharp spines that keep animals away from their water. Most plants in Joshua Tree survive by hoarding water, and then producing seeds quickly when there is any rain. The kangaroo rat survives without water, getting its moisture from its diet of seeds. Scorpions are nocturnal, and have developed a waxy coating that helps them retain water. Even wildflowers are adapted to this environment. If there isn't enough moisture, wildflowers will not bloom. Mike and Caryn invite us to learn from the desert, to challenge ourselves to consume less and adapt to the more extreme conditions of our increasingly inhospitable world and climate

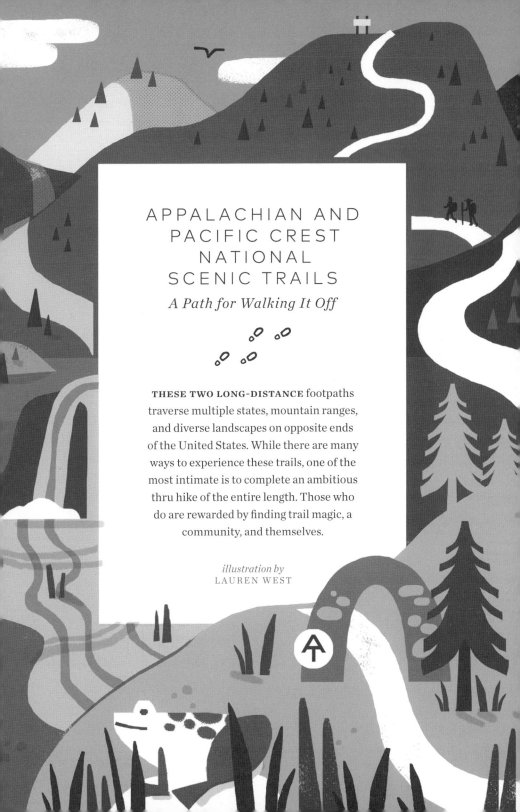

APPALACHIAN AND PACIFIC CREST NATIONAL SCENIC TRAILS

A Path for Walking It Off

THESE TWO LONG-DISTANCE footpaths traverse multiple states, mountain ranges, and diverse landscapes on opposite ends of the United States. While there are many ways to experience these trails, one of the most intimate is to complete an ambitious thru hike of the entire length. Those who do are rewarded by finding trail magic, a community, and themselves.

illustration by
LAUREN WEST

he Pacific Crest Trail (PCT) runs approximately 2,650 miles along the West Coast of North America from Mexico to Canada, passing through California, Oregon, and Washington in the United States. The Appalachian Trail (AT) is a hiking-only footpath stretching 2,190 miles along the Eastern Seaboard of the United States from Georgia to Maine. Both are national scenic trails crossing public and private land through multiple states—and the ancestral lands of twenty-two Native nations' traditional territories—that take you up and down mountains, across meadows and rivers and streams, through the scorching hot deserts of Southern California, or deep through the old-growth forests of Tennessee, and at times passing close to towns.

Both trails are for all to enjoy and do not require fees, memberships, or permits to walk on the trails themselves. That is unless you intend to stay overnight or do a long-distance hike, which do require permits. Depending on where you stay, you may pay a fee for shelters or campsites in the various state and national parks, forests, and public lands along the way. The Appalachian Trail Conservancy and Pacific Crest Trail Association are nonprofits that, with the help of volunteers, directly maintain the footpaths, advocate for their protection and expansion, provide education and resources, and promote their trails.

There are so many ways one can wind up on or choose to experience these trails. For some, they are the trail closest to home. There are some who happen to be enjoying a different trail and end up on the AT or PCT, sometimes without even realizing it. There are the weekenders who hike what they can during the day, but are primarily out for a "buddy trip"—to escape, unwind, relax, get away and catch up with each other. Then there are the special-interest groups—Girl Scouts, Boy Scouts, college or religious groups—with the intentional goal of achieving, learning, or experiencing something together. There are also those who go out on a lark, perhaps after reading *A Walk In the Woods* by Bill Bryson (featured in our last book) or *Wild* by Cheryl Strayed (featured in this book), and spend a day or a weekend hiking the trails, getting excited to experience them in person but not interested or able to spend the next five to six months hiking them. Then you have your "diehards," the long-distance hikers that make up a small percentage of trail visitors who aim to complete the entirety of the trail, whether by doing a thru hike, a section hike, a flip-flop, or a yo-yo. They can choose to go NOBO or SOBO. They can do it alone or with a buddy. Or find buddies along the way. Oh, and they can also choose a new identity through their trail name.

The secret to completing a long-distance hike on either trail is finding a "tra-mily" (trail family) along the way, with its own distinct language and way of being. Here's a little glossary to bring you in:

- Thru-hiker: A trail hiker who completes the entire trail in a single season
- Section-hiker: A trail hiker who completes the trail in a series of separate trips
- Flip-flopper: A trail hiker who completes the entire trail but in a non-contiguous manner
- Yo-yo hiker: A trail hiker who completes the entire trail in one direction, and then immediately turns around and hikes their route in reverse
- NOBO (NOrthBOund): Thru-hikers who walk north on the trail
- SOBO (SOuthBOund): Thru-hikers who walk south on the trail
- Trail name: A name one chooses on the trail (e.g., ours are Mama Pajama and Snacks, though we've never thru-hiked the AT or PCT)
- Trail magic: Assistance from strangers through kind actions, gifts, and other forms of encouragement

And that's just the tip of the iceberg. As one AT thru-hiker shared, "The trail took me one hundred and fifty days. I maybe spent five days absolutely by myself. At night, I'm usually with the friends I've known for thousands of miles." Another section hiker shared with us, "You meet people from all walks of life and from all different backgrounds and regions. You have a once-in-a-lifetime experience meeting people each night, sharing a lean-to." They are looking for something within or outside of themselves, whether they're taking a gap year, going through a midlife crisis or divorce, lost a job or a loved one, recently retired, or are trying to achieve something on their bucket list. And while you might start as strangers, long-distance hikers tend to get to know each other *really* well through their shared experiences on the trail. As Shawnté Salabert, PCT section hiker and one of our contributors, puts it: "There are three things most long-distance hikers talk about on trail: the day's mileage, the day's poop, and food—what you ate, what you wish you were eating, what you will never ever ever eat again."

So often, we see a hike in the wilderness as a solitary journey. But that idea, at least for the AT and PCT, just isn't the case on these trails. As one thru-hiker put it, "The camaraderie is such a big part of it—continually seeing people, hanging out with people all the time, taking care of each other. There is always someone there who can fix things and support you. I should have assumed it, but I wasn't expecting to find a family." The communities of people who gather to enjoy, care for, support, and preserve these trails is remarkable—the togetherness is an essential part of them. And that is what is so special about these places. While each trail features unique and challenging landscapes, they share something immensely important to the experience of being there and that's . . . *people*. The monuments and landmarks of this "park" are the moments of finding your confidence, your purpose, your people. Walking off the hard stuff and into whatever your next journey may be, as a new person. It's about finding yourself.

The idea for the Appalachian Trail is attributed to Benton MacKaye, an American forester, planner, and conservationist. In 1921, he published an article titled "An Appalachian Trail: A Project in Regional Planning," which laid out the practical and emotional benefits of an East Coast trail system. He advocated for leisure and spare time for laborers and World War I veterans. He talked up the job opportunities a trail like this would create, and how it could revitalize communities along it. What he didn't address is the role his grief played. "But living has been considerably complicated of late in various ways—by war, by questions of personal liberty, and by 'menaces' of one kind or another. There have been created bitter antagonisms," wrote MacKaye. "This situation is world wide—the result of a world-wide war." Earlier that year, MacKaye's wife, Jessie Hardy "Betty" Stubbs, had died by suicide. And the first person to thru-hike the AT, Earl Shaffer, was a veteran who took on the trail to "walk the war out of [his] system." The AT has always been a place where one confronts their grief or hardships. As Hannah Andry, one of the authors in this chapter writes, "This trail and area holds promise and change for many; a change to shed an old version of yourself, to try to be brand-new, to redefine how you want to exist in the world."

On the other side of the continent, the Pacific Crest Trail System Conference was organized by Clinton C. Clark, chairman of the Mountain League of Los Angeles, to promote the idea of building a trail that stretched the length of the West Coast. For this, Clark is known as the "Father of the Pacific Crest Trail," but before him, there was a "Mother of the Pacific Crest Trail." Inspired by an article about the Appalachian Trail, Catherine Montgomery, a Washington school teacher, shared her vision of a hiking trail along the ridges of the Pacific coast in 1926 and soon after, all the mountain clubs of the Pacific Northwest would begin planning the trail.

Struggle is often the impetus for many to leave everything behind to do a long distance hike, but can be a part of the trail experience, too. A thru-hiker shared,

"It hurt me a lot in the beginning. In the first nine miles I thought, I'll let the trail tell me where I need to be. I had no idea how hard that first part was going to be. Eventually a ten-mile day was huge to me—that was my biggest day in the beginning. By the end of the hike, I was doing ten-mile days by noon." The AT takes approximately six months to complete, and the PCT about five months. And not all of those are sun-shining, blue-sky days. Some hikers experience rain, hail, multiple feet of snow, and hurricane-strength winds. Yet, many find a way to persevere and find the bright spots. "Even though it rained a lot in 2004, I found joy. I think it's a Zen thing. Walking in the rain . . . it's just another texture." Common ailments include blistered feet, broken toenails, and a hobble caused by too much walking. Food goes from indulgence to necessity to fantasy. Many long-distance hikers lose a lot of weight while on the trail, unable to match the calories in with the calories out, and develop a ferocious hunger—torturing themselves for days with the fantasy of their next meal in the next town. Hiking for so long means pushing oneself to the absolute physical limit, sleeping it off, and waking the next day to do it again. But sometimes walking is the only way through.

And through all that struggle, many find absolute joy and bliss in the simplicity of putting one foot in front of the other. A thru-hiker described to us, "You need to *think small*. Most of us don't have experience dealing with the enormity of what a thru hike is. I focused on where I wanted to end up that night. I enjoy the day and I enjoy the next day. I celebrate the days and before you know it, those days translate into a straight line. The beauty of moving through space. You will let go of all that is happening in the world and you will bask in that simplicity. I found myself uncontrollably singing out loud to the trees . . . and I don't have a singing voice!" Pure joy comes in the form of trail magic, too. "There are a lot of boring times, don't get me wrong—but then there are these little moments of bliss and happiness, catching up with friends you haven't seen in a while or when trail magic happens. Like when I was absolutely dying and I saw a mountain in the distance and I thought, as soon as I get to the town, I'll get a Coke. And right there was a cooler someone had left with reenergizing food, water, ice—'magic water.'" That is the work of a trail angel—somebody who offers snacks, a cold drink, a ride, a place to shower or stay for a night, and other acts of hospitality and kindness.

But the second greatest gift of the trail, beyond finding yourself and your people, is perspective. "You can look up at the dappled light and listen to the birdsong. You can let go of the burden and just go." Many have described the wisdom of the ancient mountains—whether the Sierra Nevada, Cascades, Appalachians—and recounted the aura of the trail that leads people who hike them to transformative experiences that last a lifetime. "There are bad and there are good—it's a little bit more cerebral. There are times on the trail when there are perfect moments when everything aligns and it touches deeply. The breeze freshens, the temperature is comfortable, the scenery is beautiful, the smells are perfect, and you are making good miles. When you're done with the hike, you will be in your backyard and you will experience the same things and all of the sensory experiences about that original moment will come back to you."

The trail is just the trail. It doesn't need you to hike the whole thing to give you new perspective, or a new community. A day or a weekend or six months, the trail will offer its healing power of nature to anyone who walks its path. But as you'll see in the stories of this chapter, though painful and challenging, the trail will always give back more than what you put into hiking it.

Wild

Excerpt from *Wild: From Lost to Found on the Pacific Crest Trail*

CHERYL STRAYED

The trees were tall, but I was taller, standing above them on a steep mountain slope in northern California. Moments before, I'd removed my hiking boots and the left one had fallen into those trees, first catapulting into the air when my enormous backpack toppled onto it, then skittering across the gravelly trail and flying over the edge. It bounced off of a rocky outcropping several feet beneath me before disappearing into the forest canopy below, impossible to retrieve. I let out a stunned gasp, though I'd been in the wilderness thirty-eight days and by then I'd come to know that anything could happen and that everything would. But that doesn't mean I wasn't shocked when it did. My boot was gone. Actually gone.

I clutched its mate to my chest like a baby, though of course it was futile. What is one boot without the other boot? It is nothing. It is useless, an orphan forevermore, and I could take no mercy on it. It was a big lug of a thing, of genuine heft, a brown leather Raichle boot with a red lace and silver metal fasts. I lifted it high and threw it with all my might and watched it fall into the lush trees and out of my life.

I was alone. I was barefoot. I was twenty-six years old and an orphan too. An actual stray, a stranger had observed a couple of weeks before, when I'd told him my name and explained how very loose I was in the world. My father left my life when I was six. My mother died when I was twenty-two. In the wake of her death, my stepfather morphed from the person I considered my dad into a man I only occasionally recognized. My two siblings scattered in their grief, in spite of my efforts to hold us together, until I gave up and scattered as well.

In the years before I pitched my boot over the edge of that mountain, I'd been pitching myself over the edge too. I'd ranged and roamed and railed—from

Minnesota to New York to Oregon and all across the West—until at last I found myself, bootless, in the summer of 1995, not so much loose in the world as bound to it.

It was a world I'd never been to and yet had known was there all along, one I'd staggered to in sorrow and confusion and fear and hope. A world I thought would both make me into the woman I knew I could become and turn me back into the girl I'd once been. A world that measured two feet wide and 2,663 miles long.

A world called the Pacific Crest Trail.

I'd first heard of it only seven months before, when I was living in Minneapolis, sad and desperate and on the brink of divorcing a man I still loved. I'd been standing in line at an outdoor store waiting to purchase a foldable shovel when I picked up a book called *The Pacific Crest Trail, Volume I: California* from a nearby shelf and read the back cover. The PCT, it said, was a continuous wilderness trail that went from the Mexican border in California to just beyond the Canadian border along the crest of nine mountain ranges—the Laguna, San Jacinto, San Bernardino, San Gabriel, Liebre, Tehachapi, Sierra Nevada, Klamath, and Cascades. That distance was a thousand miles as the crow flies, but the trail was more than double that. Traversing the entire length of the states of California, Oregon, and Washington, the PCT passes through national parks and wilderness areas as well as federal, tribal, and privately held lands; through deserts and mountains and rain forests; across rivers and highways. I turned the book over and gazed at its front cover—a boulder-strewn lake surrounded by rocky crags against a blue sky—then placed it back on the shelf, paid for my shovel, and left.

But later I returned and bought the book. The Pacific Crest Trail wasn't a world to me then. It was an idea, vague and outlandish, full of promise and mystery. Something bloomed inside me as I traced its jagged line with my finger on a map.

I would walk that line, I decided—or at least as much of it as I could in about a hundred days. I was living alone in a studio apartment in Minneapolis, separated from my husband, and working as a waitress, as low and mixed-up as I'd ever been in my life. Each day I felt as if I were looking up from the bottom of a deep well. But from that well, I set about becoming a solo wilderness trekker. And why not? I'd been so many things already. A loving wife and an adulteress. A beloved daughter who now spent holidays alone. An ambitious overachiever and aspiring writer who hopped from one meaningless job to the next while dabbling dangerously with drugs and sleeping with too many men. I was the granddaughter of a Pennsylvania coal miner, the daughter of a steelworker turned salesman. After my parents split up, I lived with my mother, brother, and sister in apartment complexes populated by single mothers and their kids. As a teen, I lived back-to-the-land style in the Minnesota northwoods in a house that didn't have an indoor toilet, electricity, or running water. In spite of this, I'd become a high school cheerleader and homecoming queen, and then I went off to college and became a left-wing feminist campus radical.

But a woman who walks alone in the wilderness for eleven hundred miles? I'd never been anything like that before. I had nothing to lose by giving it a whirl.

It seemed like years ago now—as I stood barefoot on that mountain in California—in a different lifetime, really, when I'd made the arguably unreasonable decision to take a long walk alone on the PCT in order to save myself. When I believed that all the things I'd been before had prepared me for this journey. But nothing had or could. Each day on the trail was the only possible preparation for the one that followed. And sometimes even the day before didn't prepare me for what would happen next.

Such as my boots sailing irretrievably off the side of a mountain.

The truth is, I was only half sorry to see them go. In the six weeks I'd spent in those boots, I'd trekked across deserts and snow, past trees and bushes and grasses and flowers of all shapes and sizes and colors, walked up and down mountains and over fields and glades and stretches of land I couldn't possibly define, except to say that I had been there, passed over it, made it through. And all the while, those boots had blistered my feet and rubbed them raw; they'd caused my nails to blacken and detach themselves excruciatingly from four of my toes. I was done with those boots by the time I lost them and those boots were done with me, though it's also true that I loved them. They had become not so much inanimate objects to me as extensions of who I was, as had just about everything else I carried that summer—my backpack, tent, sleeping bag, water purifier, ultralight stove, and the little orange whistle that I carried in lieu of a gun. They were the things I knew and could rely upon, the things that got me through.

I looked down at the trees below me, the tall tops of them waving gently in the hot breeze. They could keep my boots, I thought, gazing across the great green expanse. I'd chosen to rest in this place because of the view. It was late afternoon in mid-July, and I was miles from civilization in every direction, days away from the lonely post office where I'd collect my next resupply box. There was a chance someone would come hiking down the trail, but only rarely did that happen. Usually I went days without seeing another person. It didn't matter whether someone came along anyway. I was in this alone.

I gazed at my bare and battered feet, with their smattering of remaining toenails. They were ghostly pale to the line a few inches above my ankles, where the wool socks I usually wore ended. My calves above them were muscled and golden and hairy, dusted with dirt and a constellation of bruises and scratches. I'd started walking in the Mojave Desert and I didn't plan to stop until I touched my hand to a bridge that crosses the Columbia River at the Oregon-Washington border with the grandiose name the Bridge of the Gods.

I looked north, in its direction the very thought of that bridge a beacon to me. I looked south, to where I'd been, to the wild land that had schooled and scorched me, and considered my options. There was only one, I knew. There was always only one.

To keep walking. ✦

About This Story

No chapter on the Pacific Crest Trail (PCT) would feel complete without Cheryl Strayed. With her hugely successful book *Wild: From Lost to Found on the Pacific Crest Trail*, and the 2014 film adaptation, Cheryl placed "thru-hiking" into popular culture.

Shortly after the release of the book, *Outside* magazine reported a 30 percent bump in long-distance hikers on the PCT, and Trail Information Manager Jack Haskel from the Pacific Crest Trail Association (PCTA) shared that the film had an even greater effect. In 2006 three hundred people attempted to walk the entire route; more than one thousand hikers set out in 2014—with only half of them making it. "*Wild* is the largest media event ever for the PCT, and millions are hearing about it now and are being inspired."

And it's not just the volume of hikers, it's the demographics, too. According to Haskel, anecdotal observations suggest more women are hitting the trail. Before *Wild*, fewer than 10 percent of hikers were women, but after *Wild*, that figure rose to 30 percent.

Some aren't too happy about the popularization of the trail, and Cheryl's role in it. But we find her writing to be both deeply observed and deeply emotive, and it has redefined and invited many more people into the sport of thru-hiking. Due to the increase in hikers, the PCTA launched a campaign with the hashtag #responsiblywild to promote safety and leave no trace principles so those who feel the call to the wild know how to properly prepare and care for themselves and the land, too.

I Wanted to Tell You

KITTY GALLOWAY

There's so much I wanted to tell you.

I wanted to tell you about the desert. About the Laguna Mountains and Anza-Borrego and San Jacinto and the Mojave. About how the hills and mountains and shrubs and ants and spiders and snakes and sand and sagebrush and wildflowers and cacti and trail markers and days all started to meld together. How they blended and blurred, how they flowed into one long day in which I woke up one morning and hitched to the trailhead in the rain, and how it rained and rained and then stopped raining, and from then on I walked and walked and walked. It was early April when I started. And the day flowed on until August.

I wanted to tell you how sometimes, in the beginning, for miles and miles there was no water. How it felt to carry seven liters of water on my back for thirty miles. To do that daily. How some nights were so cold I shivered despite my down bag, did sit-ups for hours to try and stay warm, but how by eight in the morning the sun was so hot it burned. About how for weeks I never saw a snake, and then one time, five days in a row, I saw a rattler.

I wanted to tell you about how many mornings I would wake up under the stars. How I'd wake at three a.m. and lie in my sleeping bag, trying to remember how to make myself move again. How in the quiet and the dark my mind would be dark, too, but how I'd pull myself out and up anyway, pack my bag and clothes and tent anyway, huff my way up and up and up a mountain as the sun rose, slow, stop to eat second breakfast and make coffee and blow into my hands at the top, then stand there and watch as the moon arced down, the sky lightened, the sun arced up, higher and higher above the horizon. How I'd stand there and count the moments before the sun made its final pull over the ridge. How it felt to be finally, and first, touched by that warmth.

I wanted to tell you about how often I would spend all day, every day, writing. How the trail became so natural, the navigation so simple, that all I had to do all day was dream. How the words flowed like steps, and the letters and notes and poems wrote themselves. How hundreds of words all strung together, hundreds of lines of words, hundreds of pages of lines. In my head. How I would write and write as my feet moved under me, my body finding her own pace, and the miles passed by like water. Like a river. How the words would flow out and form and settle for brief moments like dust. Some days one phrase repeating over and again. Other days whole stories shaping and forming. Yet how somehow, in the end, I'd never write a single word down. How as quickly as those words would settle, they would fly away again. And how I worried about this, still do. Worry about those words without homes.

I wanted to tell you about the quiet. How it's possible to walk long enough and think hard enough that eventually you stop thinking, but keep walking. About how one day in the desert my body was so tired she just broke. How as I walked I found myself crying, and soon it was clear there was to be no end to the crying. So eventually and instead, the only thing to do was stop walking. To curl up under a tree and wait for the storm to pass.

How another day, all that existed was joy. Manic, unquenchable. How I walked and walked, eight thousand feet up, six thousand feet down, thirty miles and then more, hours and hours up ridgelines and down passes and that day I could have gone forever. Could have just kept going. How the beauty in those moments lay not only in the quiet but the contrast. In the listening. In moments like the one when I was standing on a ridge and the wind was whipping and the grass and the trees and the wildflowers were all blowing sideways, and suddenly a crow dropped down into the current, hanging there so close I could almost reach out and touch her. How her eyes and feathers and feet were so vivid. So bright. So near. How we stayed there, together, me looking, her coasting, her wings almost motionless as the wind pushed and held them. And how I felt in that moment like it was almost enough. Like if I could learn to listen, hard as I possibly can, then maybe that would be enough.

I wanted to tell you what it felt like. To believe that.

There's so much more I wanted to tell you. About the desert, and then all the miles after that. Hundreds of miles, then thousands. About crossing the High Sierra early, and in snow. What it felt like to barely see trail for weeks, buried as it was beneath winter holding on—to wake up at three a.m. again every morning, this time no longer to beat the desert heat but rather so we could cross passes on ice, not slush. So we could cross the snow and keep our footing. How the rivers at that time were high and got higher. What it felt like to be so small in those tall, remarkable mountains and what it felt like to at times feel so damn alone. I wanted to tell you what it meant to get through that, by walking. To just keep walking. Walking north.

I wanted to tell you about how strong my body got. In those miles, in all that snow, day by day. How twenty-five miles a day turned to thirty, which turned to thirty-five. And how I learned to pace myself by snacks—Starburst, Cheetos, Probars, Snickers, cheese, chips, Pop-Tarts. Prebreakfast, first breakfast, second breakfast, snacks, first lunch, second lunch, third, snacks. How it felt to always be hungry.

I wanted to tell you about the trail. How it went up and over mountains and down, and up, and around, never straight. And how sometimes I would stand on a ridge and see where I was going, just there, a few miles away, and how I would see a road or a path, so direct, straight shot on pavement, but how the trail always seemed instead to go the hard way. The high way. The up and down way. The roundabout way. To get anywhere. I wanted to tell you about how often I almost took those easier ways. The road ways. The ride-from-a-car ways. But how I decided one day I wouldn't. And what that meant.

I wanted to tell you how the names flowed over me like wind. How sometimes I felt I was moving so fast, I couldn't hold each place long enough to breathe in. To take note or remember. Lake Morena, Walker Pass, Kennedy Meadows. Timberline, Snoqualmie. Glacier Peak. Stehekin. The forests, the peaks, the passes, and the towns—border to border, they began to blur. They started to slip by so quick, I couldn't hold them in my head. I wanted to tell you how I regretted that, even as my feet pushed me on.

I wanted to tell you how later, I realized how much more even I didn't know. How these lands were home to the Paiute, Shoshone, and Miwok People. The Mono and Washoe and Cocopah and Wintu People. The Shasta and Umpqua, Chelan and Kalapuya People. The Salish People. The Klickitat People. The Molalla, Chinook, and Yakama People. The Okanagan and Wenatchi and Sauk Suiattle and Nlaka'pamux People. And I'm missing about a hundred names here. A hundred times a hundred names. Band names and tribe names and family names and place names. This trail crosses through the ancestral lands of so many people—land they got pushed off of or away from. Land that was home or was sacred, and still is. Was and still is sacred, or home.

There's so much I wanted to tell you. Of those I met along the way and the community that holds this trail up. The trail angels who open their homes and the hikers that become family. The black bears that scrambled up into trees when they heard me coming, or the elk sparring by a lake off trail, far below as I walked by. There were the birds, which seemed at times to inhabit every tree and bush and bit of sky. Pinyon jay, grouse, and grebes. Juncos, kingbirds, chickadees. There were magpies and meadowlarks, warblers and wrens. There were tanagers. There were orioles. There were sparrows, swifts, and swallows. There were the hot days when vultures circled, and cool evenings that sounded like the thrum of a nighthawk wing, or the low, close hoots of an owl. And then there was that bobcat I saw one early morning, predawn. Walking down the trail quiet and in my own head as I was, she didn't see me—she just walked out into the trail ahead, stretched, crouched, peed. She straightened up slow, almost lazily, stretched again, then padded off down the trail ahead of me. Only then, suddenly, did she see me and startle. Flattened herself to the ground and army-crawled away. Low and tense, moving fast and into the trees. I remember watching her go, wondering.

I wanted to tell you about the mama bear and her three cubs, who I saw months later, a thousand miles north, on a pass in the North Cascades. How I felt the rumble of their paws on the ground beneath my feet as they thundered away into the trees just as I crested the rise and saw them. What it was to feel their quick, heavy footsteps, echoing up through my own feet like that. How it was a resonance. A reminder.

There's so much I wanted to tell you. About the trail, but really about walking. About walking all these miles: this year, this trail, but also all of these years. All of these walks. That lasted an hour, or a day, or a week, or months. About the miles upon miles upon miles of footsteps. Miles strewn across mountainsides and roadsides and riversides and forests. Footsteps through cedar groves and ponderosa pines, larches and subalpine fir, barrel cactus and saguaro. Cliff edges and talus fields. Footsteps across beds of moss, carpets of pine needles, patches of duff. Slick granite slides, smooth basalt. Crumbling sandstone. Footsteps tip-toeing through cryptobiotic soil. Footsteps crunching across snow. Sliding across ice. Pacing across glaciers. All those footsteps on trail and all those footsteps off.

I don't know what all this walking has been for. But it has something to do with patience. And I wanted to tell you that it's saved me. ✦

About This Story

Kitty Galloway's story begins on an island in the Puget Sound. Although her parents weren't into camping, friends would bring home tales of hiking the mountains around the Sound, and Kitty herself found that hiking long distances gave her a grounding she hadn't known before. At the age of nineteen, Kitty received a grant that allowed her to walk about a thousand miles of the Camino de Santiago from Le Puy-en-Velay, France, to Cape Finisterre, Spain, and she has been hiking with pen and paper ever since.

In 2016, Kitty hiked the 2,650 miles of the Pacific Crest Trail. She had already logged over 3,000 trail miles between the Camino and the Pacific Northwest Trail. "I didn't start the PCT to change my life," Kitty told us. To her, thru-hiking was a path to slow down and pay better attention—to the world around her and to her own voice. "I've found long walks to feel similar, after many miles, to meditation . . . the words and writing style [of this piece] were born out of the actual pace and cadence of walking." Kitty said of her PCT hike, "I spent a lot of time worrying that the trail had gotten too popular. But that was pretty biased. Because the other two trails I walked were fairly solitary in nature and very different from the PCT, I didn't realize how much the community of the trail has the potential to enrich and deepen the experience." Though she hiked the PCT alone, the need for human connection pulses just under every word of this essay.

Kitty would later go on to meet her husband on this hike, but that's a story for another day. What remains true is that walking the PCT is not a walk away from a community, it's a walk to find it.

1100 Miles

Excerpt from *1100 Miles: A Poetic Journey on the Pacific Crest Trail*

ALLIE "TAOGOI" DONALDSON

2 · 23 · 2019
Push hard knowing when to rest

Healing is the only way
To pass this test

Slow down, enjoy the view

No one can experience it
Quite like you

3 · 4 · 2019
Higher than the helicopters
Painted Ladies flutter, blanketing

Mountain sides as the
Desert wildflowers bloom

4 · 11 · 2019
My body is shifting
Apart from me

What is worth all
This strain and pain?

Meaningful mouthfuls or
Thousands of miles

I'll still gain smiles
Whichever it may be

5 · 6 · 2019
Sweeping valleys of gold
Hum a tune of stories untold

We truly are bold
To walk this world

5 · 19 · 2019
Incredible how
Such vivid blue skies

Come after
Storms of white

5 · 23 · 2019
Rushing rivers
Remind me of home

Always green and gleaming
When you roam

Mountain roads lead
Desert to snow

To pick up hikers
As they walk to grow

7 · 4 · 2019
Morning sun
Great Blue Heron

In this life
I'm the heroine

7 · 17 · 2019
When you no longer
Desire to speak

Go and find
Where trees creak

They sing softly
If you'll listen

Ancient songs
Gone unwritten

8 · 4 · 2019

Velvet indigo transforms to
Lilac against the fiery

Golden light of morning

The sky surrenders the stars
To bring slumbering life

Once more

8 · 20 · 2019

Giant bouquets growing
In these burned out stumps
Honoring the past cycle of life

Everything flourishes knowing
The volcano can awaken
At any moment ✦

About This Story

When we came across Allie Donaldson's book *1100 Miles: A Poetic Journey on the Pacific Crest Trail*, we were excited by the idea of bringing our readers along for the trail experience through her powerful, minimalist vignettes. We reached out to Allie, a.k.a. Taogoi (or The Art of Getting Over It) for background on her journey and poems. Having grown up in wet, evergreen western Washington, Taogoi expected the beginning of her hike in the desert to be harsh and beige, that she would see only sand, sage, and cacti. So she was surprised by the abundant colorful life she discovered, often in the form of butterflies and wildflowers.

Just over two months after her start in the desert, we find her in the Sierras in the poem from 5-23-19, which reminds her of home in the Cascade mountains. What we don't read here is the excruciating pain in her feet, bundled in trail runners and three pairs of socks, suffering from frostbite and toes "popping" with every step. She would later learn from a podiatrist that the popping was her thawing blood cells bursting as she walked. Homesick and suffering agonizing pain, she recognized home might be the better place to heal, and a cheaper option than a hostel. But after three weeks recovering at home, Taogoi felt called to get back to the trail, and did so with the 7-4-19 poem, written at Fish Lake Resort, mile 1,780 of her hike.

In these poems, we see Taogoi push herself physically—as she feels the strains that the landscape and miles put on her body, from being sunburned and scraped by brush while being stalked by mountain lions in the California desert to frostbitten feet after eleven days hiking straight up the Sierra mountain range. Taogoi also evolved internally, learning to live in the present and heed lessons from the ancient landscapes full of wisdom surrounding her. She shares, "Walking through burned areas reminds me of the fragility and resilience of life. Fire rages through the dry timber, destroying thriving life. With all the decay rotting in the rain, it breeds new life. After many years of sprouting life, wildflowers and fireweeds will help the soil become fertile enough to help the fire-activated seeds breathe life into the area again. As everything seeks to grow, the power of the volcanoes that loom are not forgotten. We are all aware that we are at their mercy when they awaken in dramatic fashion."

On Trail, We Dream
of Enchiladas

SHAWNTÉ SALABERT

On the Pacific Crest Trail, all you have is time.

Time to hike, to commune with nature, to futz with your backpack, to curse your gear, to swim in alpine lakes, to lounge on desert rocks, to slosh through creeks, to outrun thunderstorms, to glissade snow slopes, to crest passes, to wander meadows, to count miles, to filter water, to journal, to snap photos, to scout campsites, to apply sunblock, to dig catholes, to smell yourself, to chat with others, to talk to yourself, to laugh, to cry, to move in silence while pondering exactly why it is that you're out here in the first place.

All you *want*, however, is food.

It was while hiking the trail through the southern Sierra that my daydreams began to shift. Once the sole purview of hot showers and soft beds, my fantasies became dominated by thoughts of enchiladas. Once my brain locked on to the seductive image, it would not unlatch. My hours, days—dear lord, *weeks*—filled with acid-trip visions, desert peyote mirages of slender, cheese-filled, mole-draped bundles of heaven. It was a lovelorn sort of ache that quickly eclipsed the more corporeal kind that had already settled into my muscles.

Day after day, I plundered the depths of my backpack, like so many kitchen cabinets, wishing for a miracle:

Please contain one steaming enchilada,
I willed the cylindrical depths of my bear canister.

No,
came its silent, stubborn reply.

Not just impervious to ursine attacks, but also apparently unyielding to human desires, these devices. *Hmpf.* Absent any dairy-filled miracles, I had to make do. Survival, you see, requires many calories, even if they are not beautiful, life-affirming enchilada calories. This, then, is what I ingested out there:

To begin the day, one medium-roast Starbucks VIA packet,
Tossed straight into my gullet,
Washed down with water that tasted of cows, cigarettes, or algae
Because I am not a heathen

For my emotional health, there were sweets—

A daily clutch of Swedish Fish candies (red-colored only)
At least a dozen Payday bars (breakfast only)
Half a peeled orange, gifted by someone who hadn't so much as considered soap in weeks
A few chewy Japanese candies pressed into my trembling palm by concerned weekend backpackers
Something dredged from the bottom of my bear canister that might have been chocolate or might have been a small bit of dried mud
(it does not matter)
Several packets of "blue raspberry"–flavored Gushers candies, a product I thought went extinct in the late '90s, but resurfaced in the absolutely timeless freebie buckets lined up at the Muir Trail Ranch hiker resupply stop

[Here, a small interlude to explain that the Official Hiker Nutrition Pyramid* states, in no uncertain terms, that items with fruits and vegetables in their names or flavor profiles absolutely count, emotionally, as one and the same.]

This does not exist

How can one appreciate the sweeter things in life if not for the more salty ones? That is to say—you sweat a whole bunch out there.

You crave salt so much that after a hard day of hiking, you could lick your arms, your back, the hollows of your clavicle, and even those little nooks behind your knees and never, ever be satisfied.

And so I ate—

Crushed Pringles, flavored with the slight residue of crushed dreams
The charred remains of a solitary square of over-fried SPAM (RIP Army surplus pan)
Instant mashed potatoes topped with Cheetos
Instant mashed potatoes topped with Fritos
Fritos topped with Cheetos
—all of which I washed down with packets of apple cider spiked with whiskey topped off with electrolyte tablets mixed together with exhaustion.

Dinnertime is when the enchilada pangs loomed the strongest.
Oh, my heart's desire!
For better or worse, I quenched thee with—

Cheap tuna packets seasoned with a gourmet mélange of salt, taco mix, and guilt
Ramen swirled with peanut butter, tamari, sriracha, and unintentional dirt sprinkles
The contents of an industrial-size container of refried bean flakes as marketed toward Doomsday survivalists, separated into 1.5-cup servings and topped with powdered cheddar cheese wetted with tears of joy
Occasional freeze-dried meals, despite the knowledge that I would emit flatulence that smelled of dinner for about 24 hours afterward

Oh—and a double cheeseburger,
Followed by another double cheeseburger,
Despite the fact that I hadn't eaten red meat in over a decade
And my body withers under the weight of gluten.
(The next 36 hours were spent in service to my trowel.)

I'm sorry to say that I also devoured:

> Multiple unidentified winged creatures, raw
> Occasional cat hairs
> Costco-size amounts of ibuprofen
> Wisps of forest fire smoke
> Small bits of fingernail, on accident
> Fragments of that stupid paper they wrap around ginger chews, also on accident
> Absurd amounts of Beano

The closest I ever drew to my beloved enchiladas was a pair of quesadillas conjured from sun-melted Kraft singles, canned chicken, and stale tortillas. A feast fit for hiker trash!

By that time on trail, however, I must admit—my cheesy, sauce-filled fantasies had all but faded, replaced by the deep desire to wear something, anything other than the same clothes I'd been hiking in for the better part of two months. The heart wants what the heart wants, they say—well, until the heart has to pull on a pit-stained, sweat-starched, foul-smelling button-down for the fiftieth day in a row. ✦

About This Story

If you're looking for a good story to read out loud around the campfire and get some laughs ... folks, this is it. We love this piece from Shawnté not only because it made us legitimately laugh out loud throughout, but her perspective on food on the trail gave us such immense insight into the long-distance trail experience.

Shawnté literally wrote the guidebook for the PCT, *Hiking the Pacific Crest Trail: Southern California*, which covers the first 942.5 miles of the trail, beginning at Campo, California, at the border with Mexico, to Tuolumne Meadows in Yosemite National Park, California. Over the course of two years developing the book, she spent many weekends covering sections of the trail, until she finally was able to take a two-month sabbatical to hike a full five hundred miles through the High Sierra to her end point in Yosemite. Shawnté is so full of stories about her time on the PCT that even our email exchanges contained multiple stories.

One of our favorites was about the end of her two-month hike, which concluded on her birthday in Tuolumne Meadows in mid-July. "As I approached Highway 120, the unceremonious, paved end to my hike, I was overcome with emotion and stopped to let out a good cry on a log before making those final steps. When I stood up again, none other than Alex Honnold walked right past me and held out his very giant hand for a high five, which I gave right before hitting the road. Talk about surreal!" Alex Honnold, for those that don't know, is a *big deal* in Yosemite National Park and the climbing world—he's known for his record-breaking ascents of America's largest cliffs, and dazzled the world when he completed the first free solo (meaning, *no ropes*) of Yosemite's El Capitan in 2017.

When it comes to food on the trail, Shawnté had so much more to say. "I started having tater tot fantasies around the three-week mark," which prompted long potato-centric food fantasy talks with a hiking buddy and an insatiable craving for potatoes of any kind, only to have that wish fulfilled after arriving at a stopping point along the trail: french fries, number three on her list. Sometimes to fill your hunger on the trail, you have to get creative and harness new skills. "Another common affliction of the hungry, hungry hiker is that you develop 'Yogi' skills—that is, the ability, much like the famous cartoon bear, to sort of sidle up to day hikers and backpackers and bat your dirt-crusted eyelashes and casually mention how hungry you are after hiking *so many miles.*" Shawnté shares that nine times out of ten, fellow hikers will offer you food. Her most memorable time was when she met a group that was on a four-day hike of the Rae Lake Loop. At the sight of her very casually dumping what was left in her nearly empty bear canister, a classic Yogi move, they offered for her to join them around their campfire. "They of course took pity and invited me to join in their dinner, which was homemade gnocchi with sage and mushrooms and fresh cheese. They also made me scrambled eggs and bacon before I took off in the morning. I ate like a queen!!!"

So, if you find yourself in trail towns along the PCT or AT and see crusty long-distance hikers tossing back liters of sodas, pints of ice cream, whole pizzas, and family-size bags of chips, consider being a trail angel and throw in a little something extra to ensure full hearts and full bellies along their journey.

Connective Tissue

KIM O'CONNELL

I t's a pink-gray early morning, and I'm heading north on the Appalachian Trail. I can feel the sun more than I can see it, brightening behind the marbled clouds over my right shoulder. Deep as I am in the southern district of Shenandoah National Park, at this hour I have the trail all to myself. I know that's not true, not really, not on this footpath that stretches from Georgia to Maine, but it feels that way in this moment. I take a deep breath and keep going.

After a while, I begin descending along the slope of Loft Mountain. The sun is now high overhead, having broken through the hazy clouds. Bouquets of violet hepatica flowers—each with six perfect petal-like sepals surrounding a cluster of white stamens—catch my attention on the edge of the trail. Fallen logs on either side erupt with mushrooms. Leafy mountain laurel abounds, not quite a tree, but more than a shrub. As I walk, I hear nothing but the wind murmuring in the trees and my own steady breathing. Eventually I come to a small, picturesque stream. Everything seems to burst with life and energy—from the fuzzy, chartreuse moss on the tree trunks to the water burbling over and between the rocks.

There was a time when I might have been nervous to hike alone in these mountains, but not anymore. Every bend in the trail brings a new view of the seemingly endless ridges, cloaked in a kaleidoscope of greens. And yet somehow, despite its wildness, it feels familiar and comforting, too.

In 1921, Benton MacKaye, a forester and conservationist, was grieving the loss of his wife to suicide when he conceived of the idea of a marked trail along the entire spine of the Appalachians. In a manifesto called "The Appalachian Trail: A Project in Regional Planning," MacKaye envisioned a trail that would provide the urban denizens of the East with the same access to wild mountain vistas that people were extolling in places like Yosemite and Yellowstone. His goal was to provide access to the mountains for recreation—hiking and camping, mostly—but also for study and art and play.

"These mountains, in several ways rivaling the western scenery, are within a day's ride from centers containing more than half the population of the United States," MacKaye wrote. "The region spans the climate of New England and the cotton belt; it contains the crops and the people of the North and the South." Its wildness, MacKaye seemed to be saying, was tangible and close.

In the century since MacKaye's grand vision, the 2,200-mile Appalachian Trail has been accessible to both thru-hikers and day hikers, to solo travelers and to families and groups. Completed in 1937, the trail is managed by the National Park Service, the US Forest Service, and the nonprofit Appalachian Trail Conservancy, as well as several state agencies and untold thousands of dedicated volunteers. For the three million people who set foot on the trail each year, it's become a place for connection and community, and yet also a haven for solitude and silence. Guided by the trail's famous white blazes, AT hikers tend to discover something essential and profound—the exhilaration of freedom, an appreciation for beauty, and an awareness of their own power.

The Appalachian Trail can be experienced on two scales—one remarkably vast, the other exquisite and small. On the trail, you are walking on the crest of an ancient mountain range, one that has stood for 480 million years. These are lands where countless Indigenous peoples lived out their lives, Cherokee and Lenape and Abenaki and others, for millennia. It's where the Cherokee knew the grand Clingmans Dome in the Great Smoky Mountains as Kuwahi, and where the Abenaki called New Hampshire's Mount Washington Agiocochook. The names are different now, but the sense of walking among ancestral mountains and people remains.

And yet, on the AT, the scale shrinks, too. Your eyes focus. You notice small things. Bright white blood root, pushing up between rocks. Bear scat packed with berries, or claw marks high on a tree. An orb-weaver spider resting on its web. The trickle of a stream or a glassy pond. A woodland bog, shrouded amid the hills. The trail forces you to think about transitions as well—to consider how things change from one mile or one day or one state to the next. How forest gives way to meadow, or how a pine-needled trail becomes edgy with rocks, or how a hot and humid morning can suddenly turn wet and cold. The wildness of the Appalachian Trail may not be as much about its remoteness but its changeability.

This experience of the wild is one that's nonetheless becoming less common for many people. Although the lure of the wild has always drawn people toward the mountains, in the last decade, the United States has lost nearly two hundred thousand acres of tree cover to pavement each year. Worldwide, wildlife population sizes have dropped by an average of 60 percent in our own lifetimes. Children in urban areas are increasingly disconnected from places where they can roam and let their imaginations soar.

With every passing year, conserving wild areas like the Appalachian Trail becomes more necessary for people, plants, and animals alike. Preserving the trail and the open space that surrounds it maintains its recreational opportunities, provides economic benefits to local communities, ensures essential habitat for many species, and provides resiliency against the effects of climate change. The Appalachians have long been an important route for migratory birds, for example. Thousands of broad-winged hawks and other raptors depend on mountain updrafts to make their way to and from their nesting grounds in South America each year. Other birds, such as the cerulean warbler, are ever more dependent on the trail for habitat as their numbers dwindle throughout their historic range. Once found in abundance along the Eastern Seaboard, the cerulean warbler population has declined by more than 70 percent over the past fifty years. Yet they still fly—and find refuge—along the AT.

I have found refuge there, too.

I grew up in the suburbs of Washington, DC, the daughter of a single father. My parents had gone through an acrimonious divorce when I was seven, and my father had been given primary custody. Under court orders, I went back and forth between my father's house during the week and my mother's apartment every other weekend. And in between, introverted kid that I was, I spent a lot of time alone. I loved nothing more than to walk in the brambly patch of woods behind my father's house, or lie on my belly in the backyard, watching bugs go about their business in the grass. One time I brought home a box turtle shell, sad that it was empty but happy for my prize. Another time I found a toad and tied a string to its leg, holding it captive in the hopes that it could be my pet, until my appalled father set it free.

Born and raised in the Midwest, my father loved the outdoors. He was a canoeist and hiker; he read me stories from *The Call of the Wild* and *Paddle-to-the-Sea.* One day, my father told me about the trail that ran along the Appalachians, and how people hiked the entire route. Maybe he had an article about the AT from *National Geographic* or some other magazine; I can't remember. But from that moment, the Appalachian Trail loomed large in my imagination. I wondered what it would be like to hike the entire length of the trail, or what even possessed people to do so. It took on an almost mythical quality in my mind—a primeval path from another time, like something out of Narnia—a realm for other souls more adventurous than me. I was a shy, quiet girl who rarely spoke up in class. I didn't think of myself as brave. The trail seemed too long, too remote, and too hard to have relevance to me.

I couldn't foresee there might ever be a time when I would be drawn to this trail myself. Or that, just as the path creates a kind of cartilage or connective tissue for the Appalachian Mountains, it would do the same for me—offering a way to strengthen my body and mind, and be reminded of all the forces at work in the universe that were greater than myself.

As an adult, I had put away childish things. I no longer lay in the grass and studied the bugs. I did what the world expected me to do. I developed a career and bought a house and started a family. I paid my bills and fed my cats and put out the recycling. For a while, the Appalachian Trail remained as mythical and distant to me as it had ever been.

Then, my father died, in the house where I'd first discovered the natural world. The big-hearted adventurer who had read me stories was gone. In my grief, I realized that I needed to start carving space for myself again, to reclaim a bit of the wanderer and dreamer I had been as a child. And so the Appalachians beckoned me. I started hiking solo whenever I could, taking on sections of the Appalachian Trail here and there. Although I hiked many different trails in other places, I always came back to the AT. Maybe because I had built it up in my mind as a child, every time I stepped onto the trail and saw one of those iconic white blazes for the first time, I felt a thrill, a sense that I was exactly where I belonged. Hiking on the AT gives me the space to breathe, to think, and to move in ways that my everyday life does not. Perhaps most importantly, it allows me to remember the man who raised me, the stories he told, and the person he helped me to be.

· ✦ ·

Continuing my hike, I pass boulders as large as SUVs and trees as tall as office buildings—maples, hickories, and ash. Each time I pass a white blaze, it feels like a beacon, an arrow—telling me to keep going. Traversing the largest uninterrupted forest corridor on the East Coast, the AT acts as a bulwark against the effects of carbon dioxide emissions and climate change. Trees act as carbon sinks, capturing as much as forty-eight pounds of carbon dioxide per tree per year, according to some estimates, while sequestering carbon for the duration of the tree's lifespan. Trees also give the AT its "green tunnel" effect, luring us into the woods. I have hiked through bare woods in winter, where everything is brown and gray. I've hiked in late spring when the tulip poplars are in a bloom of yellow and orange. I've hiked in summer when trees are sometimes charred black from lightning and fire. And I've hiked in the fall when the deciduous leaves turn riotous and most conifers drop their cones. On the Appalachian Trail and elsewhere, I find that everything comes back to earth.

And yet, the experience of the Appalachian Trail also includes the wild sky. Because of artificial lighting, the earth is becoming brighter at a rate of about 2 percent each year. Light pollution disrupts internal circadian rhythms and disturbs the normal activities of nocturnal wildlife. It also prevents our engagement with the sky our ancestors knew, one where the glittering light from thousands of stars was enough to fill us with awe and show us where to go. Camping at one of the AT's famous shelters or in a tent under a dome of sparkling stars, or stopping at a mountain overlook after sunset, we can still find places to experience the wonder and thrill of true natural darkness. I'm not quite brave enough to hike the AT in the dark, but I know people who do, and I envy them. For now, it's enough for me to know the possibility is there.

So, I keep coming back to the trail to hike sections, mostly in Virginia, Maryland, and Pennsylvania. Sometimes, I've hiked the AT with friends and family, but most of the time I have walked alone. To date, more than twenty thousand intrepid souls have completed the trail either in sections or in one trip, according to the Appalachian Trail Conservancy. It doesn't bother me that I've never thru-hiked it and have no plans to do so; the trail doesn't judge. But unlike when I was a child,

I think I finally understand now why people do it—why they take six months out of their lives and carry what they need on their backs like a box turtle, why they throw in their lot with strangers they pass on the trail, bound together in a common purpose.

"The trail itself is merely a means of access," MacKaye once said of the trail that would form his legacy. "When this is done, the real job can commence: indeed it need not wait on this—it can begin with the building of the trail. The real job is to develop a particular environment in each particular wilderness area penetrated by the trail." This has happened, in every mountain town that has benefited from the trail, in every habitat that has been protected, and in the trailheads that lure people to take the first step.

In these wild and welcoming mountains and valleys, I like to imagine other solo hikers who are out there on this green trail, each of us like a star in the wild sky, a constellation stretching from Georgia to Maine. When each of us walks alone, we are together still, supporting each other by claiming our time in the woods as a fundamental right, a necessity for living, and a reason for being. With every new section of trail I hike, every rock scramble, every stand of serviceberry trees or mountain laurel, every open vista stacked with Appalachian ridges almost glowing beneath the sun, I find myself feeling stronger and braver. Like the leaves and cones and petals, like feathers and berries and dew, I return to the earth again. ✦

About This Story

Kim O'Connell was brought to the trail by grief, just as Benton MacKaye, the so-called father of the Appalachian Trail, had been more than a century ago. After the death of her father, Kim was drawn to the very trail he had once told her about. Her frequent visits to hike sections of the trail connected her to the identity forged with her father—as an intrepid explorer, dreamer, and lover of the outdoors. Intended or not, the legacy of grief continues to resonate across generations of people who are walking off, or walking toward, some version of themselves on the trail. "The trail," Kim reminds us, "doesn't judge."

Vertigo

DERICK LUGO

The nebulous figure advances out of the pitch blackness of my nightmares. A lifelong enigma is finally revealed to me. With every slow blink that I take, my surroundings gradually darken as the cruel truth is made clear. My mind is slipping, yet now it all makes sense.

I should have known . . . I should have . . .

Two months earlier . . .

After hiking nearly seven hundred miles of the Appalachian Trail and with roughly fifteen hundred miles to go, this long-distance trail continues to astound me with its spectacular mountain views that reward me after a well-earned elevation hike. I'm hiking up Cove Mountain, near Catawba, Virginia, with fellow thru-hiker Big Foot, who I call Biggie. He's the size of the Frankenstein monster, with the heart of the little girl who is tossed in the pond by the flat-headed beast.

Ready to embrace everything this journey has to offer, Biggie and I take a side trail for 0.1 mile to Dragon's Tooth, a thirty-five-foot rock monolith of Tuscarora quartzite that offers a 360-degree view of the nearby mountains of Virginia.

We reach the rock spire, its highest point closest to us. I stare at the tall stone structure, trying to make out its shape. I'm no dental hygienist of dragon teeth, but to me, this rock formation looks more like a ship's bow, an ancient shipwreck finally exposed after being lost to the world for centuries.

It appears to be a simple climb, and I'm mad keen on reaching the top for what is promised to be an epic view. I drop my backpack beside Biggie, who chooses to stay with our bags. He's not interested in trudging his big stature up the narrow climb to the top of the tall standing stone.

I run to the other side of the monolith, where it slopes down for easier access to its spine. I don't hesitate to scramble up and over large rocks. As I make my way near the top, my vision suddenly sways up to the sky, taking with it my equilibrium. I instinctively crouch down, onto the boulders that form this tooth of a dragon. The surface I now cringe on begins to turn me around and around, like a thrown frisbee. I pause, waiting for the violent spinning to halt. This helpless spinning sensation is no stranger; I've faced it before.

Not now, my inner voice screams, *not now, please!*

I attempt to push my body up, away from the stone surface, but a strong force pushes my head down, down into the mouth of this dragon's teeth made of rocks. What feels like a knee presses hard on my back. I try moving my head away from the hand gripping my face. Its long, dark fingers obstruct my view. I'm unaware of who or what is doing this to me, although somehow, I know it's humanoid, yet not human at all. Its head is inches from the back of my ear. I attempt to stand myself up again, but the heavy weight on my body is stationed in place, as if anchored to this massive stone. I continue my attempt to wiggle myself loose. Fear prevents me from surrendering to the dark oppressor. I'm nauseated by the rotation of the sky, yet my desperate struggle for freedom from this brute does not relent.

"Stay down, fool," a hollow voice whispers into my ear.

Hot breath covers the side of my face. Sweat rolls down the ridge of my nose, yet instantly disappears as the hot breath blows over with an icy finish. I'm disoriented, yet the spinning begins to subside, and just like that, the world stops moving, my vision clears, my stomach settles, and the dark force keeping me immobilized is gone. I crawl down Dragon's Tooth with my face sliding against the rocks. I reach the ground like a cowering dog.

"What the . . . " I let out a long, tired breath instead of the colorful demonstrative word I had intended to utter. I'm shaken, yet relieved to be on solid ground.

This dark figure, I know it well; it has lingered in my life since childhood. Still, this is the first time it has spoken to me.

Why now? I wonder.

Although I didn't process it until adulthood, my earliest memory of this menacing presence was when I was eight years old. It was also the first time I experienced vertigo. At such a young age, I didn't know that the sensation of whirling and loss of balance when looking down from a great height came with a name.

I was hanging with my little homies, Rodney and Jason. Like many children our age, we had an endless amount of energy, and we felt the need to climb whatever seemed scalable to us. On this particular day, we had our sights set on a tree with many low branches. I was the first one up, quickly reaching a height that allowed me to see the top of our two-story apartment complex. I didn't realize the scope of my distance from the ground until I looked down and saw Rodney just starting his climb up the tree. My vision shot back and forth, like seeing through a camera lens as you're zooming in and out. I swayed from side to side, trying to balance myself on the branch I stood on. As I reached for a branch to steady my wild and treacherous movement, I slipped. I frantically attempted to grab at anything that would stop my descent, and then, from the corner of my eye, I saw a black figure. At that moment, my back somehow hit the bark of the tree, I threw my arm around the closest branch and stopped my fall, but not before the dark figure moved swiftly past me with a cold touch across my bare arm, and then disappeared.

I was pushed.

During my brief despair, when the world moved aimlessly around me, I was pushed by . . . *what was that?* If the bark of the tree was not directly behind me, I would have fallen and broken a bone or two, or worse. However, being the scatter-brain kid that I was, I brushed off the episode and continued burning the energy I had to spare without another thought of the near-fatal fall.

I moved on with my play, yet the fear of heights stayed with me, and the shadowy sighting lingered, hidden in my subconsciousness.

A few decades have passed without an appearance from that dark figure.

So, why now, why on Dragon's Tooth, and why did it speak? "How was the view?" Biggie asks.

"I don't . . . I don't know," I thoughtlessly respond as I pass my giant friend.

I heave my pack and my heavy thoughts back to the Appalachian Trail, away from the Dragon's Tooth fright.

"What's eating you?" he says as he follows close behind me.

I have never shared my first childhood sighting of the dark figure, and I don't share what just happened to me with my monster-size friend. I don't dare. Maybe if I continue to ignore it, it will stay away for a couple more decades. That will surely work, right?

Today . . .

After a restful night at Palmerton, a small town 1.5 miles off the Appalachian Trail in the rocky state of Pennsylvania, I start my hike up a steep ascent out of Lehigh

Gap. It's a stifling summer day, and the temperature is pushing one hundred degrees. The sun, unencumbered by clouds, unleashes its might on my sweaty person, and the lack of trees contributes to the sun's brutal attack.

Clouds, trees, even an umbrella hat, with a battery-operated fan . . . I'd give my resupply for relief from the sun.

The hot spell is doing a number on my cognitive skills. My scrambled mind can't grasp a clear thought. I need some form of shade from this oppressive heat and this uncooperative trail. From the moment I started moving away from the gap, the trail was littered with large, small, and sharp rocks that I swear were born to turn my ankle. I'm not moving farther north from the gap, along the trail—instead, I'm going farther up in elevation.

I look down at the Lehigh River and the bridge the Appalachian Trail runs across. From this thousand-foot height, what I see is scaled down to a smaller size; the bridge looks like a ruler placed across a puddle. I turn my focus to my fingers as they work overtime, clinging and gripping the rocks above me. I reach a section of the trail that levels off, but is narrow. I have boulders to my right and a steep rock face of the gap I just climbed to my left. I place my right hand on the large stone, then sweep a quick glance down to my left, something I instantly regret.

Oh . . . no . . .

At that moment, my vision of the world, of the river, and of the bridge below spins uncontrollably. I stagger and nearly plunge toward the distant river. I hold on to the nearest boulder, which now feels like it's hanging over the trail, out into nothing but the bottom of the gap. I brace my entire body on this single rock and hold for dear life. My back feels exposed, and this rock is the only thing stopping me from toppling over. With my vision distorted, my only relief is the coolness on my cheek against the boulder, and I cling to this release from the sun's scorching stranglehold. The part of my brain seeking relief from this wobbling nightmare holds onto the cool sensation. Tears and sweat distort my sight. I blink several times to clear my vision, and that's when it makes itself seen. It's difficult to make out, like looking up into the surface of a pool while underwater. Nonetheless, I know it's there; a dark long wraith hovering over me. I lose my grip, but instinctively grab the rock with my other hand. I feel like an astronaut holding on to the outside of a spaceship, trying not to float away into the ether. The black deity storms at me with arms stretched. I push away and let space pull me away from its reach.

Falling, I dread the moment my body will hit something solid; I expect it, and it doesn't take long. My left shoulder slams into a sharp rock, and then my forehead scrapes on what feels like a steel grinder. I taste the blood that covers my face as I continue my descent. My ability to see is impaired, leaving my surroundings pitch-black. I plunge back into space, my body flailing aimlessly. I desperately swing my limbs in hopes of grabbing something to stop my speeding fall. I hear loud cracks, like burning wood in a campfire, but there are no trees, no fire, no burning wood, just bones.

It all stops when something unyielding meets the back of my head, torso, and limbs.

Pain? Where's the pain?

I wait for it, but nothing. All is black, yet I suck in air.

So I'm not in outer space.

I can't move my left arm; it's stuck behind the weight of my body. I hear a humming sound, no, it's . . . a garble, like someone trying to talk while drowning.

"Ge . . . elp . . . ge elp!"

What are you saying?

I squeeze my eyes tight, remembering that it worked when I was a kid, trying to wake from a nightmare. I slowly open my eyes, afraid of what I may see. The dark figure hovers over me . . . no, wait . . . it's actually Biggie. I look past him, up at where I once stood on the trail, where I was holding on tight, not wanting to forfeit my life.

"Get help! Get help!" Biggie screams.

Oh, that's what you're saying.

I stare at my hysterical friend, and then back up the gap. I try moving my free yet shattered arm, with no success. I desperately want to point in the direction of the dark creature that did this to me. Biggie follows my wild gaze, turns his head upward, where I stare.

"Yeah, I . . . I sa . . . saw her . . . ." He struggles to form a sentence. My heart hurts for him. I wish he wasn't seeing this.

"She was reaching out . . . trying to catch you," he continues, "but you pulled away. She let out an alarming scream . . . and that's when I saw you fa—" He chokes on the last word.

Wait . . . what?

"She's getting help, I think. I don't see her, but she seemed distraught and stormed off," Biggie adds, trying his best to keep it together, but I see his anguish.

This is my fault; I was wrong about the dark figure, I now understand. The answers to my vertigo mystery rush over me, as if a blindfold has been removed.

It wasn't the bark of the tree that saved me as a kid, I was too far out on the limb. On Dragon's Tooth, her words were a warning, not a threat. She was holding me still, so I wouldn't topple over. It all makes sense now.

I blink several times as if trying to clear my mind as well as my vision. The dark figure suddenly appears behind Biggie. He doesn't notice her presence, even when she steps in front of him. She looks down at me.

"I'm sorry," I want to say, but only a bubble of blood forms between my lips.

I finally see her face . . . I finally see who she really is.

She reaches down. This time I don't move, I can't move. My limbs refuse to listen to me. The dark figure doesn't say a word as she reaches through my chest. She doesn't need to; I know what's happening. I feel my mind falling again into space. I blink once, I stare at the sky, past the gap, past the Appalachian Trail. I blink one last time and my vertigo is gone for good. ✦

About This Story

We were first introduced to Derick Lugo, trail name Mr. Fabulous, by Jennifer Pharr Davis, an AT thru-hiker who herself set the overall fastest time on the Appalachian Trail in 2011, completing it in forty-six days, at an average pace of forty-seven miles a day. Derick is the author of *The Unlikely Thru-Hiker*, his story of hopping the train to Georgia as a Brooklyn-born New York City urbanite and telling a cab driver to drop him off at the beginning of the Appalachian Trail, having never hiked or camped a day in his life. We were immediately drawn to Derick's bright energy, so when he said he wanted to do something "a bit dark," we were intrigued and said, "Please!" Derick describes it as "a combination of what happened to me on the AT during my thru hike—a story that didn't make it into my published memoir—and a dark fiction tale of a fear of heights, where a shadow figure appears at the 'peak' of a frightening point (pun intended) throughout my life."

While some might think of the Appalachian Trail and the mountains of the East Coast as relatively flat, the trail features over 450,000 feet of elevation change between Georgia and Maine—enough to have summited Mount Everest sixteen times. If you have a fear of heights, there are several points on the trail that might make you weak in the knees. The iconic

Clingmans Dome in Great Smoky Mountains National Park is the highest point on the trail at 6,643 feet, followed by Mount Guyot at 6,621 feet and Old Black at 6,370 feet, also within the park. Many thru-hikers describe other vertigo-inducing views along the trail, Dragon's Tooth included: McAfee Knob atop Catawba Mountain and the bluff-tops at Tinker Cliffs, both in Virginia; sections of the Lehigh Gap near Palmerton, Pennsylvania; Wildcat Cliffs in New Hampshire (considered by some as the steepest mile on the AT); and lastly, the finish line at the summit of Katahdin, standing at 5,267 feet and the longest sustained elevation gain of the trail (4,000 feet over five miles of hiking). Fear of heights, however, shouldn't exclude you from the experience. While these points can be frightening, many northbound (NOBO) thru-hikers share that the pace of the trail gradually prepares you for these ascents, and that the dedication to make it to Katahdin carries you through.

Mountaineer Manifesto

EARL V. SHAFFER

You can go back to your city,
Back to your factories and mills
Where everything's smoky and gritty.
But I'll go back to my hills.

You can go back to your fancy home,
Back to your tailored togs.
I'll go back where the wild deer roam,
Back to my cabin of logs.

You can go back to your swimming pool,
Back to your troublesome bills.
I'll swim again in a streamlet cool
Back in my peaceful hills.

The evenings you'll spend on a dance floor
I'll spend out under the stars,
And find in my solitude once more
A balm for my wounds and scars.

I'll purge all my hatred or try to
Live as a free man again:
Do as I like when I want to;
Go where I choose to and when.

No offered position could lure me.
No chance for gain or renown
Could ever beguile or detour me
To coop myself up in a town.

You may take wide spacious highways
To offices, factories, and mills,
But I'll take the trails and the byways
That lead to my peaceful hills. ✦

About This Story

After returning from army service following World War II, Earl Shaffer began hiking the AT to "walk the war out of [his] system." In 1948, he walked from Georgia to Maine in 124 days with worn boots, no stove, and no tent. At the time, completing the entire trail in one trip was not considered feasible. But after initial skepticism, and then careful review by the Appalachian Trail Conservancy, he was officially recognized as the AT's first thru-hiker.

Naturally, Earl wasn't done. In 1965, he hiked from Maine to Georgia, becoming the first person to complete a thru hike in both directions. And in 1998, fifty years after his first thru hike, Earl tackled the route again, becoming, at seventy-nine, the oldest person to thru-hike the Appalachian Trail.

We celebrate Earl as a pioneer who popularized the trail, both for veterans and for the general public. This manifesto gives us insight into what continued to drive him to the trail for so much of his life. Today, you can find his journal and hiking boots in the Smithsonian National Museum of American History. At the Appalachian Trail Museum of American History in Pine Grove Furnace State Park in Pennsylvania, you can see a trail shelter he built; it was painstakingly disassembled at its original site on Peters Mountain and reassembled at the new museum. More of Earl's mountain musings can be found in *Not Too Distant Trails*, a collection of his poetry, songs, and meditations.

Walk Yourself Home

HANNAH ANDRY

Notes on the Appalachian Trail in Massachusetts,
Vermont, and New Hampshire sections
Journal entries, rambling thoughts, and some poetry.

Williamstown, Massachusetts

eep breath. One more. *Begin.*

It's evening on the trail, midsummer, Massachusetts heading into Vermont. Just outside of Williamstown and north of Mount Greylock's breathtaking sunsets and just south of Clarksburg State Forest, which flirts with the border of the Green Mountain State. An orchestra of imperceptible critters are cooing and croaking, settling down for sleep. The odd bullfrog makes itself known, and the owls come alive for their nightly concerto. The warm breeze floats the scent of pine and campfire smoke through the air. Tired hikers are setting up camp in various patches of dirt for the night, the air buzzing with the frequency of a day well walked.

I set up my little stove to get closely acquainted with some noodles and flip open my journal when someone walks up to me and asks, *"What are you writing?"*

I turn to a stranger's voice, and am faced with a timid smile and tired eyes, far away but not void of mysticism. These eyes have seen truth.

I ask in return, *"What do you think is worth writing about?"*

We start to chat, his name is Oliver. He's from Maine, hiking the trail because he didn't want to go to college and needed some time to think about what came next.

That was ten years ago.

I ask him, *"When is the right time to listen to your heart?"*

The question seems to carry him somewhere else, another lifetime perhaps. The evening sun shines on his coarse red hair, highlighting the silver strands of stories that have made their home there over the years.

He looks at me kindly and says softly, *"Soon and always. It's all a part of life's rich tapestry."*

He smiles and walks away, or perhaps to walk toward something else.

I pack up the next morning, eager to meet more thru-hikers and experience the trail a little more. My hiking boots are duct-taped at the right heel, I'm eating a granola bar and some dried mango for breakfast, and I haven't smiled so hard in years.

As I continue heading north, I stumble upon a group of jovial twentysome-things, bantering about trail names and liberal politics. Eyeing my ever present journal, they too ask me, *"What are you writing?"*

Again I respond, *"What do you think is worth writing about?"*

I watch their eyes ignite with rainbow hues in the late-afternoon sunlight, sparkling at the notion of an invitation to be vulnerable.

They reveal to me in the space that exists between candidness and oversharing that *EVERYTHING* in fact, is worth writing about. Silly me, I should have known.

Two of them have come out on the trail, one of them is now openly nonbinary or gender nonconforming and the other identifies as Pansexual. One of the group members, Alice, is running away from home; one of them, Phoenix, is walking until they can feel something again; two others, Mac and Conor, want to see how long they can go without their cell phones. There is a dog with the group, named Pistachio. One of the other group members, Belle, turns to me and says,

"Humanity; that's what we find out here. Community. The trees don't judge us for who we love or what our pronouns are, and the mountains don't criticize us for walking away from our lives or toward our truth, the dirt doesn't analyze our skin tones. Maybe here is where we can actually start to live. It's where we don't have to hold our breath for being ourselves, you know?"

I know. I know far too well the binds that tie us underwater in the shallow pool of expectation. Belle smells like cinnamon, and reminds me of good things.

It all spills out here on the trail. Breadcrumbs formed by human connec-tion and energy. Campsites morphing into communities of deep empathy and understanding. The stars turn into freckles on hikers' faces. The wind starts to sound like your favorite song.

Here on the trail, you don't have to hold your breath because no one is trying to drown you. You even stop trying to drown yourself. The trail teaches you to swim.

To tremble with courage is extraordinary.

When it feels like you don't have a place in this world, you belong here.

You belong here.

You belong where the water meets the sky,

Where constellations tell your story in threads of stars that fall onto your skin,

where the loons call and the Northern wind beckons you forward.

You belong where the wild things are, you belong amongst these things that will strengthen your precious budding wings.

You belong here because you are the wild thing. Keep walking.

The wildflowers, blueberry bushes, and thick grasses hug the dirt footpaths, and I walk step over step. After some reflection, I keep trudging onward, asking questions, thanking trail angels who are handing out potato salad and soda, and wondering:

Who are you in your moments alone?

Are you familiar and friendly with the company you keep?

Do you speak to yourself like you would a friend?

Do you allow grace to flow through you like water in a creek?

Is your resilience written into the lines of your palms like trails on a switchback?

Is the salt in your veins the same as the sea that swells far to the East?

When you touch the cold, hard earth, does it feel holy? Does it feel like a promise?

When you look at the White Mountains ahead, do you tremble or rise to meet them?

Do you kiss the sunbeams when they dance on your arms and do you howl at the moon when she rises?

Your thunder belongs in the sky as much as it belongs in your heart.

When time stands still, do you trust who you have become?

Are you brave enough to know you will change?

You are the rock, the flower, the fly. You are reflected in the world out here.

There are also worlds inside of you. The universe would be desolate without both.
These mountains will lift you if you let them, the soft dirt will humble you and
silence your ego, and the wind will gently whisper, "Keep going . . ."
And when you arrive where you are, exactly how you are, gazing out over a valley
of bright green leaves and a painted blue sky, Calm will open her arms to greet
you and say, "You are right on time."
If Chaos is cousins with Clarity, and stars can explode and fall, and the moon can
pull the sea, then you can learn to love who you are in your moments alone.
Your soul will grow deeper the more you lean in, your eyes brighter with every
sunrise you seek; if mountains and valleys can be shaped by water, you will learn
to love the company you keep.
It is the only thing that is ever truly yours.

Somewhere in Vermont

Out here on the trail, we don't have the luxury of wishing parts of us didn't exist.
I don't wish for my body to be smaller and my feelings to be less intense.
I don't wish my thoughts away, I take their hand and walk with them down the
trail until they can stumble forward on their own.
I smile at my stretch marks on my thighs that turn into topographic maps.
Out here, my crooked smile reminds me of the jagged mountain slope, and my
knees cracking feels like thunder on the inside.
Out here, my nervous stutter is perfect and honest. My chipped tooth is a
weathered cliff.
Out here, the crows' feet around my eyes hold wisdom, and that one misspelled
tattoo on my left arm is now my own personal trail marker.
Out here, I am a human being. Not a human doing.

White Mountains, New Hampshire

I laugh at the idea of my walk in the woods turning into a manifesto of sorts. The
Presidential Traverse in the White Mountains lies ahead of me, and I quiver
thinking about the winds on the exposed rock. I sip some hot cocoa in the early
morning light, the dew lingering gently on the grass around me. I think about
what I would want somebody to find and read if a gust of wind took my journal
to its next life, if my words were to fall before someone else's eyes.

I begin to write a letter to whoever that somebody may be. Maybe it's you.

"Dear Somebody,

I'm glad you found me. Maybe you'll find you, too.

There are smoke, echoes and scars on this trail and in life. I hope you find them all.

Your broken heart will be stitched together with good intentions and fiber threads of sunbeam.

You'll find lingering questions, memories and heartache out here. You will also find joy.

You will tremble with emotion and paint it across the sky; a mastery.

The answers will lie still in your veins like ice until the sunrise melts them and they flow, neatly presenting themselves to you at a summit of some strange peak.

I hope you write out here, and stop apologizing. I hope you walk until it doesn't hurt anymore, or until it does. Sing and dance and ask people questions. Know that out here, you can smile at chaos, even welcome it.

You will hug trees and tear pages out of your books and yell those words from mountaintops. You will feel your torment turning into art, a fierce gentleness and radical empathy redefining what you thought love was.

Out here, you'll find the sunrise in someone's eyes. Things don't have to last forever to be meaningful. The trail won't last forever. But still, I hope you believe someone when they tell you that you're beautiful and wild.

You'll start to dismantle your walls and morph into your unabridged, uncensored, whole self. You'll memorize the switchbacks like they are poetry, and then find them in the curves of your body.

You'll need help, and I hope you discover that hands have spaces between fingers for other fingers to fit into. Shoulders are sturdy because they are meant to be leaned on.

I hope you trace your own veins like they are the map back to a place you didn't know was lost.

I hope out here, you'll amplify someone else's voice. You should ask everyone what their story is. Share yours. You will miss people out here. It is okay to miss people.

Your body keeps the score out here, so take care of it the best you can. Health will look different on different days. Food and rest are not the enemy.

The distance is up to you. It is okay to outgrow and alter expectations.

Out here, the cheap black coffee from diners will soothe your soul, and you'll learn the weight of the word forgiveness.

On the trail, I hope you discover that the most intimate relationship you'll ever have is the one with yourself. It will be painful. It will be raw. It will be honest. It will, at times, be inexplicable. Go out and make it beautiful and don't settle for less. Set your soul on fire and give yourself chills thinking about the person you are becoming. Allow anger to come and go. Be sure to allow it to go. See it out the door and thank it for teaching you. Being a mystery isn't always in your favor, let people in at your own pace. We all have our own clocks. We all walk our own trails.

Honor your disposition and question everything. Trust yourself. Trust other people. Tell others how they make you feel. Give compliments, say thank you when you receive one. Break your own heart and fall in love every day out here. Never apologize for your enthusiasm. You will attract who you are, not what you want.

I hope on the trail you treat people how they want to be treated; if you don't know, ask. Hold space for disagreement out here, but always keep each other safe and secure.

I hope you make mischief before it finds you. I hope you packed bubbles and chocolate. Pick up the piece of trash on the trail. When joy arrives on your path, don't question if you deserve it, you do.

No one else will complete you, you will complete you. You will hurt people, and you will make people fall in love. Allow grace to become a part of you like a salt that your body needs. Let passion flow in your bloodstream but use it wisely. Be humble and celebrate differences, acknowledge injustice and yell about it. Be a human on fire. Use the ashes to paint a more inclusive picture.

Hold everyone in a positive regard out here, have conversations with people you disagree with and try not to judge their motives. Know that you set the example of how others are allowed to treat you by how you treat yourself. Believe in magic.

Forgive your family and the people who have hurt you. Release it to the trees. Forgive yourself for not always being gentle. Thank the madness that drove you to hike this trail. Forgiveness doesn't mean consent, it means peace for your soul. Silence booms on the trail. Let it. Keeping the peace on the outside does not always lead to peace on the inside.

Place your hands against the earth when you walk gently on it, and let the mud stay under your nails. Splash pond water in your hair. Lean into the wind and know it holds stories. Sleep under the stars as many nights as you can. Love stories exist between the summits and the valleys.

It is okay to be someone who feels deeply in a messy world. Life is not linear out there, nor is it tidy out here. Choose your mess, but quit trying to tidy it.

· ✦ ·

The last person I meet on the trail is a four-foot-nine woman, setting up camp and happily eating chocolate. She is petite in stature, but grand in courage. Her presence is magnetic. Her name is Morgan. I notice she is camping solo and I ask her,

"*Are you scared of being out here alone?*"

She pauses, looks up at me and says,

"*You're asking me if I'm scared of being alone out here? On the trail?*"

I nod to clarify.

She smiles, as if she knows answers to questions I have yet to ask.

She challenges me with, "*Have you ever really felt alone out here?*"

Not for one moment.

Deep breath. One more.

Begin. ✦

About This Story

Hannah Andry is one of our travel stipend recipients and a military veteran. As a teenager, Hannah told herself that she would "do every hard thing possible" and created a bucket list that included joining the military and working for Outward Bound. We were drawn to her story immediately, and also to her proposal to section-hike the AT—a less glamorized way to experience the beauty of the trail. Hannah has always found a sense of healing in the woods, which helped her as a young teenager feeling like an outcast, or after leaving the military with PTSD. She shared with us a visceral memory of arriving at Logan Airport upon leaving the military, and immediately putting her hands in the dirt outside. Soon, Hannah returned home to Boston and her dream job with Outward Bound.

The Appalachian Trail was built as a place where veterans could "walk off the war," but this was never on Hannah's radar until she joined Outward Bound, where she learned its history. She shares that her PTSD was paralyzing, and the only way she could talk about her feelings was by being out in nature. It took Hannah a long while to publicly identify as a veteran, unsure if it was shame or fear, but in learning this place was built for veterans, she described it as healing, kinesthetic, and cathartic. Nature allowed her to feel most herself and "walk herself home" to who she is: a lesbian, queer, nonbinary military veteran. Hannah shares, "The trail is the space to say really hard things out loud," and in her work with Outward Bound and her own efforts focused on diversity, equity, inclusion (DEI), and social justice, she strives to invite others into that space, too. In talking about her work with students on expeditions, she says, "I'm not good at technical skills like tying knots, but I *can* talk about feelings."

"This trail and area holds promise and change for many," describes Hannah. "A change to shed an old version of yourself, to try to be brand-new, to redefine how you want to exist in the world." Hannah dreamed of hiking the AT as a young kid, but as she got older realized a long thru hike wasn't for her and thought, "What if I could section-hike?" And so she went to "walk it off," step over step, exploring different regions along the footpath of the AT. For this piece, Hannah visited sections of the trail over long weekends. From this experience, she takes away that "the Appalachian Trail is a symbol of what could be changed. More than other long-distance trails, it's immensely populated. There are a lot of people there. There are conversations and connections that create this energy, paired with the natural world. The trees are listening. People are listening. I love that it runs through different states, through these invisible boundaries. I mean, you can meet people from around the world in a few hours."

Acknowledgments

This book would not have been realized without the support, encouragement, and enthusiasm of our wonderful community of friends, family, mentors, and supporters. We'd like to take a moment to say thank you and express our gratitude.

First, to our **friends and family** who continually encourage and support our creative endeavors without question. To Diane Shapiro, or "Rah Rah" to the girls, for spending many weekend days spoiling them while we focused on creating this book. To Sheldon Shapiro, who always thought our book was "pretty slick," and showed off the first volume to all who cared for him until his final days. To Meg Talley, for getting Ilyssa out of the house and away from children to work on the book in the company of friendship and ice cream for breakfast.

To our **Kickstarter backers**—your support gave us courage and confidence, as well as the means to commission new works for this ambitious project. We'd especially like to acknowledge backers who contributed at the "Fund a Writer" level, which provided travel stipends to six writers to travel to a national park and create a piece for the book: Peter Olsho, Jane Wilkie, Laurie Lee, Sheldon Shapiro, and Lauren and Joel Smith—who made their contributions "in support of people breaking barriers and making exploration of the outdoors more inclusive for all."

We'd like to acknowledge and share our gratitude for Ruth Nolan, who not only contributed a piece for the book but went above and beyond to support our research into Joshua Tree and the thriving writing community there.

Our sincerest thanks to Ben Camp, artistic director for Team Sunshine Performance Corporation, a Philadelphia-based theater and dance company, and former camper and camp counselor who helped us develop the storytelling tips for telling your best campfire story.

We could not have pulled any of this off without Melissa McFeeters, whose talent is the reason this book is so beautifully and meticulously designed—and who helped us grow the Campfire Stories brand into a collection of books and interactive card decks that inspire people to tell their own stories.

All of this would not be possible without our publisher, **Mountaineers Books**, who trusted this little idea from two unknown "not even writers" and launched it into the stratosphere. We'd especially like to thank Kate Rogers, who always keeps us focused, on time, and excited—while also gracefully managing and supporting (most of) our one thousand ideas.

We also acknowledge the **Indigenous Peoples and Nations** who have stewarded the lands and waterways for generations in all of the national parks featured in this collection, and were displaced for the creation of some of them. We honor and respect these communities, past, present, and future, who continue to advocate and care for their ancestral lands, and keep their history and culture alive.

And lastly, we're thankful to our **readers** for their enthusiasm and support of these collections and our national parks.

Permissions and Sources

Grand Canyon National Park

PERMISSIONS

Bohlman, Melisa Jane. "Woven Canyon." Printed with the permission of the author.

Emerick, Mary. "Rescue Below the Rim." Printed with the permission of the author.

Gavin, Thea. "At the Intersection." Printed with the permission of the author.

Gavin, Thea. "Nearly Impossible?" Printed with the permission of the author.

Rakha, Naseem. "Everything is Stardust" was first published in *Why We Boat: Running Rivers on Our Own*, Vishnu Temple Press, 2018.

Savoy, Lauret Edith. Adapted from Lauret Edith Savoy, "The View from Point Sublime" from *Trace: Memory, History, Race, and the American Landscape*. Copyright © 2015 by Lauret Edith Savoy. Reprinted with the permission of The Permissions Company, LLC on behalf of Counterpoint Press, counterpointpress.com.

Taffa, Deborah Jackson. "Canyon Dreams." Printed with the permission of the author.

Villareal, Laura. "The God of Monsoon & Her Clay Ship." Printed with the permission of the author.

Watahomigie-Corliss, Ophelia. "We Are the Land, We Are the Water." Printed with the permission of the author.

SOURCES

"Grand Canyon National Park: Geology." National Park Service, US Department of the Interior, 17 Oct. 2021, www.nps.gov/grca/learn/nature/grca-geology.htm.

History.com Editors. "Grand Canyon." History.com, A&E Television Networks, 2 Dec. 2009, www.history.com/topics/landmarks/grand-canyon.

The Voices of Grand Canyon. Grand Canyon Trust, 20 Oct. 2020, www.grandcanyontrust .org/advocatemag/fall-winter-2020/voices-grand-canyon.

Everglades National Park

PERMISSIONS

Douglas, Marjory Stoneman. Reproduced from *Everglades River Of Grass Revised Edition* by Marjory Stoneman Douglas, published by Pineapple Press. © Pineapple Press 60th Anniversary Edition, 2007, reproduced by arrangement with Globe Pequot.

Gottlieb, Andrew. "Naming the Everglades." Printed in 2015 as a limited-edition letterpress broadside for Everglades National Park; designed by Jim Cokas and printed by Sandy Tilcock of Lone Goose Press.

Jones, Sylvia. "Signs of Wildlife." Printed with the permission of the author.

Jumper, Betty Mae. "The Corn Lady." In *Legends of the Seminoles*. Pineapple Press, 2021.

Kaminski, Leah Claire. "What Used to Be the Everglades." Printed with the permission of the author.

Karetnick, Jen. "Slough Slogging in the Dry Season." Printed with the permission of the author. Previously published in *Crab Orchard Review*.

Karetnick, Jen. "Searching for the Florida Panther, I Find Only Signs." Printed with the permission of the author.

Luria, Rachel. "Living Jewels of the Everglades." Printed with the permission of the author.

Rogers, Hannah. "Dear National Park Service." Printed with the permission of the author.

Woodcock, Diana. "Beggar in the Everglades." Printed with the permission of the author.

Woodcock, Diana. "In the Company of Alligators." Printed with the permission of the author.

SOURCES

"Developing the Everglades." National Park Service, US Department of the Interior, 20 June 2020, www.nps.gov/ever/learn/historyculture/development.htm.

"Draining and Development of the Everglades." Wikipedia, Wikimedia Foundation, 24 Sept. 2021, https://en.wikipedia.org/wiki/Draining_and_development_of_the_Everglades.

"Green Corn Dance." Semtribe, www.semtribe.com/stof/culture/green-corn-dance.

"Indian Resistance and Removal." Semtribe, www.semtribe.com/stof/history/indian-resistance-and-removal.

Kocelko, Melissa. "A Short History of the Liguus Tree Snails Collection." National Park Service, US Department of the Interior, 24 June 2021, www.nps.gov/articles/a-short-history-of-the-liguus-tree-snails-collection.htm.

Olympic National Park

PERMISSIONS

Clark, Ella Elizabeth, ed. "Nahkeeta: A Story of Lake Sutherland" reprinted from *Indian Legends of the Pacific Northwest*, University of California Press, 1953; permission conveyed through Copyright Clearance Center, Inc.

Lawrence, Lace. "Erasing Legends." Printed with the permission of the author.

McNulty, Tim. "A Mountain Blessing." Appeared in *Ascendance, Poems* by Tim McNulty, Pleasure Boat Studio, New York, 2013. Used with permission.

Miranda, Gary. "Still Lifes: Hoh Rain Forest." Originally appeared in *Poetry* magazine. It is reprinted by permission of Gary Miranda.

Moon, Harvest. "Glukeek Legend." Printed with the permission of the author. Harvest Moon would like to credit her father and mother, John and Ida Brozina, her sons, Mark, Keith, Cory, Jason Christopherson, and her mentor, Mr. Lelooska, and all her teachers.

Priest, Rena. "Before Clocks." Printed with the permission of the author.

Priest, Rena. "Syncing Up at Sol Duc." Printed with the permission of the author.

Royale, Rosette. "Under the Spell of Roosevelt Elk." Printed with the permission of the author.

Semanco, Anja. "One Square Inch." Printed with the permission of the author.

SOURCES

"Elwha Klallam Historical Timeline." Lower Elwha Klallam Tribe, 28 Oct. 2019, www.elwha
.org/culture-history/elwha-klallam-historical-timeline.

"Olympic National Park: Learn about the Park." National Park Service, US Department of the
Interior, 30 Nov. 2016, www.nps.gov/olym/learn/index.htm.

Park Archives: Explore Olympic National Park, 20 Mar. 2022, http://npshistory.com/publications
/olym/index.htm.

"River Restoration." Lower Elwha Klallam Tribe, 3 July 2018, www.elwha.org
/departments/river-restoration.

Glacier National Park

PERMISSIONS

Alcosser, Sandra. "What Makes the Grizzlies Dance." Printed with the permission of the author.

Aranda, Sara. "When We Visit." Printed with the permission of the author.

Gladstone, Mariah. "Wolf Trail." Printed with the permission of the author.

Grinnell, George Bird. "The Crown of the Continent." In *The Century Magazine*. September 1901,
660–72.

Mansolino, Ann. "Glacial Flow." Printed with the permission of the author.

Muth, Bob. "Earth Prayer From the McDonald Valley." Printed with the permission of the author.

Muth, Bob. "Hiking Up the Dry Fork in the Two Medicine Valley." Printed with the permission of
the author.

Randall, Cassidy. "Going-to-the-Sun." Printed with the permission of the author.

Williams, Terry Tempest. "Glacier National Park, Montana." In *The Hour of Land*. 333–47. New
York: Sarah Crichton Books/Farrar, Straus and Giroux, 2016.

SOURCES

"Glacier National Park: How to See a Glacier." National Park Service, US Department of the Interi-
or, 4 Aug. 2021, www.nps.gov/glac/learn/nature/how-to-see-a-glacier.htm.

Robinson, Donald H., et al. Through the Years in Glacier National Park: An Administrative History.
Glacier Natural History Association, Inc. in Cooperation with the National Park Service, 1973.

Taliaferro, John. The Secret Life of George Grinnell, One of America's Greatest Conservationists.
Pacific Standard, 3 June 2019, https://psmag.com/ideas/the-secret-life-of-george-grinnell-one
-of-americas-greatest-conservationists.

Joshua Tree National Park

PERMISSIONS

Anderson, Cynthia. "Pinto Basin." Appeared in the book *Desert Dweller* by Cynthia Anderson, Pencil Cholla Press, 2014.

Anderson, Cynthia. "Split Rock Loop." Appeared in the book *Waking Life* by Cynthia Anderson, Cholla Needles Press, 2017.

Austin, Mary. "The Land of Little Rain (excerpt)." 1–21. *The Land of Little Rain*. Boston and New York: Houghton Mifflin Company, 1903.

Cipra, Mike, and Caryn Davidson. "Tales of Desert Symbiosis." Reprinted with the permission of the authors.

DelBianco, Rae. "Coyotes." Printed with the permission of the author.

Lee, Ed Bok. "Asleep In An Old Ranger Station In Joshua Tree, CA." Printed with the permission of the author.

Nolan, Ruth. "Joshua Tree Imprimatur." Printed with the permission of the author.

Patencio, Francisco, and Margaret Boynton. "The First New Plants." 22–26. *Stories And Legends of the Palm Springs Indians*. [2d. ed.]. [Palm Springs, CA]: Palm Springs Desert Museum, 1943.

Rosenthal, Ed. "Salvation Canyon (excerpt)." *Salvation Canyon: A True Story of Desert Survival in Joshua Tree*. Los Angeles, CA: DoppelHouse Press, 2020.

Winslow, Sheree. "Wonderland of Rocks." Printed with the permission of the author.

SOURCES

"Artist-in-Residence Program." National Park Service, US Department of the Interior, 29 Mar. 2022, www.nps.gov/jotr/getinvolved/supportyourpark/air.htm.

"Joshua Tree National Park: Nature." National Park Service, US Department of the Interior, 31 Jan. 2017, www.nps.gov/jotr/learn/nature/index.htm.

"Lewis DeSoto." Sand To Stone, 2016, www.sandtostone.org/artist-lewis-desoto.htm.

Murphy, Heather. *Are 1,818 Airbnbs Too Many in Joshua Tree? The New York Times*, 7 Apr. 2022, www.nytimes.com/2022/04/07/travel/joshua-tree-california-airbnb.html.

Zarki, Joe. "A Park for Minerva." National Park Service, US Department of the Interior, 28 Feb. 2015, www.nps.gov/jotr/learn/historyculture/mhoyt.htm.

Appalachian National Scenic Trail & Pacific Crest National Scenic Trail

PERMISSIONS

Andry, Hannah. "Walk Yourself Home." Printed with the permission of the author.

Donaldson, Allie a.k.a. Taogoi. "1100 Miles (excerpts)." *1100 Miles: A Poetic Journey on the Pacific Crest Trail (Excerpts)*. Reprinted with the permission of the author.

Galloway, Kitty. "I Wanted to Tell You." Printed with the permission of the author.

Lugo, Derick. "Vertigo." Printed with the permission of the author.

O'Connell, Kim. "Connective Tissue." Printed with the permission of the author.

Salabert, Shawnté. "On Trail, We Dream of Enchiladas." Printed with the permission of the author.

Shaffer, Earl V. The poem, "Mountaineer Manifesto" for which permission to reprint is hereby granted, is included in the book *Not Too Distant Trails: Appalachian Trail Poems, Songs, Meditations* by Earl V. Shaffer, Nancy Shaffer Nafziger, Editor. Earl Shaffer Foundation Inc. 2018.

Strayed, Cheryl. "Prologue" from *Wild: From Lost To Found on The Pacific Crest Trail* by Cheryl Strayed, copyright © 2012 by Cheryl Strayed. Used by permission of Alfred A. Knopf, an imprint of the Knopf Doubleday Publishing Group, a division of Penguin Random House LLC. All rights reserved.

SOURCES

"Appalachian Trail Histories." Omeka RSS, https://appalachiantrailhistory.org/exhibits/show /builders/bmackaye.

MacKaye, Benton. *An Appalachian Trail: A Project in Regional Planning*. Appalachian Trail Conservancy, 4 Jan. 2022, https://appalachiantrail.org/our-work/an-appalachian-trail-a-project-in -regional-planning/.

Mann, Barney Scout. *The Hidden History of the Pacific Crest Trail*. The Mountaineers, 7 Sept. 2021, www.mountaineers.org/blog/the-hidden-history-of-the-pacific-crest-trail-3.

Young, Elizabeth. "Catherine Montgomery." *Badass Womxn in the Pacific Northwest*, University of Washington Bothell and University of Washington Libraries, 10 June 2019, https://uw .pressbooks.pub/badasswomxninthepnw/chapter/catherine-montgomery.

Park Communities

Each national park attracts its own unique ecosystem of people. Here are just some of the friend groups, park advocates, and artist residencies that work to celebrate, preserve, and protect the national parks featured in this collection.

Grand Canyon National Park

GRAND CANYON CONSERVANCY

As the official nonprofit partner of Grand Canyon National Park, their mission is to inspire generations of park champions to cherish and support the natural and cultural wonder of Grand Canyon. They provide support for projects such as trails and historic building preservation, educational programs for the public, and the protection of wildlife and their natural habitat, and also operate the retail shops within the park.
www.grandcanyon.org

GRAND CANYON TRUST

The trust was established in 1985 to protect the air, water, and wildlife of the slickrock canyons, fragile deserts, and forested mesas of the Grand Canyon. They work on issues from grazing to forest restoration to uranium mining—as well as protecting tribal life and Indigenous knowledge across the Colorado Plateau by supporting small businesses and Native entrepreneurs, facilitating the Colorado Plateau Intertribal Gatherings, and standing behind tribes as they reclaim the authority to manage their ancestral lands and protect cultural landscapes from commercial development.
www.grandcanyontrust.org

HAVASUPAI TRIBE

For over one thousand years the remote village of Supai, Arizona, an eight-mile hike down into the Grand Canyon, has been home to the Havasu 'Baaja, People of the Blue-Green Water, or as they are known today, the Havasupai Tribe. Just above the village, a hidden limestone aquifer gushes forth life-sustaining blue-green waters that nourish fields of corn, squash, and beans that have allowed the Havasu 'Baaja to thrive in the harsh desert landscape deep in the Grand Canyon for centuries.
www.theofficialhavasupaitribe.com

NPS ARTIST-IN-RESIDENCE PROGRAM (AIR)

This newly revived and restructured program hosts artists on the South Rim with the support of Grand Canyon Conservancy, providing accomplished professional artists time and space to explore and develop significant work. Its new focus is on substantial projects that benefit the public and the park by enhancing our fundamental understanding of the canyon and its communities.
www.nps.gov/grca/getinvolved/supportyourpark /air.htm

Everglades National Park

ARTISTS IN RESIDENCE IN EVERGLADES (AIRIE)

In partnership with the Everglades National Park, AIRIE empowers artists to think creatively and critically about their relationship to the environment, with a mission of revealing new paths forward.
www.airie.org

FRIENDS OF THE EVERGLADES

This nonprofit was founded in 1969 by renowned journalist, author, and environmental activist Marjory Stoneman Douglas. To this day it is dedicated to preserving, protecting, and restoring the only Everglades in the world by compelling government agencies to comply with existing environmental laws and resist any efforts to weaken such laws, encouraging politicians to recognize the long consequences of their actions, and spreading awareness of the importance of the Everglades to the South Florida ecosystem.
www.everglades.org

LOVE THE EVERGLADES MOVEMENT

LTEM's mission is to implement evolving strategies across the full spectrum of being that address the environmental, structural, cultural, and spiritual problems plaguing the Florida Everglades by raising awareness and organizing positive community engagement at the local, regional, national, and global levels.
www.lovetheeverglades.org

THE ALLIANCE FOR FLORIDA'S NATIONAL PARKS

As the official philanthropic partner for Everglades, Dry Tortugas, and Biscayne National Parks, as well as Big Cypress National Preserve, the Alliance for Florida's National Parks works relentlessly to ensure that Florida's greatest natural ecosystems are preserved and protected for generations to come. They've created and supported diverse programs that provide meaningful experiences and educational opportunities in an effort to lay the foundation for lifelong stewardship.
www.floridanationalparks.org

SEMINOLE TRIBE

We Seminole have lived in Florida for thousands of years. Our ancestors were the first people to come to Florida. Our ancestors were connected by family and culture to others across North America, from the Atlantic coast to the Mississippi River, from the Gulf of Mexico to the Great Lakes.
www.semtribe.com

Olympic National Park

FRIENDS OF OLYMPIC NATIONAL PARK

This friends group works to preserve the park's natural, cultural, and recreational resources for the benefit of present and future generations. Their mission is to promote understanding of the park's ecological, educational, economic, and recreational importance and work with Olympic National Park on special projects. They cosponsor programs like lecture series, nature walks, and tours guided by park rangers, and coordinate volunteer opportunities to enhance the park.
www.folym.org

LOWER ELWHA KLALLAM TRIBE

The Lower Elwha Klallam Tribe is a sovereign, federally recognized Indian Nation, with its own constitution and government. Not only does the Tribe govern itself, but many tribal administrative departments oversee the everyday function of the reservation and provide for tribal members.
www.elwha.org

LUMMI NATION

Today the Lummi Nation is a nationally recognized leader in tribal self-governance and education. We understand the challenge of respecting our traditions while making progress in a modern world—to listen to the wisdom of our ancestors, to care for our lands and waterways, to educate our children, to provide family services, and to strengthen our ties with the outside community.
www.lummi-nsn.gov

QUINAULT NATION

We are among the small number of Americans who can walk the same beaches, paddle the same waters, and hunt the same lands our ancestors did centuries ago. The Quinault Indian Nation (QIN) consists of the Quinault and Queets tribes and descendants of five other coastal tribes: Quileute, Hoh, Chehalis, Chinook, and Cowlitz.
www.quinaultindiannation.com

WASHINGTON'S NATIONAL PARK FUND

As the official philanthropic partner to Mount Rainier, North Cascades, and Olympic National Parks, WNPF raises private support to preserve and protect Washington's cherished national parks. They fund scientific research, youth and family experiences, and projects that will keep these parks strong and vital now and forever, for everyone.
www.wnpf.org

Glacier National Park

BLACKFEET NATION

The Blackfeet Indian Reservation is home to the 17,321-member Blackfeet Nation, one of the ten largest tribes in the United States. Established by treaty in 1855, the reservation is located in northwest Montana.
www.blackfeetnation.com

BLACKFEET OUTFITTERS

This full-service hunting, fly fishing, packing, outfitting, and eco-tours business provides a unique experience for clients to discover Montana's splendor and gain insight into the Blackfeet Native American people and culture. Explore, discover, and experience Montana's grandeur on the ancestral lands of the Blackfeet Indians.
www.blackfeetoutfitters.com

GLACIER NATIONAL PARK CONSERVANCY

As the official fundraising partner for Glacier National Park, GNPC raises private funds for vital projects and programs that preserve and protect the park. Additionally, the conservancy operates nonprofit bookstores to support park interpretation and education activities and programs. Projects funded include trail restoration, field trips, and citizen science in future years.
www.glacier.org

GLACIER INSTITUTE

As the official education partner of Glacier National Park and Flathead National Forest, the institute provides a wide range of innovative outdoor educational programs and field-based experiences, from personalized tours to week-long focused courses that connect individuals with the natural world and provide unforgettable experiences.
www.glacierinstitute.org

NPS ARTIST-IN-RESIDENCE PROGRAM (AIR)

The Glacier National Park Artist-in-Residence program offers artists four weeks of focused time to creatively explore the natural and cultural resources of this inspiring landscape while pursuing their artistic goals. The program seeks artists whose work is related to the park's interpretive themes and supports the mission of the National Park Service and conservation of these public lands. It also allows artists the opportunity to share their work with an international audience through educational programs.
www.nps.gov/glac/getinvolved/air.htm

Joshua Tree National Park

AGUA CALIENTE BAND OF CAHUILLA INDIANS

The Agua Caliente Band of Cahuilla Indians is a historic Palm Springs–based, federally recognized Native American Tribe with more than five hundred members. The Tribe is steward to more than 31,500 acres of ancestral land. The cities of Palm Springs, Cathedral City, and Rancho Mirage, as well as portions of unincorporated Riverside County, span across the boundaries of the Agua Caliente Indian Reservation.
www.aguacaliente.org

FRIENDS OF JOSHUA TREE

FOJT is a nonprofit organization dedicated to preserving the tradition of climbing in Joshua Tree National Park. They advocate, communicate, and encourage ethical and environmentally sound climbing practices, and work to shape park policy on climbing and climbing-related issues. They act as the liaison between the climbing community and the National Park Service.
www.friendsofjosh.org

FUND FOR PEOPLE IN PARKS

As an official philanthropic fundraising partner of the National Park Service, the fund provides private funds and other resources for projects that enhance visitor experience and cannot be accomplished with federal funding alone. These projects present lesser-known narratives and fresh perspectives through oral histories, films and television specials, educational signs, visitor center exhibits, ship reconstruction, and informational brochures and books. Wayfinding projects such as tactile relief maps, trail improvements, guide brochures, and compass roses allow visitors to better understand the landscape and their place in it.
www.peopleinparks.org

JOSHUA TREE NATIONAL PARK ASSOCIATION

The park's primary nonprofit partner since 1962, JTNPA works with Joshua Tree National Park to help it achieve programming goals in education and interpretation, along with scientific and historical research and activities. They operate four park stores that are often the first stop for visitors from around the world; offer a field institute with classes taught by experts in natural sciences, cultural history, and the arts; and raise funds for programs and projects within the park.
www.joshuatree.org

MOJAVE DESERT LAND TRUST

In its mission to protect the Mojave and Colorado desert ecosystems and their natural, cultural, and scenic resource values, MDLT has conserved more than one hundred thousand acres of prime desert habitat, forever weaving together national parks, national monuments, wilderness areas, and wildlife corridors. The organization works closely with a broad range of desert community members and visitors, as well as with local, state, and federal agencies. MDLT offers hands-on learning and volunteer opportunities to residents of and visitors to the desert.
www.mdlt.org

NPS ARTIST-IN-RESIDENCE PROGRAM (AIR)

This artist residency program is open to visual artists, performing artists, musicians, and writers who'd like a one-month stay in the fall or spring to focus on their art practice. Artists are invited to explore Joshua Tree and pursue their creative work while also sharing their unique perspective

through a visitor outreach experience such as a short hike, a performance, or answering visitor questions at a public location.
www.nps.gov/jotr/getinvolved/supportyourpark/air.htm

Pacific Crest National Scenic Trail & Appalachian National Scenic Trail

PACIFIC CREST TRAIL CONSERVANCY

Since 1977, the PCTA mission has been to protect, preserve, and promote the Pacific Crest National Scenic Trail as a world-class experience for hikers and equestrians, and for all the value provided by wild and scenic lands. Their vision is to ensure the entire PCT corridor is permanently protected, well maintained, and effectively managed, and that the trail is renowned as a rare opportunity to travel exceptionally scenic, remote, primitive landscapes. The PCTA is widely recognized as the trail's champion and steward, and achieves its work through the strength of its partnerships, staff, volunteers, and the rest of the PCT community.
www.pcta.org

APPALACHIAN TRAIL CONSERVANCY

Since 1925, the mission of the ATC has been to protect, manage, and advocate for the Appalachian National Scenic Trail. With a focus on education, they prepare and educate millions of visitors each year as they explore the natural and cultural wonders of the trail, promote outdoor ethics to minimize the impact visitors have on the environment, and engage supporters on issues important for protecting the AT experience. Their efforts ensure that the trail is protected forever through public engagement, broader landscape protection, and best trail-management practices. They also manage more than 250,000 acres that protect fresh drinking water, culturally and historically significant landscapes, threatened and endangered species, and recreation-driven economies. Lastly, to empower the next generation of AT stewards, they engage youth and rally local communities to help protect the trail. Through their programs and partnerships, they support over six thousand volunteers that maintain and care for the AT and its surrounding lands.
www.appalachiantrail.org

EARL SHAFFER FOUNDATION

The nonprofit Earl Shaffer Foundation celebrates the life, times, and creative works of Earl V. Shaffer of Pennsylvania (1918–2002), writer, poet, naturalist, photographer, and dedicated environmentalist.
www.earlshaffer.com

About the Contributors

J. Drew Lanham
Birder, naturalist, essayist, poet, and recipient of a 2022 MacArthur Fellowship, J. Drew Lanham is the author of *The Home Place: Memoirs of a Colored Man's Love Affair with Nature*. His writings have appeared in anthologies as well as periodicals including *Orion* and *Audubon*. Lanham is an Alumni Distinguished Professor of Wildlife Ecology at Clemson University. He lives in South Carolina.

Grand Canyon National Park

Melisa Jane Bohlman (she/ella/ela) is a Sonoran desert dweller, from the saguaro forests and summer magic monsoons. She is humbled to use her writing to amplify those who have been historically silenced and their connections to the land on this beautiful spinning planet. She shares her big smile and height from her fourth-generation New Jersey father and her big, brown "pechiche" eyes and belly laugh from her Ecuadorian-Chinese madre. She is honored to work with Campfire Stories.

Thea Gavin became a wilderness first responder and instructor with the Grand Canyon Conservancy Field Institute after a life-changing stint in 2011 as artist in residence at the North Rim. A retired creative-writing professor, she continues to lead writing workshops in wild places, including her local Orange County, California, foothills. Thea's blog, "Barefoot Wandering and Writing," chronicles over eleven years of barefoot adventures, including many shoeless miles above and below the rim at Grand Canyon.

Mary Emerick is the author of the novel *The Geography of Water* and two memoirs, *Fire in the Heart* and *The Last Layer of the Ocean*. She lives in a log cabin in eastern Oregon and spends all of her free time in the mountains.

Naseem Rakha is a geologist, educator, storyteller, and award-winning author and journalist whose novel *The Crying Tree* earned international acclaim for its frank examination of crime, punishment, sexual identity, and forgiveness. Naseem's commentaries can be found in *The Guardian*, and she was a contributor to National Public Radio. She is currently working on a collection of short stories and essays, but when not writing, Naseem spends her time hiking, climbing, rafting, and photographing throughout the American West. She lives in Oregon with her husband.

Lauret Edith Savoy is the author of *Trace: Memory, History, Race, and the American Landscape*, winner of the 2016 American Book Award from the Before Columbus Foundation and the 2017 ASLE Creative Writing Award. She coedited *The Colors of Nature: Culture, Identity, and the Natural World* with Alison Hawthorne Deming, compiled and edited *Bedrock: Writers on the Wonders of Geology* with Eldridge and Judy Moores, and coauthored *Living with the Changing California Coast* with Gary Griggs and Kiki Patsch. Lauret's essays and other writings have appeared in the *Georgia Review*, *Gettysburg Review*, *Huffington Post*, *Travel & Leisure*, *ArtForum*, *Christian Science Monitor*, and *Orion* magazine. She is the David B. Truman Professor of Environmental Studies and Geology at Mount Holyoke College, a photographer, and pilot. Winner of Mount Holyoke's Distinguished Teaching Award and an Andrew Carnegie Fellowship, Lauret has also held fellowships from the Smithsonian Institution and Yale University. She is a fellow of the Geological Society of America.

Deborah Jackson Taffa (Quechan/Laguna Pueblo) is the director of the MFA in creative writing at the Institute of American Indian Arts. She is passionate about promoting Indigenous voices and values. Her work can be found in the *Boston Review, A Public Space*, the *Best American* series, and other places. She wishes to thank her supporters: PEN America, MacDowell, Hedgebrook, Tin House, Kranzberg Arts Foundation, the University of Iowa, Washington University in St. Louis, and the Ellen Meloy Fund.

Laura Villareal earned her MFA at Rutgers University-Newark. Her writing can be found in print and online at places such as *AGNI, Black Warrior Review*, and *Waxwing*. She is the author of *Girl's Guide to Leaving* (University of Wisconsin Press, 2022).

Ophelia Watahomigie-Corliss is a member of the Havsuw 'Baaja, the People of the Blue-Green Water, better known to the public as the Havasupai Tribe, located at the bottom of the Grand Canyon, whose land makes up what is now known as Grand Canyon National Park. Ophelia holds two bachelor's degrees from Northern Arizona University and is a proud mother to a sweet Supai girl.

Everglades National Park

Marjory Stoneman Douglas (1890–1998), the "Guardian of the Glades," is the author of *Everglades: River of Grass*, which was published

in 1947 after five years of research and writing, the same year Everglades National Park was founded. She continued her advocacy for the Everglades through environmental activism following the book's publication, and at the age of seventy-nine in 1969, Douglas helped establish the Friends of the Everglades and served as its first president. Her first novel, *Road to the Sun*, came out in 1951, and she went on to publish eight other books, culminating in her 1987 autobiography, *Voice of the River*.

Andrew C. Gottlieb's work has appeared in many places including *Best New Poets, Denver Quarterly, Ecotone, The Flyfish Journal, Mississippi Review, Orion*, and *Poetry Northwest*. He's been writer in residence in a number of wilderness locations, including three national parks.

Sylvia Jones is an editorial fellow at *Shenandoah* literary journal and the 2021–22 Stadler fellow at Bucknell University. She lives in Baltimore with her partner, Agata, and their buff tabby. She serves as a reader for *Ploughshares* and a volunteer for the PEN America Prison Writing Program. Her most recent writing can be found in *DIAGRAM, Spilt Milk, Ponder Review*, the *Santa Clara Review*, and elsewhere. She recently received her MFA from American University.

Betty Mae Jumper was born in South Florida's Indiantown. She was the first Seminole to earn a high school diploma, and the first female chief of the Seminole Tribe of Florida. Jumper was also the Seminoles' first Health Director and is known as the tribal storyteller. She edited the *Seminole Tribune*, is the author of two books: *And With the Wagon – Came God's Word* and *Legends of the Seminoles*.

Leah Claire Kaminski holds degrees in poetry from Harvard University and UC Irvine's programs in writing. Born and raised near Homestead, her writing is steeped in South Florida's natural world. She was a resident artist at Everglades National Park in 2018. Recent work can be seen in *Prairie Schooner, Fence, Vinyl,* and *ZYZZYVA*, among others. Her chapbook *Peninsular Scar* was released in 2019, and *Root* is forthcoming from Milk & Cake Press in 2022.

Jen Karetnick is a Miami-based poet, writer, and author/coauthor of twenty books. Her award-winning work has appeared in *The American Poetry Review,* TheAtlantic.com, *Guernica,* the *Miami Herald, The Missouri Review, Michigan Quarterly Review,* on NPR, and she has been an artist in residence in the Everglades and a Deering Estate fellow. She is cofounder of SWWIM (Supporting Women Writers in Miami), a nonprofit that raises the voices of women poets worldwide, and is managing editor of its online poetry journal *SWWIM Every Day.*

Rachel Luria is an associate professor at Florida Atlantic University's Wilkes Honors College. In June 2018, she was the artist in residence in the Everglades, where she composed original fables inspired by the wilderness around her. Her nonfiction was named a Notable Essay of 2015 by the editors of *The Best American Essays,* and her work has appeared in *Arts & Letters, CRAFT, The Normal School, Phoebe, Dash Literary Journal,* and others.

Hannah Star Rogers grew up in rural Alabama and earned a PhD from Cornell University and an MFA from Columbia University. She received a Solitude fellowship at the Akademie Schloss in Stuttgart, Germany, and is a visiting scholar at the University of Edinburgh, Scotland. Her poems and reviews have appeared in the *Kenyon Review,* the *Boston Review,* the *Los Angeles Review of Books, Tupelo Quarterly,* and the *Carolina*

Quarterly. Her artist residencies include Tofte Lake Center in Ely, Minnesota; the Arctic Circle in Finland; the Djerassi Artist Residency in Woodside, California; and National Park Service residencies in Acadia, Maine, and the Everglades, Florida.

Diana Woodcock is the author of four poetry collections, including *Facing Aridity* (2020 Prism Prize for Climate Literature finalist) and the forthcoming *Holy Sparks* (2020 Paraclete Press Poetry Award finalist). She received the Vernice Quebodeaux "Pathways" Poetry Prize for Women for *Swaying on the Elephant's Shoulders.* She holds a PhD in creative writing from Lancaster University, where she researched poetry's role in the search for an environmental ethic, and currently teaches at VCUarts Qatar.

Olympic National Park

Ella Elizabeth Clark (1896–1984) was born in Summertown, Tennessee, and educated in Illinois, at Northwestern University. She was on the English staff of Washington State University from 1927 to 1961. Her interest in Indian folktales began when she was a lookout for the Forest Service in the mountains of western Washington during World War II. In her life, she visited many Indian reserves, where she was fortunate enough to sit at the feet of some of the last of the old generation of Indian storytellers.

Lace Lawrence (Yakama) is a nature lover, writer, and nonprofit consultant with a passion for utilizing storytelling to diversify and decolonize outdoor recreation. Born into a long line of storytellers, Lace was raised on the Yakama Reservation riding horses, exploring deer trails, and swimming in rivers. She now resides in Fall City, Washington, with the love of her life and two adventure dogs but can often be found exploring new places in Aurora, her lime-green mini-campervan.

Tim McNulty is a poet, essayist, and natural history writer. He is the author of three poetry collections: *Ascendance*, published by Pleasure Boat Studio, *In Blue Mountain Dusk*, and *Pawtracks*, and eleven books on natural history, including *Olympic National Park: A Natural History* and *Washington's Mount Rainier National Park*. Tim has received the Washington State Book Award and the National Outdoor Book Award.

Gary Miranda was born in Bremerton, Washington, and raised in the Pacific Northwest. His poems have appeared in the *New Yorker*, the *Atlantic Monthly*, *Poetry*, the *American Poetry Review*, and elsewhere. His poetry is widely anthologized, and he has published four collections, one of which—*Listeners at the Breathing Place*—won the Princeton Contemporary Poetry competition. He also published a well-received translation of Rainer Maria Rilke's *Duino Elegies*.

Harvest Moon (Quinault) is a renowned storyteller and honored historian. Her stories portray vivid images that transport audiences of all ages to another world. A heartfelt traditional storyteller, Harvest's expressive recitation is an oratory forum of pure essence. Nothing is stronger than water and the words of women.

Rena Priest (Lummi) is a poet and an enrolled member of the Lhaq'temish (Lummi) Nation. She has been appointed to serve as the Washington State poet laureate for the term of April 2021–23. She is a Vadon Foundation fellow and recipient of an Allied Arts Foundation Professional Poets Award. Her debut collection, *Patriarchy Blues*, was published by MoonPath

Press and received an American Book Award. She holds an MFA from Sarah Lawrence College.

Rosette Royale is a Seattle-based writer and storyteller whose work has appeared in the *Seattle Times*, *Psychology Today*, *Portland Monthly*, and on Rollingstone.com. He's a newbie to the world of backcountry hiking and camping, and he's currently working on a book about his wilderness experiences in the temperate rain forests of Olympic National Park.

Anja Semanco lives along the Central Salish Sea in Bellingham, Washington, where she works for a small environmental advocacy organization. Her essays have been nominated for the Pushcart Prize and Best American Science and Nature Writing. She received her MA in journalism from the University of Colorado, Boulder in 2017 and has worked to capture the stories of our human and nonhuman relationships ever since.

Glacier National Park

Sandra Alcosser is a poet, writer, and creative-writing professor whose poems have appeared in the *New Yorker*, the *New York Times*, *Paris Review*, *Ploughshares*, *Poetry*, and the *Pushcart Prize Anthology*. She received two individual artist fellowships from the National Endowment for the Arts, and her books of poetry, *A Fish to Feed All Hunger* and *Except by Nature*, received the highest honors from the National Poetry Series, the Academy of American Poets, and the Association of Writers & Writing Programs. She founded and directs San Diego State University's MFA each fall, edits *Poetry International*, and served as Montana's first poet laureate.

Sara Aranda is a writer and endurance athlete based in the mountainous West. She obtained her BA in creative writing, with an emphasis in poetry, from the University of California, Riverside. A variety of her work has been published in *Alpinist* magazine, *The American Poetry Review*, *The Climbing Zine*, and *Boulder Weekly*, among others. One of her essays made the *Best American Essays* Notables list for 2019.

Mariah Gladstone (Blackfeet, Cherokee) grew up along the Backbone of the World near the Blackfeet Reservation. She graduated from Columbia University and returned home, where she developed Indigikitchen to revitalize traditional Indigenous foods. She lives in Babb, Montana, and spends her summers sharing Blackfeet stories and swimming in cold mountain lakes.

George Bird Grinnell (1849–1938), known to some as the "The Father of American Conservation" and to others as the "Father of Glacier National Park," was an anthropologist, historian, naturalist, and writer who published many books on Native American customs and oral traditions, including *Pawnee Hero Stories and Folk-Tales*, *Blackfoot Lodge Tales*, *The Cheyenne Indians: Their History and Ways of Life*, and *By Cheyenne Campfires*. For decades, Grinnell was also editor and contributor to *Forest and Stream* magazine, as well as cofounder, with Theodore Roosevelt, and key member of the Boone and Crockett club, which advocated for ethical hunting.

Ann Mansolino is a writer and visual artist whose work explores the relationship between the internal self and external ideas of place. She was the artist in residence at Glacier National Park in September 2020. Ann has taught at colleges and universities in the United States, Canada, and Singapore, and has exhibited her artwork internationally. She currently lives in Blairmore, Alberta, Canada.

Bob Muth is a retired junior high English teacher, poet, and author. He works as a volunteer backcountry ranger in Glacier National Park. He lives with his wife, Laurie, and their Australian shepherd, Rainy, on a small farm near the park.

Cassidy Randall is a freelance writer telling stories on environment, adventure, and people exploring human potential. She's occasionally on her own adventures when not hunched over her computer.

Terry Tempest Williams is a naturalist and fierce advocate for freedom of speech and has been called "a citizen writer," a writer who speaks out eloquently on behalf of an ethical stance toward life. The recipient of many awards and honors, Williams is known for her impassioned and lyrical prose. She is the author of the environmental literature classic *Refuge: An Unnatural History of Family and Place*; as well as *An Unspoken Hunger: Stories from the Field*; *Desert Quartet*; *Leap*; *Red: Patience and Passion in the Desert*; *The Open Space of Democracy*; and *Finding Beauty in a Broken World*. She is a columnist for the magazine the *Progressive*, and her writing has appeared in the *New Yorker*, the *New York Times*, *Orion* magazine, and numerous anthologies worldwide as a crucial voice for ecological consciousness and social change. In 2009, she was featured in Ken Burns' PBS series on the national parks, and in 2016, her book *The Hour of Land: A Personal Topography of America's National Parks* was published to coincide with and honor the centennial of the National Park Service.

Joshua Tree National Park

Cynthia Anderson has been a California resident and poet for over forty years and is the author of eleven books. Her poems have been published widely in journals and anthologies, and she has received multiple nominations for Best of the Net and the Pushcart Prize. She is coeditor of the anthology *A Bird Black As the Sun: California Poets on Crows & Ravens*. Cynthia makes her home in the Mojave desert near Joshua Tree National Park.

Mary Austin (1868–1934) wandered the desert territory for more than a decade after her family came across the Tehachapi Mountains and into the San Joaquin Valley, north of Bakersfield, in 1888. She published *The Land of Little Rain* in 1903, part travelogue, part memoir, part ethnography. She went on to write thirty-three other books, including *A Woman of Genius* and *Experiences Facing Death*, and even collaborated with famed photographer Ansel Adams on *Taos Pueblo*. Particularly passionate about women's rights and birth control, many of Austin's later works recounted the struggles of independent-minded women in a repressive society.

Mike Cipra has lived and written in landscapes ranging from the salt flats of Death Valley and the cliff dwellings of Mesa Verde, to the monzo-granite boulders and blooming yuccas of Joshua Tree National Park. He's a former park ranger and lifelong conservationist whose short stories and poems have appeared in *Dark Mountain*, *saltfront*, *Awkward One* and *Awkward Two*, *Danger City*, and *The Whirligig*.

Rae DelBianco is the author of internationally acclaimed novel *Rough Animals*, a western thriller that garnered comparisons to Cormac McCarthy, Denis Johnson, and Ron Rash, with praise from *Vogue* to *Outside* and many others. In 2019, she was awarded the Joshua Tree Highlands Artist Residency. An avid naturalist, hunter, and self-taught taxidermist, DelBianco lives in Mississippi at work on a second novel, *The Taxidermist*, based on her experiences as a rural LGBTQ+ woman.

Caryn Davidson worked in the education branch of Joshua Tree National Park for twenty years. She also served as the program manager for the park's artist-in-residence program until retiring in 2017. She was the director of environmental education at Big Morongo Canyon Preserve, and now leads hikes for Road Scholar and Joshua Tree National Park Association's Desert Institute. She holds a master's degree in French literature from UCLA. She enjoys hiking, yoga, and creative writing.

Ed Bok Lee is the author of *Real Karaoke People*, *Whorled*, and *Mitochondrial Night*, recipients of the American Book Award, Asian American Literary Award (Members' Choice), Minnesota Book Award, and PEN/Open Book Award. Lee attended kindergarten in Seoul, South Korea, and lives in Minneapolis, Minnesota.

Ruth Nolan, Mojave Desert Literary Laureate (2021–23), is a former wildland firefighter who fought fires in Joshua Tree National Park. She's curator of *Fire on the Mojave: Stories from the Deserts and Mountains of Inland Southern California* and editor of *No Place for a Puritan: The Literature of California's Deserts*. She is professor of English at College of the Desert, teaches for the Desert Institute at JTNP, and is a fierce desert defender.

Francisco Patencio served as ceremonial chief of the Agua Caliente Band of Cahuilla Indians from 1925 to 1939. He is the author of *Stories and Legends of the Palm Springs Indians,* which was published in 1943.

Ed Rosenthal, commercial real estate broker and poet, reads his poetry at official ceremonies and special events in LA. In 2010, a vacation hike turned into a harrowing near-death experience on the Mojave desert. After his rescue, he was a guest on *Bear Grylls: Escape from Hell.* In 2013, Moonrise Press published his poetry manuscript, *The Desert Hat,* and in 2020, DoppelHouse Press published his memoir, *Salvation Canyon.* Rosenthal is working on *The Projects,* about New York housing projects of the 1960s.

Sheree Winslow (Northern Cheyenne) was given the name Many Trails Many Roads Woman by the medicine man of her Northern Cheyenne tribe and embraces a life of wonder and wander. She has received many honors for her writing about travel and place. Her work has appeared in numerous publications including *Brevity, Midway Journal, Passages North,* and the *Changing Tides* anthology. She is a graduate of Vassar College and received her MFA from Vermont College of Fine Arts.

Appalachian National Scenic Trail & Pacific Crest National Scenic Trail

Hannah Andry (she/hers) is a New England local who enjoys long walks in the woods, spending time with loved ones, and asking the deeper questions in life while staring at the stars. She formerly worked for Outward Bound, which sparked her love for the entanglement of the natural world and emotion. Hannah believes in the power of compassion and nature as her guiding forces, and does her best to share those experiences with others.

Allie Donaldson, a.k.a. Taogoi, had no experience backpacking prior to her hike. After her grandmother died, she decided she would go on a long-distance hike on the Pacific Crest Trail. She decided to document the extraordinary experience through poetry and discovered her trail name—Taogoi (The Art of Getting Over It). Her life experiences so far could not compare to learning the lessons of the trail, pushing through pain and having to grow up fast in an intense year.

Kitty Galloway is a writer and educator based on a small farm in Frenchtown, Montana. She holds a BA in sustainable agriculture and education and an MS in environmental writing. She's hiked over five thousand miles of long-distance trails, much of that time solo, and is currently hard at work on her first book, which is about healing, walking, and what can come of slowing down.

Derick Lugo's forte is storytelling: he's the author of *The Unlikely Thru-Hiker,* a memoir of his six-month hike of the entire Appalachian Trail, he's written articles for outdoor magazines, contributed short stories to various books, and is a keynote speaker and adventurer.

Kim O'Connell is based in Arlington, Virginia, and has published articles and essays in national and regional publications, including the *Washington Post,* the *New York Times, Ladies' Home Journal, Huffington Post, National Geographic News, National Parks Traveler, AT Journeys, National Wildlife, Landscape Architecture,* and more. Kim has been a writer in residence at Shenandoah and Acadia National Parks, and she teaches nature writing and other topics for Johns Hopkins University's graduate science writing program.

Shawnté Salabert is a Los Angeles–based freelance writer interested in the connections between humans and the natural world. Her work has appeared in *Adventure Journal, AFAR, Alpinist, Backpacker,* the *California Sunday Magazine, Condé Nast Traveler, Outside,* and *Sierra.* She is the author of *Hiking the Pacific Crest Trail: Southern California.*

Earl Shaffer (1918–2002) was a York, Pennsylvania–born outdoorsman, poet, musician, and writer who, in 1948, following four and a half years of combat in WWII, became the first person to thru-hike the two-thousand-plus-mile Appalachian Trail. He was corresponding secretary for the Appalachian Trail Conference and cofounder of trail maintenance organizations, and led the construction of four AT shelters. In 1998, his final AT thru hike made him, at seventy-nine, the oldest person to achieve that goal at that time.

Cheryl Strayed is the author of the #1 *New York Times* bestselling memoir *Wild,* the *New York Times* bestsellers *Tiny Beautiful Things* and *Brave Enough,* and the novel *Torch. Wild* was chosen by Oprah Winfrey as the first selection for Oprah's Book Club 2.0. Strayed's books have been translated into nearly forty languages and have been adapted for both the screen and the stage. Strayed is the host of the *New York Times* hit podcast *Sugar Calling* and also *Dear Sugars,* which she cohosted with Steve Almond. Her essays have been published in *The Best American Essays,* the *New York Times,* the *Washington Post Magazine, Vogue, Salon,* the *Sun, Tin House,* the *New York Times Book Review,* and elsewhere. Strayed holds an MFA in fiction writing from Syracuse University and a bachelor's degree from the University of Minnesota. She lives in Portland, Oregon.

About the Illustrators

Grand Canyon National Park

Simone Martin-Newberry is an illustrator and graphic designer whose work is guided by a love of color, texture, movement, and rhythm. She has created art for the *New York Times*, the *Guardian US*, Chronicle Books, Random House, and many others. Originally from Los Angeles and based in Chicago for many years, she currently lives and works on the road, seeking out rocky canyons and green mountain trails along the way. *www.heysimone.com*

Everglades National Park

Dominique Ramsey is an award-winning freelance illustrator from North Carolina who loves all things animal and nature. She strives for uniqueness using bright colors, cultural patterns, and shapes to catch the viewer's eye. When

not illustrating darker themes, she is working on character designs for animation and children's media. *www.dominiqueramsey.com*

Olympic National Park

Levi Hastings is an experienced illustrator and visual storyteller based in Seattle, Washington. His work reflects lifelong obsessions with natural science, travel, and history. His published books include *The Spirit of Springer*, *Galloping Gertie*, and *Big Wig*. *www.levihastings.com*

Glacier National Park

Sarah Gesek is an artist and illustrator located in Seattle, Washington. The inspiration for her paintings comes from the world around her, nature being the main catalyst. She frequently paints whimsical interpretations of her travels near and far. *www.sarahgesekstudio.com*

Joshua Tree National Park

Pavonis Giron is an author and illustrator with a love of bold colors and a taste for exploration, whether in the great outdoors or between city blocks. Currently based in Milwaukee, Wisconsin, Pavonis grew up among the sunbleached rocks of the Mojave desert, which still inspire their work today. In addition to writing and illustrating books for children, Pavonis has also worked in product and game design. *www.pavonisgiron.com*

Appalachian and Pacific Crest National Scenic Trails

Lauren West is an illustrator, muralist, and designer who now lives in Vermont after over eighteen years in Philadelphia. Her work explores humor, nature, and everyday life with a focus on simple forms, bright colors, and dynamic spaces. Her combination of humor and simplicity pushes her work into a world between strange and playful, but always cheerful. Lauren sees art as a way to communicate with the world and tries to make her work as visually accessible and vibrant to everyone who experiences it. *www.laurencatwest.com*

CAMPFIRE STORIES DESIGNER & ILLUSTRATOR

Melissa McFeeters is an independent illustrator and graphic designer in Philadelphia. She partners with clients who are passionate about making the world a better, more beautiful place. She is currently a full-time freelancer working on branding, publication design, infographics, and illustration from her studio in Fishtown. In addition to designing our books and card decks, she also created the iconography seen throughout each volume. *www.melissamcfeeters.com*

About the Editors

Ilyssa Kyu is a design researcher focused on inclusion at frog, a global creative consultancy, and the founder of Amble, a sabbatical program for creative professionals to take time away with purpose in support of nature conservancies. She has a degree in industrial design and previously worked as a designer at the City of Philadelphia Office of Sustainability, and as a UX designer and design researcher at creative studios in and around Philadelphia. As a facilitator, convener, researcher, and strategist, she applies design thinking to find clarity in the chaos and unconventional, creative ways of solving problems.

Dave Kyu is a socially engaged artist, writer, and project manager. Born in Seoul, South Korea, and raised in the United States, he explores the creative tensions of identity, community, and public space in his work. He has managed public arts projects for the Mural Arts Program, Asian Arts Initiative, and the City of Philadelphia. His own creative projects have found him commissioning skywriting planes to write messages ten thousand feet over Philadelphia, and doing everything Facebook told him to do for a month.

Together, they created *Campfire Stories: Volume I, Campfire Stories Card Deck, Campfire Stories Card Deck—For Kids!* and were artists in residence at Independence National Historic Park as part of the Imagine Your Parks grant—a collaboration between the NEA, National Park Service, and Mural Arts Program—which resulted in "I Will Hold You in the Light," an event that brought together six diverse performers responding to the theme of "The Pursuit of Happiness." They live outside of Philadelphia with their two daughters and pup Alder, and are always seeking adventure and connection in the outdoors.

recreation • lifestyle • conservation

MOUNTAINEERS BOOKS is a leading publisher of mountaineering literature and guides—
including our flagship title, *Mountaineering: The Freedom of the Hills*—as well as adventure narratives,
natural history, and general outdoor recreation. Through our two imprints, Skipstone and Braided
River, we also publish titles on sustainability and conservation. We are committed to supporting
the environmental and educational goals of our organization by providing expert information on
human-powered adventure, sustainable practices at home and on the trail, and preservation of
wilderness.

The Mountaineers, founded in 1906, is a 501(c)(3) nonprofit outdoor recreation and conservation organization whose mission is to enrich lives and communities by helping people "explore,
conserve, learn about, and enjoy the lands and waters of the Pacific Northwest and beyond." One
of the largest such organizations in the United States, it sponsors classes and year-round outdoor
activities throughout the Pacific Northwest, including climbing, hiking, backcountry skiing, snow-
shoeing, camping, kayaking, sailing, and more. The Mountaineers also supports its mission through
its publishing division, Mountaineers Books, and promotes environmental education and citizen
engagement. For more information, visit The Mountaineers Program Center, 7700 Sand Point
Way NE, Seattle, WA 98115-3996; phone 206-521-6001; www.mountaineers.org; or email
info@mountaineers.org.

Our publications are made possible through the generosity of donors and through sales of 700 titles
on outdoor recreation, sustainable lifestyle, and conservation. To donate, purchase books, or learn
more, visit us online:

MOUNTAINEERS BOOKS
1001 SW Klickitat Way, Suite 201 • Seattle, WA 98134
800-553-4453 • mbooks@mountaineersbooks.org • www.mountaineersbooks.org

An independent nonprofit publisher since 1960

More from Mountaineers Books

Campfire Stories

Dave Kyu and Ilyssa Kyu
An anthology of stories and myths
from six of America's favorite
national parks

Campfire Stories Deck

Dave Kyu and Ilyssa Kyu
A deck of 50 cards featuring storytelling prompts to help you connect
with friends and family

Campfire Stories Deck for Kids!

Dave Kyu and Ilyssa Kyu
Fifty cards with illustrations to
encourage kids to create and tell
their own stories

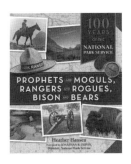

**Prophets and Moguls,
Rangers and Rogues,
Bison and Bears**

Heather Hansen
An engaging and accessible
account of the first one hundred
years of the National Park Service

**Earth Almanac: Nature's
Calendar for Year-Round
Discovery**

Ken Keffer
Highlights natural history to
celebrate throughout the seasons;
illustrations by Jeremy Collins

**Bears Don't Care
About Your Problems**

Brendan Leonard
The creator of Semi-Rad's hilarious
take on outdoor adventure